# TRACING Y
# KENT
# ANCESTORS

# FAMILY HISTORY FROM PEN & SWORD

Tracing Secret Service Ancestors
•
Tracing Your Air Force Ancestors
•
Tracing Your Ancestors
•
Tracing Your Ancestors from 1066 to 1837
•
Tracing Your Ancestors Through
Death Records
•
Tracing Your Ancestors Through
Family Photographs
•
Tracing Your Ancestors Using the Census
•
Tracing Your Ancestors' Childhood
•
Tracing Your Ancestors' Parish Records
•
Tracing Your Aristocratic Ancestors
•
Tracing Your Army Ancestors – 2nd Edition
•
Tracing Your Birmingham Ancestors
•
Tracing Your Black Country Ancestors
•
Tracing Your British Indian Ancestors
•
Tracing Your Canal Ancestors
•
Tracing Your Channel Islands Ancestors
•
Tracing Your Coalmining Ancestors
•
Tracing Your Criminal Ancestors
•
Tracing Your East Anglian Ancestors
•
Tracing Your East End Ancestors
•
Tracing Your Edinburgh Ancestors
•
Tracing Your First World War Ancestors
•
Tracing Your Great War Ancestors:
The Gallipoli Campaign
•
Tracing Your Great War Ancestors: The Somme
•
Tracing Your Great War Ancestors: Ypres
•
Tracing Your Huguenot Ancestors
•
Tracing Your Jewish Ancestors
•

Tracing Your Labour Movement Ancestors
•
Tracing Your Lancashire Ancestors
•
Tracing Your Leeds Ancestors
•
Tracing Your Legal Ancestors
•
Tracing Your Liverpool Ancestors
•
Tracing Your London Ancestors
•
Tracing Your Medical Ancestors
•
Tracing Your Merchant Navy Ancestors
•
Tracing Your Naval Ancestors
•
Tracing Your Northern Ancestors
•
Tracing Your Pauper Ancestors
•
Tracing Your Police Ancestors
•
Tracing Your Prisoner of War Ancestors:
The First World War
•
Tracing Your Railway Ancestors
•
Tracing Your Royal Marine Ancestors
•
Tracing Your Rural Ancestors
•
Tracing Your Scottish Ancestors
•
Tracing Your Second World War Ancestors
•
Tracing Your Servant Ancestors
•
Tracing Your Service Women Ancestors
•
Tracing Your Shipbuilding Ancestors
•
Tracing Your Tank Ancestors
•
Tracing Your Textile Ancestors
•
Tracing Your Trade and Craftsmen Ancestors
•
Tracing Your Welsh Ancestors
•
Tracing Your West Country Ancestors
•
Tracing Your Yorkshire Ancestors

# TRACING YOUR KENT ANCESTORS

## A Guide for Family Historians

David Wright

Pen & Sword
**FAMILY HISTORY**

First published in Great Britain in 2016
PEN & SWORD FAMILY HISTORY
an imprint of
Pen & Sword Books Ltd
47 Church Street,
Barnsley
South Yorkshire,
S70 2AS

ISBN 978 1 47383 802 4

A CIP catalogue record for this book is
available from the British Library.

Typeset in Palatino and Optima by CHIC GRAPHICS

Printed and bound in England by
CPI Group (UK), Croydon, CR0 4YY

Pen & Sword Books Ltd incorporates the imprints of Pen & Sword
Archaeology, Atlas, Aviation, Battleground, Discovery, Family History,
History, Maritime, Military, Naval, Politics, Railways, Select, Social History,
Transport, True Crime, Claymore Press, Frontline Books, Leo Cooper,
Praetorian Press, Remember When, Seaforth Publishing and Wharncliffe.

For a complete list of Pen & Sword titles please contact
PEN & SWORD BOOKS LTD
47 Church Street, Barnsley, South Yorkshire, S70 2AS, England
E-mail: enquiries@pen-and-sword.co.uk
Website: www.pen-and-sword.co.uk

# CONTENTS

Preface     vii

Abbreviations     ix

Map of Kent Parishes     x

**Introduction: Some Kentish History and Geography**     1

**Chapter 1 Preliminaries**

A. Genealogical Introduction     18

B. Getting Started     26

C. Research Problems     36

D. My Family History: Some Warnings     40

**Chapter 2 Principal Basic Sources**

A. Civil Registration     45

B. Census Returns     50

C. Parish Registers and Bishop's Transcripts     56

D. Monumental Inscriptions     70

E. Probate Records     74

**Chapter 3 Mainly Local Records**

A. Borough     92

B. Cathedral and Church Courts     96

C. Directories     100

D. House Histories     103

E. Newspapers     106

F. Nonconformity     109

G. Parish Chest     113
     Ecclesiastical; Civil; Apprentices; Bastardy; Charity;
     Churchwardens; Constables; Enclosure; Rates; Settlement and
     Removal; Surveyors; Vestry Minutes

H. Poor Law and Hospitals     128

I. Quarter-sessions                                                        135
J. Schools and Education                                                   140
K. Maps                                                                    143
    County maps; Estate maps; Surveys; Tithe Maps; Town Maps
L. Trades and Industry                                                     148
    Banks and bankruptcy; Bell-founding; Brewing; Brick-making;
    Cement-making; Cloth-making; Coal-mining; Copperas;
    Dockyards; Fishing; Gunpowder; Iron-making; Paper-making;
    Quarrying; Silk-weaving
M.Voters                                                                   158

**Chapter 4 Mainly National Records**
A. Crime and Punishment                                                    161
B. Domesday Book                                                           165
C. Heraldry                                                                167
D. Land and its Possession                                                 171
    The Early Mediaeval Period; Final Agreements; The Four Rolls
    Series; Inquisitions Post Mortem; Bargain and Sale; Lease and
    Release; Title Deeds; Other Material
E. Manorial Records                                                        178
F. The Professions                                                         181
    Church; Coastguards; Customs; Government; Law; Medicine
G. The Services                                                            186
    The Army; The Navy
H. Tax Records                                                             195
    Association Oath Rolls; Hearth Tax; Land Tax; Lay Subsidies;
    Marriage Duty Act; Poll Taxes; Protestation Returns; Window Tax;
    Miscellaneous

**Directory of Archives, Libraries and Societies**                        201
**General Bibliography**                                                   206
**Gazetteer of Kent Ancient Parishes**                                    210
**Index**                                                                 225

# PREFACE

If your ancestors originated in the ancient, fascinating and diverse county of Kent, you will be well served by its large and rich collections of historical documents; for this county, along with the rest of the country, has not been invaded since 1066, and so its archives still retain many documents dating back a thousand years and more, along with great quantities of other items from its borough collections and 400 or so ancient parishes. Some of the earliest genealogical pioneers were Kentish and so you may consequently enjoy consulting many of the county's important indexes in the course of extending your pedigree.

The three principal archives are at Canterbury, Maidstone and Rochester, but north-west Kent also has several local archive centres, and family history societies and groups are evenly spread throughout the county offering help, advice, talks and lectures. Further afield, but easily accessible, the London Metropolitan Archives holds much material relating to those parts of north-western Kent now within Greater London, while The National Archives (formerly the Public Record Office) at Kew offers the researcher almost unlimited riches in all aspects of genealogy, perhaps most especially for the mediaeval period where some sets of records survive in unbroken sequences for nearly 800 years. Details of all of these sources can be found in the Directory at the back of the book. I have been working in archives in Kent and London for nearly forty years, and have had the pleasure of handling a great many different types of records over that long period. If you are a beginner, Chapter 2 on principal sources should set you up and gently introduce you to a mixture of original and online material. In chapters 3 and 4 I give a broad overview of the great wealth of material available in archives in both Kent and London from early mediaeval charters to modern electoral registers.

But no matter what experience you have under your belt, do first read the chapter on preliminaries and remind yourself that this fascinating hobby is not an easy one to get right: to err is human, and I certainly made lots of mistakes when first setting out on the long and never-quite-complete journey of researching my family tree. If you avoid some of the traps that I fell into, then this book will have proved its worth.

David Wright,
November 2015

*Ash (by Sandwich): a large church in an enormous parish. Perhaps thirty or more generations of many local families lie buried here. (Copyright Neil Anthony)*

# ABBREVIATIONS

| | |
|---|---|
| **BL** | British Library |
| **BRS** | British Record Society |
| **CCA** | Canterbury Cathedral Archives |
| **GOONS** | Guild of One Name Studies |
| **GRO** | General Register Office |
| **HOL** | House of Lords Record Office |
| **KAS** | Kent Archaeological Society |
| **KFHS** | Kent Family History Society |
| **KHLC** | Kent History and Library Centre |
| **LMA** | London Metropolitan Archives |
| **MALSC** | Medway Area Local Studies Centre |
| **NWKFHS** | North West Kent Family History Society |
| **ODNB** | Oxford Dictionary of National Biography |
| **SOG** | Society of Genealogists |
| **TNA** | The National Archives |

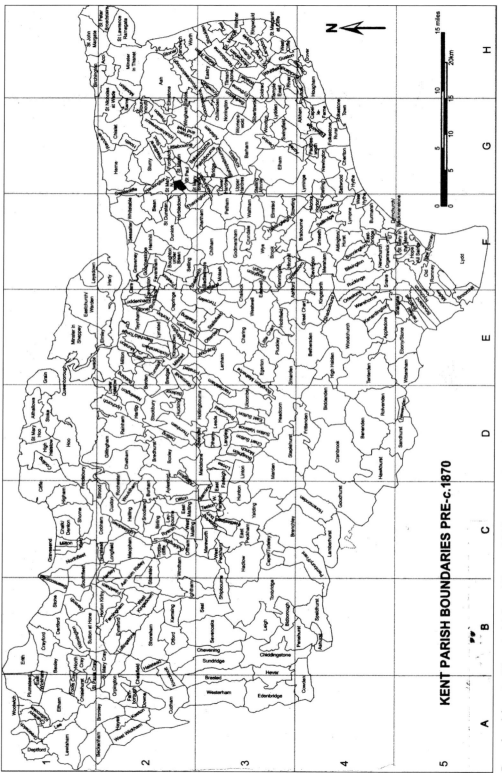

# KENT PARISH BOUNDARIES PRE-c.1870

*Reproduced from An Historical Atlas of Kent, ed. T. Lawson and D. Killingray, by permission.*

# INTRODUCTION
## Some Kentish History and Geography

At nearly a million acres Kent was the tenth largest of the English historical counties, and one that has stood nobly for centuries as the gateway to England from the Continent, with a considerable part of its bulk lying closer to France than it does to London. Many famous and picturesque towns and castles hug its long shoreline, and the disparate landscape stretches from the isles of Sheppey and Thanet to Romney Marsh to the Weald to the marshes and parishes in the north-west, these now within the M25 and fairly engulfed by the London metropolis.

National landmarks such as Dover Castle and four of the former ancient Cinque Ports have guarded its shores and welcomed or repulsed strangers for nearly a thousand years; attractive and ancient towns such as Faversham, Hythe, Sandwich and Tenterden still welcome many visitors; the two cathedrals (a nationally unique distinction) of Canterbury and Rochester lie within the two oldest dioceses; and the county town of Maidstone sits on the River Medway, deliberately chosen for its more or less exact position in the centre of the county.

Ancient borders with Sussex, Surrey and Middlesex, as well as with Essex just across the River Thames and France a mere 20 miles away, mean that genealogical and historical research can never be conducted in a vacuum. The passage of incoming and outgoing peoples has never ceased – some have come and stayed, such as the French Huguenots in Canterbury and Sandwich, but far more have gone in that great human diaspora which has taken Kentish inhabitants to reside in the farthest parts of the planet, to Australia, New Zealand, South Africa, the Americas and the Far East.

Generally rising sea levels mean that much of the Kentish coastline has changed almost beyond recognition since the Anglo-Saxon period. Thanet is now well and truly attached to the mainland, hardly at all separated by the placid Wantsum Channel which was once navigable and guarded by a Roman fort at either end. Sheppey is today a single entity now that its daughter islands of Elmley and Harty cling so closely to their ancient mother; the Isle of Oxney and the former ports of Fordwich, Romney, Sandwich and Smallhythe now all lie stranded many miles from the sea, mostly after huge landscape-changing mediaeval storms; and meanwhile, at the very southern tip, the shingle bank of Dungeness annually gains a few more yards as it stretches ever outwards towards France.

A great deal of antiquity remains, even for the casual observer. The very name of Kent itself is a Celtic one and cognate with *Cantium*, the name that Julius Caesar gave to that part of Britain lying within sight of Gaul which he would visit fleetingly in 55–54 BC. From Canterbury radiate substantially unchanged Roman roads to Reculver, Richborough, Dover and Lympne; and north-westwards strikes Watling Street (the present A2), the first link between Britain and Rome at the beginning of the Christian era. The villa at Lullingstone, the fort at Reculver and the pharos at Dover stand as just three of the many Roman antiquities within the county, dating at various times from after AD 43 when the Roman invasion of Britain commenced with its landing at Richborough under the commander Aulus Plautius. Romans roads were so well marked that they long outlived their builders, sometimes being adopted as parish or even partial county boundaries.

The Roman withdrawal began in or soon after 410, in anticipation of internal collapse in the rest of the empire. Britain had now to look to itself for security and protection. More frequent raids by Saxon and other pagan peoples meant that Kent was increasingly helpless and led to King Vortigern promising the Isle of Thanet as a reward to those Continental tribes who would come to his and the nation's aid. The initial force was led by Hengist and Horsa in 449, from a people described by Bede as Jutes. In reality they were probably a Frankish race from the middle Rhine, a fact easily evidenced by the many parish names ending in –*ing* and –*ham*, so very close to the modern German –*ingen* and –*heim*.

The reign of King Ethelbert as *Bretwalda*, or overlord of all the kingdoms south of the River Humber, saw the landing of St Augustine, the papal envoy, at Ebbsfleet in Thanet in 597 to begin the long and uncertain reconversion of England to Christianity. Early converts used St Martin's Church in Canterbury, still today substantially Roman in

*Reculver: Roman fort and Anglo-Saxon church lie cheek by jowl with much of the former now under the sea. (Copyright Neil Anthony)*

fabric and perhaps the most venerable church in all England. Thus was founded the Diocese of Canterbury with Augustine as first archbishop overseeing lands covering some two-thirds of the county as far west as the River Medway. Shortly before his death in 604, Augustine created the Diocese of Rochester to cover the rest of Kent, installing Justus as its first bishop.

This unique division would ultimately give Rochester some 132 ancient parishes and Canterbury 281, figures that hardly changed until 1845 when Deptford, Greenwich, Lewisham and Woolwich were lost, first to the Bishopric of London, and then to Southwark in 1904. In 1926, following the creation of many Victorian daughter parishes, the county total was 476.

Early Christianity struggled before flourishing. The uncertain and drawn-out process is evidenced by such sixth- and seventh-century place names as Alkham, Elham and Wye, each recalling a heathen settlement, and also Woodnesborough, preserving the pagan Wodin in its etymology. The first two English religious houses were both in Canterbury, St Augustine's Abbey, the burial place of many early archbishops, and Christ Church Priory, each founded in about 600 by

3

St Augustine. Early nunneries were established at Folkestone and Lyminge in the 630s, and at Minster-in-Sheppey and Minster-in-Thanet in the 670s. All were subject to constant Danish raids: Sheppey was overrun in 835 and Canterbury attacked in 842, although the first battle involving an English fleet gained it a victory off Sandwich in 850. There were notable over-winterings by the Vikings at Thanet in 850, on Sheppey in 854, the establishment of an encampment at Appledore in 892 and a fortress near Milton Regis in 893.

By the later eighth century the Kentish royal line had died out and the county was subsumed under the overlordship of Mercia, submitting to Wessex in 825 and finally becoming a shire county presided over by its own *ealdorman*, or earl, within the Kingdom of England. At the time of Domesday in 1086 the population of Kent was about 70,000, the largest town of Canterbury having about 5,000 inhabitants. Folkestone and its hinterland were the most densely populated with about seventeen people to the square mile, followed by the Medway Valley and much of north-east and east Kent with twelve. By far the sparsest, and indeed at this time almost empty, was the Wealden district to the south-west, where many large parishes and future iron- and cloth-making industries would not be opened up until the 1500s. By the time of the Lay Subsidy of 1334/5 the county population was around 125,000, dropping by about a quarter after the Black Death.

Following persuasive arguments by the newly elected Archbishop Lanfranc at the councils of Winchester and Windsor in 1073, the northern province of York was limited to the country north of the Humber, while the see of Canterbury now took jurisdiction over everywhere else, including Wales, to the south. Henceforth the Archbishop of Canterbury would preside at national councils with the nation's second and third men, the Archbishop of York and the Bishop of London, at his right and left hands respectively. The mother see of England maintained a visible presence, but not just at Canterbury: sixteen other archiepiscopal residences were spread widely at locations including Knole, Northfleet and Otford to the west, Gillingham and Maidstone in the centre, and Charing, Lyminge, Saltwood and Wingham to the east.

By the time of the Normans and Plantagenets Kent was well established and starting to fall into the pattern of national history. Its appellation of the 'Garden of England', familiar to most, is still borne out by the farming practices that Julius Caesar described, as well as by Mr Pickwick's three-fold horticultural description of apples, hops and cherries. King Stephen founded his great abbey at Faversham and, if buried in the town, as is generally believed, represents the only royal burial in a parish church in England. Canterbury witnessed the murder of its Archbishop Thomas à Becket in 1170 and the start of what would be the second greatest place of pilgrimage in the land, to be immortalised by Chaucer, perhaps a Kentish man himself. Dover saw the arrival of the first Dominican friars in 1220, followed shortly afterwards by a small group of nine Franciscans making their way to Canterbury in 1224. The group of four Kentish Cinque Ports flourished between about 1150 and 1350, but by the time of the Tudors only Dover remained of any consequence, the rest having lost their harbours to the continuous silting process that gradually and inexorably took the sea further and further away.

By the later eleventh century about half the cultivable land in Kent was in the hands of the Church, chiefly the archbishops of Canterbury and Rochester, and Christ Church Priory and St Augustine's Abbey, both at Canterbury. The Conqueror had granted the rest of the county to six of his Norman supporters, retaining only the enormous manor of Milton Regis and three others. It was Odo, his half-brother, Bishop of Bayeux, who received the greatest rewards in the form of some 200 manors right across the county. In the vulnerable south-east Hugh de Montfort, Constable of England, and a reliable knight and Hastings veteran, was given possession of almost the entire area excepting only the archbishop's important manor of Saltwood, which he duly held as that prelate's tenant. It was here that Hugh would consolidate his defensive position by building Saltwood Castle.

Other castles served to protect the interior and subject the inhabitants, those at Leeds, Saltwood, Tonbridge and West Malling yielding importance only to Canterbury, Dover and Rochester. Others were situated at Allington, Chilham, Eynsford and Sutton Valence. Feudalism suited a mainly rural society, but such towns as existed fitted awkwardly into its pattern: Canterbury, Dover, Faversham, Fordwich, Hythe, Rochester, Romney and Sandwich were termed boroughs and lay outside the normal manorial organisation. Little larger than a modern village, they were closely linked with the surrounding countryside, although many of the townsmen were engaged in trade.

All of them except Canterbury were favourably situated for commerce in being sea or river ports, thus affording opportunities for overseas trade (especially Dover and Sandwich) as well as taking part in the enormously important mediaeval fishing industry.

The county abounded in religious houses from 1220 until the Henrician dissolution. There were Benedictine monasteries at Canterbury, Dover, Faversham and Rochester; Benedictine nunneries at Canterbury, Davington, Higham, Minster-in-Sheppey and Malling; Augustinian canons at Bilsington, Canterbury, Combwell, Leeds, Lesnes and Tonbridge; about a dozen mendicant orders of friars widely scattered from Greenwich to Sandwich; single houses of Cistercians at Boxley and Cluniacs at Monks Horton; Praemonstratensian canons at Bradsole and Langdon; and a handful of alien houses, which mostly closed in the 1400s.

Kent differed greatly from other parts of the country in the way in which mediaeval land was divided. In the Midlands and elsewhere the open-field system prevailed whereby (1) a village or township had attached to it (usually) three large fields; (2) the owners of houses each possessed a number of strips of land in the fields which were often redistributed in order that everybody in turn got a fair share of the best and worst land; (3) from a certain date each year every owner had the right to graze a specified number of beasts in the fields; (4) the way in which the fields were used and disputes settled was supervised by the Court Baron; and (5) one of the fields was usually left fallow every second or third year. The fields were 'open' in that the strips were not enclosed by hedges, and they were 'common' in that everyone in common with his neighbours had a right to pasture his beasts in the field after a certain date. Although there are traces in Kent of small 'common' fields, and in the east there were 'open' fields, unenclosed by hedges, this was not the same as the common, open-field system. East Kent had many fields that were large and unenclosed and seemingly held in strips, but they were not common fields and there was no annual redistribution of strips and no right of pasturing beasts in common. Rather, each tenant pastured his beasts on his own lands after the harvest had been gathered and had to put up wattle fences to prevent his cattle straying on to another man's land.

Kent's famous gavelkind system of holding land differed significantly from other land tenures in that when an owner died intestate his land was divided equally between all surviving sons instead of passing solely by primogeniture to the eldest. This frequently led to endless division and subdivision of holdings and the splitting up of fields into little parcels or 'strips' to ensure that all surviving sons received a fair share of the best and worst of their parent's lands. This sometimes cumbrous practice diminished only slowly, not finally being outlawed until 1925.

Between 1750 and 1850, therefore, the only enclosure practised in Kent was that touching parts of rough common or wasteland or of marsh reclaimed from the sea or rivers. By Act of Parliament Barming Heath, Bexley Heath, Brasted Chart, Bromley Common, Coxheath, East Malling and Ditton Commons, Rhodes Minnis at Lyminge, Swingfield Minnis and Wrotham Heath were all enclosed, as were the marshes at Burham, Crayford, Erith, Queenborough and Wouldham. In spite of all these enclosures a good many common lands still survive, both small and large.

The cataclysm of the Dissolution of the Monasteries fell heavily on the two most valuable properties of Christ Church and St Gregory's priories at Canterbury, the next most valuable being Boxley Abbey, Dover Priory, Faversham Abbey, Leeds Priory, Lesnes Abbey, Rochester Priory and Tonbridge Priory. Most other houses were far poorer and often had never really recovered after the Black Death, so much so that when the king's commissioners began their inspections many of the famous houses, such as Bilsington and Boxley, contained residents barely into double figures. All the monastic possessions were transferred to the Crown, some to be granted out again immediately, others later to be sold or granted to favourites within the king's circle. At the conclusion, two-thirds remained in the ecclesiastical ownership of Canterbury or Rochester, the rest divided between eleven laymen, notable among them Sir Thomas Wyatt of Allington who acquired Boxley Abbey and Aylesford Friary, and Sir Thomas Cheyney of Minster-in-Sheppey who was granted Faversham Abbey and the priories at Davington and Minster-in-Sheppey.

Henry VIII was energetic in building castles at Deal, Sandgate, Sandown and Walmer to repel possible French and Spanish invasions along a low-lying coast. These were complemented by other coastal castles or forts at Dover, Folkestone, Gillingham, Gravesend with Milton, Sheerness and Upnor, this last-mentioned to protect Chatham

Dockyard. Later defence arrangements included a comprehensive series of Armada beacons stretched across much of the county (only at Birling could sightlines across the North Downs be maintained) and a semaphore telegraph system which ran from Deal to Chatham and on to London.

Around 1700 the largest towns in Kent were Canterbury, Deptford, Dover, Rochester, and Sandwich, followed by Chatham, Deal, Faversham, Gravesend, Greenwich, Maidstone and Woolwich. Lesser in size were Ashford, Bromley, Cranbrook, Dartford, Folkestone, Hythe, New Romney, Sevenoaks, Strood, Tenterden and Tonbridge. The 1662–4 Hearth Tax returns now suggest a countywide household total of about 33,000 and a population of perhaps 140,000.

Large numbers of defences were constructed from about 1770 in anticipation of a French invasion. A government survey of the Thames and Medway defences revealed many weaknesses, and so forts and blockhouses were built around the Hoo peninsula and particularly at Chatham, some not being completed until after Waterloo. Batteries were built at Sandwich and Dungeness, a series of twenty-seven Martello towers hugged the coast from Folkestone down to Romney Marsh, and the 25-mile Royal Military Canal stretched from Hythe to Rye and Winchelsea with a military road running alongside it for moving troops rapidly to any desired point. Beacons were now inadequate for sending messages quickly from the coast to London and back, and a new semaphore system placed on the tops of hills was introduced. There were just nine stations positioned from Dover to Shooter's Hill covering the county from east to west and relaying a message in 2 minutes.

For as long as the threat of invasion lasted there were tented troops at Barham Downs, Coxheath and Brabourne Lees, and barracks at Chatham, Dover and Shorncliffe. At Canterbury several thousand soldiers were permanently housed in barracks from 1795, and by 1800 Ashford saw a substantial magazine and barracks housing 2,000 men, all of whom were engaged in building and maintaining the network of turnpike roads between that town and the Romney Marsh.

The county's architecture is distinctive, varied and often memorable, oasthouses being perhaps the quintessential Kentish buildings. The mediaeval heritage is substantial, with many attractive Tudor 'black and white' ensembles and individual houses, Wealden villages crammed with vernacular buildings as at Cranbrook and Tenterden, and larger towns, Faversham and Sandwich chief among them, the latter probably the best-preserved small mediaeval town in England.

Proximity to London and increasing wealth in the eighteenth century saw the building of many fine new country houses, the architecture reflecting the taste and education of their owners, for example, at Bourne Park, Bradbourne, Finchcocks, Goodnestone next Wingham and Mereworth, the last-mentioned in the Palladian style, which would have been seen on the Grand Tour. Capability Brown's work is evidenced at Danson Park and Humphry Repton's at Cobham. At Tunbridge Wells the hand of Decimus Burton built the Calverley Park estate of nineteen villas and thereby established the classical style as suitable for smaller domestic architecture, leaving Gothic for larger schemes as seen, for example, at Hadlow Castle.

In common with the rest of the country, few post-mediaeval churches were built (Plaxtol of 1649 is a notable exception), although rebuilding occurred at Gravesend after a fire in 1727 and at Mereworth in 1744–6 to match the neighbouring castle. Daughter churches to cater for expanding populations may be seen at St Paul Deptford (1720–30) and St George Ramsgate (1824–7). There are rather more Non-conformist places of worship of this date, usually plain and vernacular, at Bessel's Green (Baptist, 1716), Maidstone (Unitarian, 1736) and Tenterden (Unitarian, 1746).

Other notable public buildings include almshouses at Canterbury, Dartford, Faversham and Sevenoaks; town halls at Faversham (1819), Maidstone (1764), Queenborough (1793) and Tenterden (1790); two-dozen union workhouses, that at Bridge exceptionally well preserved; and the splendid Theatre Royal at Margate (1787).

The history of the chief highways and of most roads between market towns from about 1700 to 1875 is to be found in the minutes, accounts, maps and other archives of the turnpike trusts. The extremely poor state of the road system before the age of the turnpikes, often exacerbated by wheeled traffic, meant that travel was generally only practicable between spring and autumn; such roads as there were in winter were simply not passable because of mud, flooding and broken surfaces, the deep ruts being filled up with anything to hand, which generally meant large unbroken stones awaiting wheeled traffic to break them down. From 1663 onwards interested people in a locality would seek an Act of Parliament to enable them to take over a portion of road, erect toll-gates or turnpikes, appoint salaried officers and improve the road by drainage, bridge-building and straightening out of bends; professional surveyors and bands of labourers carried out all of this work. Turnpike- or gate-keepers were leased to the highest bidder. A General Turnpike Act of 1773 ushered in the golden age of road travel for the royal mail and stagecoaches until about 1840, when the railways brought a swift and almost complete change to the way in which the public travelled. Despite this progress, even in the early 1800s there were still few practicable roads for want of skilled labour rather than legislation.

The Watling Street road from London to Dover, major coach routes and leisure places such as Tunbridge Wells were the first to receive attention. Between 1709 and 1753 ten turnpike trusts were set up to extend accessibility to more places including the road from Canterbury to the sea at Whitstable and onwards to London, and at the same time fixing charges for use of the road by horses, sheep, carriages and so on. By the late 1700s Canterbury was losing the benefit of leisure traffic to the coastal towns because of cheap water transport and so the roads to the Thanet coastal towns and to Sandwich and Folkestone were all turnpiked. But in all, some two-thirds of all the county's turnpiked roads were in the west, reflecting the proximity of London and other transport hubs such as Chatham and Maidstone. By the mid-1800s the increase in road traffic was too great for the turnpike trusts to be able to cope with, and so Parliament introduced local highway boards, although these were more or less the same bodies with the same districts.

Passengers travelling to the Continent in the seventeenth and eighteenth centuries generally sailed to and from Rye just over the county border in Sussex. Postal packets operated twice a week from Dover to both Calais and Ostend, and there were regular cross-Channel steamboat services from the 1820s. The South Eastern Railway linked its London trains to cross-Channel steamers in 1843–4, and from that date there were also regular sailings to both France and Belgium.

The fame of the commercially unsuccessful 1830 Whitstable–Canterbury railway line serves as a reminder that before 1850 the nearest town on the north coast with a train service was Gravesend. The main London–Redhill–Tonbridge–Ashford line, started in 1842, was constructed partly to pick up local Kent traffic, but also to secure the cross-Channel traffic passing through Dover; it was extended to Maidstone in 1844, to Tunbridge Wells in 1845 and through Canterbury to Ramsgate and Margate in 1846, the main eastern hub being at Ashford. Prices were not cheap at 1*d*. a mile (the majority of people who walked to work were probably unaffected), and mass travel would have to await the introduction of cheap-day excursions. Later development was rapid, financed by the South Eastern and London, Chatham and Dover companies, and by 1914 very few places were more than 3 miles from a station, although of course today the network has shrunk greatly.

There were a number of consequences of the extensive network that later developed. Many of the coastal towns from Whitstable to Dover now provided family seaside holidays. In the west other places such as Greenhithe, Snodland, Stone and Swancombe saw rapid industrialization, and Crayford, Dartford, Erith and Sittingbourne also expanded greatly. Tramways began with a route from Greenwich to Peckham in 1871, and this soon becoming an important method of urban travel within metropolitan Kent and many of the principal coastal towns. During the 1860s the towns of Birchington, Tankerton and Westgate emerged, all railway creations founded on consumer demand. Canterbury Cathedral Archives (CCA) has a good collection of railway records, supplemented by a parish index, for 1835–1901 (CCA: CC-J).

The early watering places of Kent are justly famous. In 1606 Lord North discovered bubbling waters in a distant Weald valley, word of which soon reached London and there commenced a steady stream of visitors to the 'Tonbridge' wells. After the Restoration and its consequent building boom an extensive group of lodging houses, shops and coffee houses appeared, all maintained by a regular coach service which now brought the curious and wealthy down from London in 7 hours on the county's first turnpiked road. Houses were soon being built in several waves to accommodate the increasing numbers, especially after the railway arrived in 1845, amounting almost to a garden suburb with attendant fashionable squares and crescents.

Seaside resorts emerged as Tunbridge Wells' popularity peaked and developed as the spa town waned. Margate came first by two decades, Broadstairs, Deal and Ramsgate in 1754, Dover and Whitstable in 1768, Herne Bay in 1776 and Folkestone, Hythe and Gravesend (popular because of steamboats) by the end of the eighteenth century. Their success was based on the publicised medicinal benefits of sea water, transport developments and consumer demand; all of them offered bathing in sea water as well as the drinking of it, but little else not available at the spa. Herne Bay was planned as a steamboat seaside resort but never got off the ground, as the scattering of Regency buildings shows today. Deal won fashionableness through its importance as a naval station and shipping port of call during the Napoleonic Wars. Hythe and Sandgate gained patronage from officers at Shorncliffe Barracks, an advantage also accorded to Folkestone.

But it was Thanet that gained the lion's share of visitors, and Margate that took the crown, several unique features including the earliest reference to seawater bathing (1736), the perfection of the bathing machine (1753) and the benefits of the Margate Sea Bathing Hospital (1796). Water communications with cheaper fares than road transport guaranteed visitor numbers which included the aristocracy, gentry and clergy, but also by the 1780s more humble members of society began to visit as the sailing packets could accommodate far greater numbers than coaches. It was not long before Margate's pier was built in 1824, to be followed by Deal, Gravesend, Herne Bay and Sheerness in the 1830s, and others a few decades later. In 1851, perhaps unsurprisingly, some 15 per cent of the county population resided in just nine seaside towns. A half-century later Folkestone, Margate and Ramsgate had significantly outgrown all the other resorts.

Restrictions on working hours from the 1840s and the introduction of bank holidays led to increased working class leisure, even if there were initially few theatres except in the resorts and at Canterbury, Chatham and Maidstone. Museums opened at Tunbridge Wells (1836), Dover (1849), Maidstone (1856) and Rochester (1892). The Victorian love of public amenities saw the widespread introduction of swimming baths, libraries, parks, golf courses and the like.

Public unrest was frequently at the mercy of bad harvests, the exporting of wheat in times of shortage and the wartime demands on grain stocks. The typical protest was a food riot, often preceded by grievances being nailed up in public. The Napoleonic Wars of 1793–1815 included severe shortages in 1795–6 and 1799–1801 which coincided with the threat of French invasion. As a consequence urban workers in Maidstone and the Medway towns went on strike because of rising prices and food shortages. Similar causes brought about rural unrest with attacks on mills and outbreaks of arson. The conclusion of war with France resulted in great economic and social distress. In 1830 the 'Swing' riots saw machine-breaking in east Kent, and wage-rioting and the destruction of threshing machines by agricultural labourers widely across the rest of the county, all of which was soon to spread rapidly across southern and eastern England. Mob violence escalated and the military was deployed throughout the county to support local forces of law and order, often with harsh results.

Parishes were hard-pressed to quell such behaviour. Law enforcement lay in the hands of annually elected and unpaid borsholders or petty constables, some large parishes having a high constable in command of them. The borsholders were charged with raising hue and cries and enforcing laws against vagrancy and Sabbath infringements by serving warrants and bringing offenders before magistrates. In some urban areas night watchmen were appointed to similar positions, but they were few in number and often incapable of acting efficiently. By the later 1700s local property owners, despairing at the difficulty and expense of detection, arrest and prosecution, formed associations for the prosecution of felons, and some established their own police forces or patrols. As a result a rudimentary system of policing emerged, organised through the justices at borough and parish level. Punishments included fines, whipping and branding, and prisons were soon full of those awaiting sentencing or execution, together with many debtors.

Until 1831 public executions took place at Penenden Heath near Maidstone, and thereafter in front of Maidstone gaol. The earliest prisons and bridewells were at Canterbury, Dartford, Dover, Maidstone (records 1805–53 at Kent History and Library Centre (KHLC): PC/M) and Rochester, along with several prison hulks on the Thames housing convict labour and future transportees. By the mid-Victorian period there were fifteen county-wide lock-ups with parish constables from Dartford in the north-west to Hythe in the south-east. New county prisons were built at Canterbury in 1808 and at Maidstone in 1812–18. Police stations were commonly built after 1860, usually containing cells. Despite prison reform, there was widespread hard labour and harsh regimes, and little sign of the promised rehabilitation.

The Victorian census returns afford much information. The county population doubled between 1801 and 1851, although with great regional variations. Many parishes had more people in 1850 than in 1900, but in one-third of all parishes there were fewer people in 1900 than in 1850, the most noticeable losses being in the east because of movement from countrysided to town, the seeking of work in the industrial Midlands and north or overseas emigration. Between 1801 and 1861 major towns such as Canterbury, Rochester and Maidstone doubled or trebled in size. Seaside towns generally doubled, with Folkestone and Ramsgate trebling. Industrial towns often trebled or quadrupled, notably Dartford, Gillingham, Gravesend, Sheerness and Sittingbourne. Dormitory and residential towns like Beckenham, Chislehurst and Sevenoaks showed lesser increases, although by 1921 they had all grown prodigiously.

But not everything is on such a scale, and much of the county still retains pristine countryside dotted with tiny villages, farms and churches. If you can trace your origins to such a place, then you may experience views and buildings hardly changed since your ancestors knew them and lived in them. Thanet is wide and open; the Elham Valley green and lush; the north-western marshes empty and windswept; the Wealden villages prosperous and mellow; Romney Marsh a world apart with churches, sheep and sky. And wherever you go Kent's quintessential orchards and farmland still grow hops, apples and cherries in profusion – Mr Pickwick would not be disappointed.

## Bibliography: General History

Armstrong, A., *The economy of Kent, 1640–1914* (1995)

Armstrong, J.B. and Hopkins, P.G.M., *Local studies* (1955)

Aston, M. and Bond, J., *The landscape of towns* (1987)

Banks, F.R., *English villages* (1963)

Baring Gould, S., *Old country life* (1913)

Beresford, M., *The lost villages of England* (1954)

——, *History on the ground* (1957)

Bettey, J.H., *Church and parish: a guide for local historians* (1987)

Bloomfield, P., *Kent and the Napoleonic Wars* (1987)

Blythe, R., *Akenfield: portrait of an English village* (1969)

Camden, W., *Britannia: Kent*, ed. G.J. Copley (1977)

Chalklin, C.W., *Seventeenth-century Kent: a social and economic history* (1978)

Clark, P., *The English alehouse, a social history 1200–1830* (1983)

Crowther, M.A., *The workhouse system, 1834–1929* (1981)

Currie, C.R.J. and Lewis, C.P. (eds), *A guide to English county histories* (1994)

East, G.N., *Geography behind history* (1938)

Elton, G.R., *The sources of history: England 1200–1640* (1976)

Finberg, H.P.R., *The local historian and his theme* (1952)

Finberg, J., *Exploring villages* (1958)

Fowler, S., *The workhouse: the people, the places, the life behind doors* (2014)

Friar, S., *The local history companion* (2001)

Fussell, G.E., *The English rural labourer* (1949)

Galbraith, V.H., *The historian at work* (1962)

Gasquet, A., *Parish life in mediaeval England* (1907)

Gaunt, W., *English rural life in the eighteenth century* (1925)

Glass, D.V. (ed.), *Social mobility in Britain* (1954)

Greenwood, C., *County of Kent* (1838)

Harris, J., *The history of Kent in five parts* (1719)

Hart, A.T., *The country priest in English history* (1959)

Hasted, E., *The history and topographical survey of the county of Kent* (2nd edn 1797–1801, repr. 1972)

Hobsbawm, E.J, *Labouring men* (1964)

Hoskins, W.G., *The making of the English landscape* (rev. edn 1981)

——, *Fieldwork in local history* (2nd edn 1982)

——, *Local history in England* (3rd edn 1984)

——, *The English family 1450–1700* (1984)

Howarth, K., *Oral history, a handbook* (1998)

Ingram, M., *Church courts, sex and marriage in England 1570–1640* (1987)

Jenkins, R.C., *Canterbury (a history of the diocese)* (1880)

Jessup, F.W., *Kent history illustrated* (2nd edn 1973)

——, *The history of Kent: a select bibliography* (2nd edn 1974)

——, *A history of Kent* (rev. edn 1995)

Jones, A., *A thousand years of the English parish* (2000)

Kilburne, R., *A topographie, or survey, of the county of Kent* (1659)

Lambarde, W., *A perambulation of Kent* (1576, repr. 1970)

Laslett, P., *Introduction to historical demography* (1966)

——, *The world we have lost – further explored* (3rd edn 1983)

——, Eversley, D.E.C. and Armstrong, W.A., *An introduction to English historical demography*, ed. E.A. Wrigley (1966)

Lawson, T. and Killingray, D., *An historical atlas of Kent* (2004)

Leslie, G.R., *The family in social context* (1967)

Litten, J., *The English way of death: the common funeral since 1450* (1991)

Marshall, D., *English poor in the eighteenth century* (1926)

May, T., *The Victorian domestic servant* (1999)

Mee, A., *Kent* (1936)

Melling, E. (ed.), *Kentish sources IV. The poor* (1964)

Menefee, S.P., *Wives for sale: an ethnographic study of British popular divorce* (1981)

Meredith, H.O., *Economic history of England* (1949)

Mitchell, J.B., *Historical geography* (1954)

Nissel, M., *People count: a history of the General Register Office* (1987)

Oliver, G., *Photographs and local history* (1989)

Oppenheimer, S., *The origins of the British: a genealogical detective story* (2006)

Owen, D.E., *English philanthropy 1660–1960* (1965)

Pakington, H., *English villages and hamlets* (1936)

Philipott, T., *Villare Cantianum* (1659)

Pike, W.T. (ed.), *Kent at the opening of the twentieth century: contemporary biographies* (1904)

Pine, L.G., *The story of titles* (1969)

Poole, R.L., *Mediaeval reckonings of time* (1918)

Pounds, N.J.G., *A history of the English parish: the culture of religion from Augustine to Victoria* (2000)

Prescott, E., *The English mediaeval hospital 1050–1640* (1992)

Pugh, R.B., *How to write a parish history* (6th edn 1954)

Ribton-Turner, C.J., *History of vagrants and vagrancy* (1887)

Roberts, B.K., *Making of the English village* (1987)

Rose, M., *The English poor law 1780–1930* (1971)

Russell, J.C., *British mediaeval population* (1948)

Russell-Smith, J., *Bibliotheca Cantiana or Antiquarian Kentish books* (1836, repr. 1980)

Simpson, A.W.B., *An introduction to the history of land law* (1961)

Slack, P., *The English poor law 1531–1782* (1990)

Stafford, F. and Yates, N., *The later Kentish seaside, 1840–1974* (1985)

Tait, J., *The English borough: studies on its origins and constitutional history* (1936)

Tate, W.E., *The English village community and the enclosure movements* (1967)

Thompson, E.P., *The making of the English working class* (1963)

Trevelyan, G.M., *English social history* (1944)

Victoria County History, *Kent*, 3 vols (1908–32)

Walton, J.K., *The English seaside resort: a social history 1750–1914* (1983)

Watts, M.R., *The chapel and the nation* (1996)

Weaver, F.J., *Material of English history* (1938)

*Who's who in Kent* (1935)

Whyman, J., *The early Kentish seaside 1736–1840* (1985)

Winchester, A., *Discovering parish boundaries* (1990)

Wrigley, E.A. (ed.), *An introduction to historical demography* (1966)

Yates, N., *Kent and the Oxford Movement* (1983)

——, Hume, R. and Hastings, P., *Religion and society in Kent, 1640–1914* (1994)

Zell, M., *Industry in the countryside: Wealden society in the sixteenth century* (1994)

——, *Early modern Kent 1540–1640* (2000)

# Chapter 1

# PRELIMINARIES

## A. GENEALOGICAL INTRODUCTION

The description of genealogy as 'the other oldest profession' is worth a moment's thought: the Bible is full of pedigrees, some very long indeed (far longer than most people could ever hope to construct!) and considerably older than the Greek and Roman courtesans who may be the source of this much-quoted phrase. Everybody has ancestors and all names are old, but this is no guarantee of tracing the original bearers. With luck and skill a very few English pedigrees may be taken back to the Norman Conquest or even a little before, but for the majority of people the sober conclusion will soon be reached that a large proportion of ancestors cannot be traced with any *certainty* much before the Tudor period, or even the English Civil War – a colourful pedigree chart may look resplendent hanging over a fireplace, but is every generation forged as an unbreakable link in a cast-iron chain?

Does the line relate to your surname but not your family? The irony of English genealogy is that many records used today in research were not created for that specific purpose: we constantly assume and infer that what we see is what we need, but how many family trees would stand up in a court of law where proof beyond all reasonable doubt would be the key to acceptance? The other unpalatable fact of English genealogy is that too many surnames are too common – what you think (and hope) is unusual and easily traceable may lie thick on the ground in a small area, and this allied with the conservatism of English forenames means that disentangling two or three families, sometimes in a single parish, may sometimes prove daunting, if not impossible.

Most people are fascinated by the meanings of both place names and surnames, the former being generally in existence from the Anglo-Saxon period, the latter settled on individuals by about the fourteenth century. There are many books and dictionaries on both types, but the subject is a fluid one and not too long out of its infancy. Some place names are easily understood but many are not and are open to multiple interpretations in the all-too-common want of sufficiently early written sources. The Domesday Book may help you, but in truth it is not always really early enough, so you may need to look for an Anglo-Saxon deed or charter of a few centuries earlier (the earliest written reference being always the most meaningful), which might show that two places spelled the same today were quite different a millennium ago.

The majority of surnames arose from: (1) place names (Kent, Wood, Field); (2) occupations (Butcher, Chapman, Smith); (3) relationships (Williamson, Fathers, Brotherhood); and (4) nicknames (Wise, Strong, Redhead), but there are thousands of others that defy neat classification and for which the jury may be out for much longer, pending more research into mediaeval sources. It can be dangerous to assume that similar spellings relate to the same surname or that people with the same surname in the same parish must be related – names can arise independently within a small geographical area. Early Norman-French names might change from Batteleur to Butler, or be translated from Le Blanc to White or from De La Rue to Street.

Negatives aside, the subject of genealogy is a rich and fascinating one, taking in social and economic history, geography, topography, heraldry and much else. It is difficult not to learn much as you trace back from one generation to the next, your knowledge of the English counties and their layouts will grow, and your carefully gathered ancestors begin to fit into them. You will soon learn not to move too fast, not to confuse individuals with similar names, and that in counting back 20 generations (that is, about 600 years) from yourself gives a theoretical 1,000,000+ ancestors, perhaps the equivalent of the entire fourteenth-century population of England. If you consult maps (and not just parish ones) and know the lie of the land you may apprehend that a mountain range has interposed itself into the assumed travels of your early ancestors.

Names, dates and place are the genealogist's mainstay and you will ask many hundreds of times where someone was born or married or died. It is perhaps ironic that many people today are unsure of these basic facts, even for their own parents, as evidenced by information on modern death certificates. Monied and landed people left more records behind them, but much genealogy is about the agricultural poor and no less interesting to investigate. A surname may prove to be not English and involve a sudden change of direction in searching. The whole business is fascinating and frustrating by turns. No pedigree chart is ever complete, and the construction of it should involve the most rigorous analysis and detective work, always bearing in mind that we may generally be able to discover what someone did, but not how or why – for example, how did future married couples meet and why did some families often keep moving?

England has not been invaded since 1066, and consequently has an extremely rich heritage of historical documents. The purpose of this book is to introduce you to a large range of Kentish sources, where they are kept and how they may be interpreted. Civil registration, the census and probate records will get you going, but they cannot always offer a guarantee of success, even back to the earlier Victorian age, and especially if we take into account the ever-present human faults of vanity and deception. We must always work from the known to the unknown, so do not start with your great-grandfather unless you have *indisputable* documentary evidence that he is your relation, for otherwise your genealogical house may be built on sand – did he adopt your grandfather and then silently conceal the fact so that his 'son' was blissfully unaware of it? And even then, we must occasionally beware the concrete information of certificates which at the point of registration was accepted as truth without verification. The future may have similar problems: in the 1990s some 18,000 babies were born in the UK by the *in vitro* process, most of whom do not and may not ever know the true identity of one or both of their natural parents, facts that neither civil registration nor any other public record will disclose.

Adoption can be tricky as there was no formal adoption process before 1927, and the term often meant guardianship or fostering. From that year the special General Register Office (GRO) indexes cover all legal adoptions as recorded in the Adopted Children's Register. Certificates give the child's date of birth and the adoptive parents' names but not the original birth forename or surname.

Changes of adult name are common, especially for immigrants who sometimes anglicised a foreign name but equally often took an entirely new one. No formality was necessary, but if proof was required, a deed poll was executed and lodged at court as a permanent record. These are indexed under the former name only, 1851–1903 (TNA: C 275), and under former and new name, 1903–2003 (TNA: J 18). Other name changes may be found in W.P. Phillimore and E.A. Fry, *An index to changes of name for the United Kingdom and Ireland … 1760–1901*, and perhaps also in the *London Gazette* or *The Times* newspaper.

The last two decades have seen an extraordinary revolution in the way people now conduct research, an explosion of indexes and the digitisation of vast amounts of records. This has sometimes brought mixed benefits in a surfeit of data. The days are long gone when desperate attempts were made to locate a family event as close as possible to a census year in the hope that the corresponding certificate would lead to success in the census. Now, in complete contrast, a census index may throw up many possible candidates, some of which may require the most careful handling to achieve positive identification. Nobody will dispute the extreme utility of an index, but few indexes indeed are complete. Is there a description of the purported contents? Does a transcript or index of a parish register alert you to missing years? It is now far less easy to ascertain quickly that, for example, the 1841 census returns of Herne Bay, Seasalter, Swalecliffe and Whitstable have not survived; in the absence of this knowledge and if your online search was negative, what would you assume about your quarry with a common name? Would another entry in Faversham or Canterbury fit the bill as the nearest thing and perhaps lead to the wrong death certificate?

Are you descended from royalty? The great genealogist and herald Anthony Wagner made a study of so-called 'gateway ancestors', that is, descendants of royalty who had so many descendants themselves that the blood was inevitably spread ever thinner and down to commoners. Against this is human vanity and the lengths to which some will go (including the forging of documents) to prove descent from royalty or nobility, some such spurious pedigrees appearing in early genealogical journals and books. Detailed pedigrees of British monarchs appear in *Burke's Peerage* and *Burke's Guide to the Royal Family*, and while some 50,000 legitimate descendants of Edward III are well documented, the world of mediaeval genealogy is still one where caution should be a byword, pending the discovery of new records and the more rigorous examination of existing ones.

You may be on slightly firmer ground with the peerage, as the wealth and importance of many families could vary enormously over time. Younger sons of a peer were frequently impecunious in comparison with elder siblings, and their sons and grandsons might have been farmers or in trade. *Debrett's Peerage* is more accurate than *Burke's Peerage*, the latter having relied on family information, but both should be used and compared. Innumerable marriages of younger sons and daughters of peers result in large numbers of commoners in the pedigrees, and so the chance of finding a link is perhaps quite high, but even then must be subject to rigorous verification as source material is rarely given. A better hope may lie in a descent from the gentry, or county families with no title. They are listed in *Burke's Landed Gentry of Great Britain*, and although most editions are unindexed, later ones are now searchable on subscription websites. All baronets created between the foundation of the order in 1611 and 1800 will be found in Cokayne's *The complete baronetage*, but as the knights are less well covered, see also Shaw's *Knights of England*.

---

**ORR** ( *formerly* **GODFREY-FAUSSETT-OSBORNE)**
**OF HARTLIP PLACE**

HELEN JOAN, MRS. ORR, of Hartlip Place, Kent. ; *b*. 14 June, 1908, *m*. 13 Oct. 1932, ●Lt.-Col. Oswald James Ritchie Orr, O.B.E., R.E., only son of late Oswald Scott Orr, of St. Andrews, Fife, and has issue,

●BRYAN JAMES GODFREY, *b*. 19 Jan. 1942.
●Sarah Alice Joan, *b*. 2 Aug. 1937.

**Lineage** (of OSBORNE)—The earliest of the records now preserved at Hartlip are the wills of Thomas Usberne, of Upchurch (1453), of his son and heir William Osborne, of Hartlip, and of Leysdon and Eastchurch, in Sheppey, and of Alicia his wife (dated 1433 and 1464), William appears by his wills to have been possessed of his Sheppey estates before inheriting those of Hartlip, to which he probably succeeded on the death of the above-mentioned Thomas.

THOMAS OSBORNE, of Hartlip, son and heir of the above William and Alicia (will dated 1534), was father, by Agnes his wife (*d*. 1543), of, *inter alios*,

1. JOHN, his heir, of whom presently.
2. William, whose son Stephen Osborne, of the manor of Nutts, in Leysdown, Sheppey, *d*. 1582, leaving a son and heir, John Osborne, of Nutts, who by his wife, Jane, dau. of Thomas Cobbe of Chilham, Kent, was father of
   1. Thomas, of Nutts, his heir, *m*. Margaret, yst. dau. of Sir Samuel Peyton, Bt., of Knowlton, Kent (*see* BURKE's *Extinct Baronetcies*), and *d.s.p.*
   2. William, whose son, John Osborne (who *d.s.p.*), conveyed the estate of Nutts to his sister's husband, Gilbert Brandons, 1661 (the Sheppey branch thus becomes extinct).

The eldest son,
JOHN OSBORNE, of Hartlip Place (or Place House) was Auditor of Exchequer in reigns of KING HENRY VIII, and QUEEN ELIZABETH, obtained a grant of Arms from Clarenceux King of Arms 1573. He *m*. Catherine, dau. of John London, of Graveney, Kent, and *d*. 1577, when he was *s*. by his son,
JOHN OSBORNE, who obtained a grant of arms from Clarenceux 1573 ; *m*. 1stly, Francisca, dau. of Valentine Everard, of Sarre, Kent ; 2ndly, Anna, dau. of Edmund Bardolfe, of Rattamstede, Herts ; and 3rdly, Mary, widow of — Gilbert. He *d*. 1588, and was *s*. by his son
EDWARD OSBORNE, of Hartlip Place, *m*. 1611, Marie, dau. and heiress of Robert Denne, of Denne Hill, Kent, and *d*. 1645, leaving, with other issue, his heir,
JOHN OSBORNE, of Hartlip Place, and Dane House, Hartlip, also latterly of Maidstone, who *d*. 1663, and was *s*. by his son,
THOMAS OSBORNE, Major in the Militia, who *d*. 1738, and was *s*. by his son,
THOMAS OSBORNE, who *d.s.p.* 1719, leaving his two sisters, co-heiresses,

THOMAS OSBORNE, who *d.s.p.* 1719, leaving his two sisters, co-heiresses, Mary, *m*. Rev. R. Milway, Vicar of Borden, Kent, who inherited, and soon alienated the estate of Dane House ; and Elizabeth, *m*. Richard Tylden, of Milsted, Kent, who inherited the estate of Hartlip Place, which she devised to her dau., MARY wife of the REV. THOMAS BLAND, whose son, WILLIAM BLAND, of Hartlip Place, *m*. Elizabeth, dau. of Rev. Bryan Faussett, of Heppington, Kent ; M.A., F.S.A., Fell. of All Souls, Oxford (*see* GODFREY-FAUSSETT *formerly of Heppington*), by whom he left an only son, WILLIAM BLAND, of Hartlip Place, *m*. 1stly, Sarah, dau. of Rev. Ralph Price, Rector of Lyminge, Kent, by whom he had a son, William Osborne, and a dau., Albinia Jane, who both *d*. young ; and 2ndly, Isabella, dau. of Gen. Irvine, of the family of IRVINE of Drum. Mr. Bland *d*. without surviving issue 1869, aged 81, and devised his estate to his cousin,
THE REV. HENRY GODFREY GODFREY-FAUSSETT-OSBORNE, of Hartlip Place, Vicar of Littleton, and Rural Dean of Evesham, Worcs, and a Magistrate for that co., 3rd son of the Rev. Godfrey Faussett, D.D., of Heppington (*see* GODFREY-FAUSSETT *formerly of Heppington*), assumed in 1871, the additional surname of OSBORNE ; *b*. 1824, *m*. 1854, Helen Melville (*d*. 7 May, 1913), dau. of Rev. Edwin Sandys-Lumsdaine, of Lumsdaine (*see that family*, 1937 Edn.), and *d*. 1878, having had issue,
1. Henry Fermor Godfrey, *b*. and *d*. 1855.
2. HENRY BRYAN GODFREY, of whom presently.
1. Helen Mary Godfrey, *m*. 29 Oct. 1891, Major James Andrew Colvile Wedderburn-Maxwell, of Glenlair, Dalbeattie, late 54th Regt. and Bengal Staff Corps, and *d*. 20 July, 1946, having issue (*see that family*). He *d*. 28 Dec. 1917.
2. Margaret Lilias Godfrey, *m*. 15 Feb. 1900, Col. Walter Russell, R.E., yst. son of Francis Russell, of The Red House, Wateringbury, Kent, and *d*. 2 Jan. 1931. He *d*. 4 April, 1917.
3. Maud Isabel Godfrey, *m*. 30 April, 1889, Hubert Hector John Wix, son of Rev. Joseph Wix, of Guildford Lodge, Watford, and formerly Vicar of Littlebury, nr. Saffron Walden, Essex, and *d*. 24 March, 1947. He *d*. 29 Nov. 1942.
4.●Cicely Mabel Godfrey (*Petty Place, Hartlip, nr. Sittingbourne, Kent*).

The surv. son,
HENRY BRYAN GODFREY GODFREY-FAUSSETT-OSBORNE, of Hartlip Place, Kent, District Probate Registrar at Lichfield 1904–29 ; *b*. 1 April, 1865, *educ*. Charterhouse, and Ch. Ch. Oxford (M.A. 1891), *m*. 26 April, 1906, ●Margaret Sydney (*Place Stables, Hartlip, nr. Sittingbourne, Kent*), eldest dau. of Charles Bourns, of West Hill, Oxted, and *d*. 4 Oct. 1945, leaving issue,
1.●HELEN JOAN, of whom we treat.
2.●Kathleen Margaret (7, *Mall Studios, N.W.*3) ; *b*. 27 Sept. 1911, *m*. 20 May, 1940, Edward Morland Lewis, son of late Benjamin Archibald Lewis, of Undercliff, Ferryside, Carmarthenshire. He *d*. 4 Aug. 1943.
3.●Elizabeth Ann, *b*. 11 Nov. 1912, *m*. 28 April, 1937, ●Major Richard Hubert Sams, R.E. (ret.) (*Firbeck, Tester Park, Chislehurst, Kent*), son of Sir Hubert Arthur Sams, C.I.E., of 20, Boyne Park, Tunbridge Wells, Kent, and has issue, two daus.
4.●Diana Cicely, *b*. 19 Sept. 1915, *m*. 24 Feb. 1940, ●Lt.-Col. John Theodore Stevenson Tutton, O.B.E., R.E. (47, *Maidstone Road, Chatham, Kent*), son of late Dr. Alfred E. H. Tutton, F.R.S., D.Sc., of Yew Arch, Dallington, Sussex, and has issue, two daus.
**Seat**—Hartlip Place, nr. Sittingbourne, Kent. **Residence**—Queendown Warren, nr. Sittingbourne, Kent.

*A printed pedigree: a valuable overview of six centuries, but all sources must be carefully checked.*

Tempting as rapid online searches are, it is one of the great genealogical truths that nothing can replace an examination of the original document, which may reveal further unindexed information, valuable marginalia or even handwriting on the back, all overlooked or discarded in the copying process. A personal story here: over many months a long series of Tudor parchment documents at The National Archives (TNA) had been searched for the origins of John Smith, merchant of London, without any success until when packing up the final membrane a short note on the back was spotted which declared that this 'had been prepared for John Smith Esq, merchant, late of Exeter, Devon'. Let the searcher beware. So use indexes, whether printed or online, but with great care, and indeed you may well find something that would never otherwise have come to light.

Always check what may be available in print before searching. Other than the many standard reference works itemised in this book, countless individuals and societies have produced many valuable works, often backed up with the benefit of local knowledge to overcome handwriting and other problems. Online family trees are now widespread, but will you content yourself with another's work without testing it for yourself?

## Bibliography
There are many excellent recent books on genealogy, some the first of their type on a particular subject, but also a good number of earlier classics that have yet to be superseded (and often reprinted or revised). Books on individual parishes, towns and villages are now legion and must be looked for separately.

First I will list two works that are outstanding and deserve to be thoroughly known in every way as constant companions. Steel has an excellent bibliography which includes many valuable articles, and Smith and Gardner have various recommendations for research procedures, all born of long and wise practice.

Steel, D.J. (ed.), *National index of parish registers: Vol. I. General sources of births, marriages and deaths before 1837* (3rd edn 1976);
*Vol. II. Sources for nonconformist genealogy and family history* (1973);
*Vol. III. Sources for Roman Catholic, Jewish genealogy and family history* (1974);
*Vol. IV. South East England: Kent, Surrey and Sussex* (1980)

Gardner, D.E. and Smith, F., *Genealogical research in England and Wales*, 3 vols (1956–64)

The publisher Phillimore has for many years produced numerous splendid books on all aspects of genealogy and local history, and the company's catalogue is always informative reading. The excellent series produced by the Society of Genealogists (SOG) (various authors and editions) entitled *My Ancestor was a [ . . .] how can I find out more about him?* now stretches to nearly thirty titles, and is of a predictably high and consistent standard.

## GENERAL WORKS

Adolph, A., *Tracing your aristocratic ancestors* (2013)
Bevan, A., *Tracing your ancestors in the National Archives* (7th edn 2006)
Brown, J., *Tracing your rural ancestors: a guide for family historians* (2011)
Burlison, R., *Tracing your pauper ancestors: a guide for family historians* (2009)
Camp, A.J., *Tracing your ancestors* (1972)
——, *Everyone has roots* (1978)
——, *First steps in family history* (3rd edn 1998)
—— and Spufford, P., *The genealogists' handbook* (1969)
Chambers, P., *Mediaeval genealogy: how to find your mediaeval ancestors* (2005)
Cole, J.A. and Titford, J., *Tracing your family tree* (4th edn 2002)
Currer-Briggs, N. and Gambier, R., *Debrett's family historian: a guide to tracing your ancestry* (1981)
Fitzhugh, T., *How to write a family history* (1988)
Hamilton-Edwards, G.K., *In search of ancestry* (4th edn 1983)
Hawkings, D., *Pauper ancestors* (2011)
Iredale, D., *Your family tree* (1970)
Merriman, B.D., *Genealogical standards of evidence* (2010)
Outhwaite, R.B., *Clandestine marriage in England 1500–1800* (1995)
Owen, D.M., *The records of the established church in England excluding parochial records* (1970)
Palgrave-Moore, P., *How to record your family tree* (1991)
Pelling, G., *Beginning your family history* (7th edn 1998)
Rogers, C.D., *Tracing missing persons* (1986)
—— , *The family tree detective* (3rd edn 1998)

—— and Smith, J.H., *Local family history in England 1538–1914* (1991)
Scheinfeld, A., *You and heredity* (1952)
Smith, D., *Social networking for genealogists* (2009)
Steel, D.J., *Discovering your family history* (rev. edn 1986)
—— and Taylor, L., *Family history in focus* (1984)
Wagner, A., *English ancestry* (1961)
——, *Pedigrees and progress: essays in the genealogical interpretation of history* (1975)
——, *English genealogy* (1983)
Whitehall, G., *The fine art of tracing your artist ancestors* (2004)
Wood, T., *An introduction to civil registration* (1994)

JOURNALS
*Amateur Historian* (1952–date)
*Archaeologia Cantiana* (1858–date)
*Bygone Kent* (1979–date)
*Coat of Arms* (1950–date)
*Collectanea Topographica et Genealogica* (1834–43)
*Family History* (1962–date)
*Gentlemen's Magazine* (1731–1868)
*Herald and Genealogist* (1863–74)
*Heraldry Gazette* (1957–date)
*History Today* (1951–date)
*Index Library* (1888–date)
*Journal of Kent History* (1975–date)
*Journal of the Society of Archivists* (1955–date)
*Kent Archaelogical Review* (1975–date)
*Kent Life* (1962–date)
*Kent Recusant History Journal* (1979–date)
*Local Population Studies* (1968–date)
*London Gazette* (1665–date)
*Miscellanea Genealogica et Heraldica* (1886–1938)
*Monumental Brass Society, Transactions* (1887–1914; 1935–date)
*Notes & Queries* (1849–date)
*Population Studies* (1947–date)
*The Ancestor* (1902–5)
*The Genealogical Magazine* (1897–1904)
*The Genealogist* (1877–1922)

*The Genealogists' Magazine* (1925–date)
*The Indexer* (1958–date)
*The Local Historian* (1952–date)
*Topographer and Genealogist* (1846–58)

## B. GETTING STARTED

Chance plays a hand in all genealogical research and needs to be encountered to be appreciated. My ancestor Francis Wright died in Limehouse in 1859, so only one census would reveal his birthplace, actually 150 miles away; he was indeed found in the 1851 census (after a three-month search!), but if he had died in 1850, the pedigree would have been quite blocked. Success depends on various things: an uncommon surname is a great help; a family staying in one place for many generations; better-off people owning land or property; and the survival of the necessary records.

*An original birth certificate: this copy for my paternal great-grandmother was issued on the day the birth was registered and shows the father's original signature.*

You may wish to investigate a single colourful individual about whom there are family stories, or perhaps an uncle who disappeared as a young man, but let us assume the more usual path, that is, either the maternal or paternal line, one of which is more than enough to start with. Whoever it is, try to set them in their historical context and be aware of events that may have affected their lives. Did they emigrate or immigrate, and if so, why? Is the surname a tidied up variant of an original foreign one or one that has been completely changed for reasons as yet unknown? Set as much as you know at the start on a sheet of A4, perhaps separating the definite in ink from the possible in pencil and be prepared to change it frequently or even to start all over again. The speculations of one generation as to their relationships and claims become the fixed traditions of the next, so start with certain information, that is, yourself. The convinced descendant has an answer for everything, but the researcher who approaches his quarry with an open mind and a desire for the truth, whatever it may be, will learn much about not only the past but also about the present. Listen carefully to what relatives tell you, but bear in mind that falsehoods may be repeated in all good faith: double-check everything as far as is possible.

It will be helpful to be clear about standard family relationships such as step-relations, second cousins and half-siblings. A generation works out fairly consistently at thirty years: is every ancestor on your tree old enough to have produced a child of the next generation? Have you conflated two generations because of problems with individuals' ages or similar names? Women usually had their last child at about 43, but men could become fathers at 80. John William Goodall, a London GPO clerk, was born in 1816 and by his first wife had eight children before she died at 69; he then remarried at 70 to a second wife thirty-five years his junior by whom he had five more children. At his death his eldest child was 62 and his youngest just five months, that baby having been born to a father of 82. (An extraordinary but well-documented case, and one of the most interesting in the author's files.)

You will probably know in advance if a coat of arms is attached to your ancestors, but even so, ensure it is for your family and not just for the surname. Professionals of the clergy, the law and the services are often much easier to trace; before the 1820s there were only the two English universities of Oxford and Cambridge, the alumni of which have long been in print. Never forget that families could fall as well as rise on the social scale, perhaps several times in each direction. In general the survival of English records has been far better in the south than in the north, and as this book will show, Kent is richly supplied with historical sources.

Surnames became hereditary in England by about 1400, as a glance at the list of incumbents in any parish church will show. In general, people are fascinated by the origins of personal and place names, but rush too quickly to find a meaning in them. Whilst many place names fall into large and broad patterns with repetitive common elements and meanings that are fairly securely understood, a very different situation applies with surnames, where some of the established early works and dictionaries are now beginning to show cracks in their scholarship. If you must, be prepared to accept a working hypothesis for a surname origin, but never forget that far too often the essential earliest written sources simply do not exist to offer any certainty.

It is human nature to simplify and tidy up with the passage of time, often making an unusual word resemble another familiar one. Marriage Farm near Wye, for example, has nothing to do with matrimony but hides the much earlier Anglo-Saxon description of 'boundary ridge' – anyone walking in that part of the North Downs will easily see why.

England is common in uncommon surnames, and the meanings of a proportion of them are unlikely ever to be fully ascertained. That said, unusual forenames or surnames are a distinct boon to the genealogist and will jump out of indexes and other sources. A common practice is to find a woman's maiden name given to her children as a first or subsequent forename. While this is a good general indicator, it is far from infallible and can be dangerous. The artist Turner's second forename of Mallord was actually that of his godparents, and my grandfather's middle name of Wye was the surname of family friends rather than showing any blood relationships or geographical connections with that small Kent town. Children's middle names occasionally commemorate more distant family surnames, perhaps several generations back, but the instances are few and far between. Never forget that surnames before about 1700 are far more fluid than you might imagine, and aliases abound in both the rich and the poor, sometimes because of remarriage, adoption or illegitimacy. Double-barrelled surnames appear from the later 1700s (not always with a hyphen), and along with complete changes of surname were assumed in order to gain an inheritance or property. A tablet in Godmersham church commemorating Edward Knight, Jane Austen's unmarried brother, amply proves this point.

Is your Latin up to scratch? It is an unavoidable fact that as you go back in time the more likely it is that English will disappear, and indeed it was not until 1733 that Latin was abolished for most official records (wills being a major exception). A basic working knowledge of Latin is greatly to be recommended and will get you out of all kinds of scrapes, given that many records are repetitive and written to a standard formula. This together with the fact that the earlier the record the more clearly it is likely to be written will allow you to attack Norman charters and similar material with some confidence – the art of 'diplomatic', or knowing in advance what is likely to appear being an ever-constant companion. A few days' work with photographs of documents and accompanying transcriptions will improve your skills immeasurably.

But even if your document is in English, can you read it with certainty? The English secretary hand was in common usage for the best part of two centuries before giving way to the modern 'round' hand in the later 1600s; it is not always easy to read, especially if written in a hurried cursive way, but again, practice with documents and transcripts will bring a good degree of confidence quite quickly. Thereafter it should be fairly straightforward, but some of the artificial and crabbed law and chancery hands that survived well into the 1800s can be exasperating; and most people will have experienced diabolical Victorian handwriting and the tricky and confusing pairs of copperplate capital letters. Bad handwriting is a mark of 'civilisation' and is most certainly still with us.

Has your family tree already been worked on by another relative or published somewhere? The SOG has huge collections of deposited pedigrees as well as many thousands of members' birth briefs. Many family history societies, including Kent, publish members' interests in their journals. One-name studies are immensely popular and the main Guild of One Name Studies (GOONS) society publishes an annual register of surnames being studied. Such well-known books as *Debrett's* and *Burke's* will most certainly include ample information on the aristocracy, and *Who's Who* and the *ODNB* are always good for potted biographies. The army, navy and air force have long published annual volumes of their members, and the early heralds' visitations are also in print. Victorian street and trade directories are very useful for locating your (slightly better off) ancestors. Do be aware that many published pedigrees in the nineteenth century were researched for people who paid for this service, and therefore inconvenient facts such as illegitimacy may have been ignored, or the names, dates and status of some people quietly changed. Many family history societies have collections of members' deposited charts and trees, and CCA has a large run of files of surname interests. Keep up to date as well by subscribing to one of the popular family history magazines.

Social history is another fascinating subject, and inextricably linked to our ancestors' lives as we follow them from parish to parish and generation to generation. Knowing a little about the ages at which people married and died, how they were affected by disasters such as epidemics and harvest failure, an overview of English history will add colour and realism to your work and avoid the uncomfortable feeling of searching in a vacuum. The valuable maxim 'history is meaningless without geography' should never be forgotten. Walk around your ancestral parish, get the lie of the land, the roads and lanes, the principal buildings and the neighbouring parishes; is the church well out of the centre, perhaps meaning that your ancestors may have attended one in the next parish because it was a shorter walk? The UK is rich in museums and study centres, both large and small, general and specialised. Even if they have nothing genealogical, there will almost certainly be material relating to a town, village or neighbourhood, local occupations and perhaps even individual lives.

*A family wedding: Charles Wright, my oldest great-uncle, was married at Boulder, Western Australia, in 1900.*

Let us return to our sheet of A4. Have you started with yourself by noting birth and marriage, education, employment, hobbies and so on? Better still, write a short autobiography and file it for future generations; and better even than that, make your own will now and record in it the names and birth details of at least yourself, your siblings and your parents. Now sketch out what you can of family members, both living and deceased, and follow up by sending questionnaires to the more distant ones. Talk to as many of them as you can and ask to see birth, marriage and death certificates, not forgetting to note down other snippets as they are mentioned. If your grandfather had a common name, it may be difficult to isolate the correct birth entry if the location is not certain; is one of his brothers or sisters still alive, perhaps with a more unusual name, to help? Older women tend to know a great deal; my grandfather's last sister, a fifteenth child, had an exceptional memory and helped with who had remained unmarried or died young, thereby saving much time on long marriage and death searches. Her two eldest brothers had gone to Australia before she was born, which explained gaps in family photographs. She also knew everybody's full names – a common stumbling block when so many people use nicknames or not their first given name.

Photographs are essential to any family history; perhaps you may see a strong resemblance between yourself and an eminent Victorian? The tragedy today is that so many earlier ones contain unidentifiable people, even if they can be fairly accurately dated by clothing styles. Make every effort to show yours to as many relatives as possible, and bear in mind that there may be friends or strangers in the groups as well. My just-mentioned great-aunt looked after all our family photos, and before I was 15 I had sat often at her knee and got her to write down on the reverse all that she knew – something for which I shall always be eternally grateful.

All kinds of other items may surface if family members are approached, any of which may throw up a valuable clue and avoid much speculative searching: correspondence between future married couples, copies of family wills, funeral expenses and accounts, identity cards, ration books, weddings and obituaries from local newspapers, military medals, employment records and perhaps even a family Bible, which may well record births, marriages and deaths back to the early 1800s, but beware here as surnames are sometimes

*Family memorabilia: souvenirs of my great-grandfather, Charles Elvy Wright.*

difficult to disentangle and may represent a cousin line rather than the direct one.

As a rule, older people enjoy talking about their earlier life, schooling, aunts and uncles and grandparents and so on. Once they have started, you may be hard-pressed to write down everything you are told, but questions such as did anybody marry twice, was there a family accent and where was someone buried may reveal great truths – the last of these three can be highly important as death certificates offer no clues, although family funeral cards can be useful here. You may also learn of relatives who have disappeared – lost in a war, emigrated or whose whereabouts are simply unknown, perhaps because of a change of name. Huge social mobility in the last half-century has meant that it is now often trickier to find the living than the dead, especially as family moves across several counties, perhaps over hundreds of miles, or even to another continent are now a commonplace; despite living in an age of information overload, many people are often hard-pressed to locate even first cousins.

In the orderly rush to trace the dead, do not forget the living. This type of research can be equally demanding: many people have lost touch with cousins who may now be scattered around the world, but the best family trees should strive for absolute completeness, even if coming down to the present may be decidedly more difficult than tracing backwards. Such databases as civil registration, probate records, electoral registers, street and telephone directories, and then perhaps online media should comprise the first sequence of your investigations.

Your initial investigations and results may suddenly overwhelm you in their volume and complexity. Have you quoted or paraphrased? Is everything legibly recorded and the source noted in case you need to go back and check something which is unclear? Filing and indexing are essential and far easier if you stick to one ancestral line at a time, old-fashioned card indexes still being extremely useful for this purpose.

It is now perhaps time to draw up the first working family tree in order to assess what has been found and what remains unknown. The traditional type, and perhaps the easiest to comprehend, is the drop-chart where you are at the foot, your parents above you and so on. All charts soon become overcrowded (I'm thinking of my grandfather's fourteen siblings) and you will have to rewrite onto a larger one or start separating branches or generations (or even individuals) and cross-reference them to another sheet. In the early stages small groups of people only on a chart are far easier to comprehend – your 10ft full pedigree chart is still far off!

One other popular type of chart is called a *seize quartiers*, or one where you display yourself, your parents and so on back to your sixteen great-great-grandparents without any intervening brothers and sisters. Here you would strictly record only occupations and dates of birth, marriage and death. Despite so many sources of research, it is interesting to note that many people will find this extraordinarily difficult to achieve, and if you were to attempt the next generation as well (*trente-deux quartiers*) you might well find that you had set yourself a task that could easily outlive you. (If the unimaginable were to happen, you would most certainly now prepare thirty-two separate charts for them.)

Whether or not you can interest other relatives in helping, be sure to deposit copies of your research at the SOG – you will augment their already vast collection and be able to rest assured that your vast labours will not be consigned to oblivion after your demise by an uninterested family. And better still, why not consider publication of your family history as a permanent record for all time? In it you can include pedigrees, maps, photographs and illustrations, all backed up by a comprehensive index.

The family tree must be unambiguous, which means that everybody must have a surname, with women recorded under their maiden names. Brothers and sisters must be strictly entered on a horizontal line from left to right in order of age seniority; if a date of birth is uncertain, then approximate or say 'seven in the 1841 census'. Marriage dates are generally to be inferred from the age of the eldest child (if you are sure you have found him), but deaths will present far more problems. If unknown, you may have to list the last census detail, the date of a last known child, or somebody's recollection of when he was last seen or known to be alive. There are far too many pedigree charts covered in too many people who have never died – no genealogist worth his salt should ever allow this to happen.

Your carefully prepared chart may also become complicated by children born to second and third marriages, illegitimate ones (best marked by a wavy or dotted line) and those born to a single mother who subsequently married but did not pass her new surname to her child who may be recorded under either her maiden name or that of the putative father. Keep details as concise and clear as you can, and consider separate CVs where warranted. Families may also be recorded in tabular or indented form where generations and individuals have unique reference numbers; a glance at *Burke's Peerage* or similar volume will show this.

Finally, abbreviate very sparingly, if at all; what is obvious to you at the time of writing may be quite unclear in a year's time.

## Bibliography

### LATIN AND PALAEOGRAPHY

Beal, P., *A dictionary of manuscript terminology* (2008)

Buck, W.S.B., *Examples of English handwriting 1550–1650* (1965)

Cappelli, A., *Dizionario di abbreviature latine ed italiane* (6th edn 1967)

Denholm-Young, N., *Handwriting in England and Wales* (1954)

Emmison, F.G., *How to read local archives 1550–1700* (1968)

Glover, R.F. and Harris, R.W., *Latin for historians* (3rd edn 1963)

Gooder, E., *Latin for local history* (2nd edn 1978)

Graesse, Benedict and Plechl, *Orbis Latinus* (1971)

Grieve, H.E.P. (ed.), *Examples of English handwriting 1150–1750* (1954)

Hector, L.C., *The handwriting of English documents* (2nd edn 1966)

Jenkinson, H., *Later court hands in England from 15th to 17th century* (1927)

Johnson, C. and Jenkinson, H., *English court hands 1066–1500 illustrated from the public records,* 2 vols (1915)

Kennedy, B.H., *Revised Latin primer* (1966)

Latham, R.E., *Revised mediaeval Latin word-list* (1965)

Lewis, C.T. and Short, C., *A Latin dictionary* (1880)

Parker, J., *Reading Latin epitaphs: a handbook for beginners* (1999)

Stuart, D., *Latin for local and family historians* (1995)

Westcott, B., *Making sense of Latin documents for family and local historians* (2014)

Wright, C.E., *English vernacular hands from the twelfth to fifteenth centuries* (1960)

### NAMES

Addison, W., *Understanding English place-names* (1978)

Bardsley, C.W., *English surnames* (1968)

Ekwall, E., *The Oxford dictionary of English place-names* (4th edn 1960)

Glover, J., *The place names of Kent* (1976)

Guppy, H.B., *Homes of family names in Great Britain* (1968)

Field, J., *English field names: a dictionary* (1972)

McKinley, R.A., *A history of British surnames* (1990)

Phillimore, W.P. and Fry, E.A., *An index to changes of name for the United Kingdom and Ireland ... 1760–1901* (1905)

Pine, L.G., *The story of surnames* (1965)

Reaney, P.H., *The origin of English surnames* (1967)

—— and Wilson, R.M., *A dictionary of English surnames* (3rd edn 1991)

Redmonds, G., *Names and history: people, places and things* (2004)

Wallenberg, J.K., *Kentish place-names* (1931)

——, *The place-names of Kent* (1934)

Wilson, S., *The means of naming: a social and cultural history of personal naming in western Europe* (1998)

Withycombe, E.G., *Oxford dictionary of English Christian names* (3rd edn 1977)

Yonge, C.M. *History of Christian names*, 2 vols (1878)

## C. RESEARCH PROBLEMS

Genealogy is slow, time-consuming and often fraught with pitfalls, dead ends and sudden turns. Particular classes of records throw up their own difficulties, but we will now look at some general ones.

Every line becomes blocked at some point, sometimes even barely into the nineteenth century. This may well be because the researcher has gone too hard and fast on the direct line without considering the lives of brothers and sisters, in-laws or other close family members who might reveal valuable clues. The unexpected marriage place of a cousin or burial place of a great-aunt should be the occasion for careful consideration as to why these locations have been chosen: is it because other family were in these places several generations ago? Likewise, in earlier centuries, any testator bequeathing money to a distant church may well be mindful of his parish of birth.

Before the publication of Dr Johnson's dictionary in 1755, there was no such thing as the correct spelling of any English word – an educated man might spell the same word in different ways within a single document. As few people were literate until the mid-Victorian period, it follows that any declaration was necessarily recorded as it was heard, and that if the speaker had an accent or the listener hearing problems, then words and phrases might suffer considerable distortion. Once something was written down it would generally not be corrected. Surnames above all other things are particularly at risk, and especially when indexes are being searched – Nott or Knott; Simms or Syms; Weatherly or Whetherley; Humphreys or Umfreyes – the list is endless and demands great caution, even well into the civil registration period, and especially in the census returns.

I have already alluded to the problems of forenames. Even today, many people's deaths are registered under names not agreeing with those at either birth or marriage, perhaps because they had disliked and suppressed them, or through the ignorance of an informant. People with three or more forenames are particularly subject to their being mis-ordered or reduced. Diminutives such as Molly and Bert are not easy to resolve. Although the practice of two or more forenames was uncommon before the later 1700s, it was widespread by the reign of Victoria, but this does not mean that the bearer, especially if illiterate, used them or even knew of both.

Some marriage certificates can throw up intricate problems. Ringo Starr's father was John George Parkin, the son of George Henry Parkin, who died when his son was just 6. His widow remarried a Richard Henry Starkey. The little future Beatle took his step-father's name, but when marrying was unsure of how to describe himself. In the event, he gave his name as John Alfred Parkin Starkey and said that his father was Henry Parkin Starkey. If it had not been for the family's remembrance of the true facts, the pedigree would have become untraceable, even in the twentieth century.

Place names can be frustrating. Throughout the country there are dozens of Prestons and Newtowns, both small and large, Herefordshire and Hertfordshire differ by just one letter (as do their abbreviations) and most counties have duplicated parish names: Kent has two each of Ash, Buckland, Capel, Charlton, Goodnestone, Kingsdown, Milton, Minster, Newington, Preston and Stone; some have differing suffixes, but are not always used. There are also three Hoos, four Boughtons and other confusibilia like Barham and Burham, Bexley and Boxley, Elham and Eltham, and Sellindge and Selling, all requiring great care to identify the correct parish. Not everyone gave a parish of birth or residence, even in a will, but rather a hamlet or other smaller settlement, for example, Acol, Sheerness or Sissinghurst, all in Kent but lying within another ancient parish. You will need to check maps or gazetteers, perhaps starting with Samuel Lewis's *Topographical dictionary of England* with its concise descriptions of location and activities.

More dangerous than most other things are dates. Contrary to general belief, the English calendar has not been stable but undergone many vicissitudes, even concerning such basic things as the starting date. This was 25 March (Lady Day) until 1752 so, for example, 1748 began on 25 March and ended on 24 March in the year we would now call 1749. Consequently, dates from 1 January to 24 March 1748 noted in an old record are actually later than April 1748; best practice today is to double-date them, for example, 4 February 1748/9 to indicate Old Style (OS) or 4 February 1749 New Style (NS). The matter is confusing and leads to such anomalies as an infant being buried before it was baptised. Examples of explicit double-dating may occasionally be seen on church memorials.

Following Lord Chesterfield's Act of 1751, England decided to catch up with the Continent (and also with Scotland) where the Gregorian calendar was by then eleven days ahead of the Julian one. Therefore the year 1751 ended on 31 December, and 1752 began on the next day, 1 January (the first New Year's Day of this date). But in order to catch up, the following 2 September was followed by 14 September (omitting eleven days) before 1752 ended normally on 31 December. This sequence can also cause confusion with Continental dates, and so during the Glorious Revolution of 1688 Prince William of Orange appears to have landed in Brixham on a date (5 November) earlier than he had left Holland. The loss of eleven days is still reflected in the Orthodox Christmas of 6 January and the taxman's new year of 5 April. On a tablet at Stourmouth you may read that Mr Carr Culmer was born 1 January 1735 and died 10 January 1835 – so was he nine days past 100? His life time included the loss of those eleven days in 1752, so by strict reckoning he was one day short of his century.

When searching earlier material, you will not get very far without a knowledge of regnal years. For many centuries nearly all documents were dated by these and not by calendar years. Regnal years can be quickly looked up in printed tables, but it is useful to know a few (even roughly) by heart. The death of one monarch and the accession of the next are dated to the same day, so, to take a modern example, the first regnal year of the present queen ran from 6 February 1952 to 5 February 1953 and Christmas Day of that year would be written 25 December 1 Elizabeth II. Note that the reign of Charles II was deemed to have started from 1649, the year of the execution of his father, and not from the Restoration in 1660.

This introduction must end (and not start) by mentioning the Internet. The volume of information being publicly uploaded rises exponentially, but what is emphatically true is that the Internet is a finding tool, not a research avenue, even if we are uncomfortably approaching the questionable point of completely housebound genealogical research. The breadth of sources that are now covered is inestimable and allows things to be found in previously unexpected or unthought of locations, whether from an index or a digitised original record. But none of these techniques will ever replace both checking the original entry and searching the document much more fully and widely to gain a social or historical overview of its construction and purpose: undigitised and unindexed introductory matter, marginalia and interlined entries, editorial comments, historical introductions and the like may greatly illumine both our gathering of facts and the background to them.

Almost every library, record office, organisation, society, museum and archive of interest to you to will invite searches of its website and material already uploaded and/or indexed. Beyond these are the enormous genealogical websites, such as Ancestry and Findmypast, which constantly and valiantly strive between them to include more digitised than undigitised sources. The National Archives' Discovery catalogue allows rapid access to unimaginable amounts of original source material from both its own as well as some 2,500 other national and foreign archives (see also an online list of TNA research leaflets). British History Online has many images of mediaeval documents at www.aalt.law.uh.edu, as does www.mediaevalgenealogy.org.uk. The Kent Archaeological Society (KAS) website has much valuable local material covering the whole county. Medway Archives has its CityArk image catalogue, and KHLC its CalmView archive catalogue.

Further valuable general sites are items from the SOG unique library at SOG Data Online and GENUKI, which covers all aspects of our subject and acts as a gateway to sites run by countless other individuals, societies and archives in Britain and Ireland, including thousands of pages of transcripts. Cyndi's List, a sort of yellow pages to (mostly North American) displays sites arranged by geography and subject, and similar is Rootsweb.com, hosted by Ancestry. Almost any other specialised subjects may be rapidly accessed by just Googling a few key words – the world is the genealogist's oyster.

**Bibliography**

COMPUTER GENEALOGY

Christian, P., *The genealogist's internet* (2012)

Hawgood, D., *Internet for genealogy* (2nd edn 1999)

——, *GENUKI, UK and Ireland genealogy on the Internet* (2000)

——, *An introduction to using computers for genealogy* (3rd edn 2002)

Helm, M.L. and A.L., *Genealogy online for dummies* (2014)

Morris, H., *Researching your family history online* (2012)

Paton, C., *Tracing your family history on the internet* (2011)

## D. MY FAMILY HISTORY: SOME WARNINGS

Having indicated some general problems, it may now be helpful to indicate how I got started and what early traps I fell into. My good genealogical fortune was to be an eldest child, and also the first grandchild on both sides of the family. Even more luckily, my paternal grandfather was the penultimate of fifteen children, so I grew up surrounded by venerable great-aunts and uncles, some of whom were born in the 1870s. Memories of these Victorians are still very much with me, and as I was of an inquisitive nature even before I was a teenager, I often quizzed them about their own childhoods, where they grew up, what they remembered of their parents and who all the people were in the extensive family photograph collections (now all carefully recorded).

All of this meant that I had a good basic range of details even before I had heard of the word genealogy. When I learnt that my grandfather was called Sidney Wye Wright and my great-grandfather Charles Elvy Wright unusual names suddenly began to fascinate me, the latter middle name being a quintessentially east Kent one. My grandmother showed me Sidney's birth, marriage and death certificates and, in line with a family of fifteen children, I soon found out that he been born on his parents' twenty-second wedding anniversary. I learnt that the name Wye was not in our family – it was simply the surname of some family

## Birth

**1848** Birth in the Sub-district of *Mile End Old Town* in the *County of Middlesex*

| No. | When and where born | Name, if any | Sex | Name and surname of father | Name, surname and maiden surname of mother | Occupation of father | Signature, description and residence of informant | When registered | Signature of registrar | Name entered after registration |
|---|---|---|---|---|---|---|---|---|---|---|
| 84 | Eighteenth March 1848 Frederick place Mile End Road | Charles Elvy | Boy | Robert Wright | Sarah Wright formerly Elvy | Merchants Clerk | Robert Wright Father 6 Frederick place Stepney | Twenty Sixth April 1848 | Samuel Castledon Registrar | |

CERTIFIED to be a true copy of an entry in the certified copy of a Register of Births in the District above mentioned. Given at the GENERAL REGISTER OFFICE, LONDON, under the Seal of the said Office, the *19* day of *November* 19*75*.

## Marriage

Registration District *City of London*. Marriage solemnized at *St Peters Cornhill* Church of *St Peters Cornhill* in the *City of London*

| When married | Name and Surname | Age | Condition | Rank or profession | Residence at the time of marriage | Father's name and surname | Rank or profession of father |
|---|---|---|---|---|---|---|---|
| April 7th | Charles Elvy Wright | 22 | Bachelor | Commercial Clerk | 3 Green Court Cornhill | Robert Wright | Commercial Clerk |
| | Emily Brooks | full | Spinster | | 20 Pembury Road Lower Clapton | Thomas Brooks | Manufacturer |

Married in the Parish Church according to the Rites and Ceremonies of the Established Church by Licence by me Rich'd Whittington Inc. Rector.
This marriage solemnized between us, Charles Elvy Wright, Emily Brooks, in the presence of us, William Peacock, Maria Peacock.

## Death

**1914.** DEATH in the Sub-district of *Islington, South East* in the *County of London*

| No. | When and where died | Name and surname | Sex | Age | Occupation | Cause of death | Signature, description, and residence of informant | When registered | |
|---|---|---|---|---|---|---|---|---|---|
| 221 | Sixteenth December 1914 27, Church Street | Charles Elvy Wright | Male | 66 years | Commission Agent | Heart Failure Atheroma of Coronary Arteries Natural. P.M. | Certificate received from Walter Schröder Coroner for London Inquest held Eighteenth December. 1914 | Nineteenth December 1914. | |

CERTIFIED to be a true copy of an entry in the certified copy of a Register of Deaths in the District above mentioned. Given at the GENERAL REGISTER OFFICE, LONDON, under the Seal of the said Office, the *15th* day of *February* 19*80*.

*Birth, marriage and death: the entries for my great-grandfather. Note how little information the death entry gives, not even marital status.*

friends; I then wondered if the baptism might show them as godparents but was told that the last clutch of this large family were never baptised at all.

41

I rushed to find my then most distant known ancestor in the census.

### 1911 census: Wimbledon, Surrey
Charles Wright, head, 63 (married 17 years, one child, still alive),
    land agent, born Bow, Mddx
Matilda Wright, wife, 53, born Poplar
Algernon Wright, son, 5, born Marylebone

This was the last census that I actually found Charles in (a respected accountant, freemason and freeman of the City of London), but if it had been the first, and without prior family knowledge, the Wright pedigree could have come to grief. In the 1901 census Charles is with his true wife (whom he had married in 1870) and nine of his children – that first wife died in 1938. The above 1911 census is a complete fabrication and comprises a common-law wife, for whom he deserted the mother of his fifteen children, and an illegitimate grandchild. Let the searcher beware!

Charles Elvy Wright was born in Bow in 1848, his father Robert Wright given as an East India Company clerk and his mother Sarah Wright formerly Elvy – a clear example of a woman's maiden name being perpetuated in the next generation. Needless to say, no East India Company records could disclose my humble clerk ancestor, but a longish journey to meet the Vicar of Shadwell in London's East End found his baptism there in 1816 in the Shadwell registers. He had seven younger siblings on whom many years were spent teasing out their lives with this commonest of English surnames.

Our earliest London generation was Robert's parents, Francis and Susanna Wright. They died in 1859 and 1860, and the one possible census told me (after a three-month search through the whole of Stepney) that they were both born in Wells, Norfolk – failure here would have been the end of this pedigree. But how to find their marriage? One of their sons was at the same address for several decades and by pure chance I noted an index entry for the birth of a Francis Starling Charles Wright in the right district. The certificate revealed the correct parents, and then to the marriage of Francis Wright and Susanna Starling in 1815 at St Martin-in-the-Fields. No other possibilities have come to light, so it looks as if the couple left Norfolk and arrived in Westminster to marry in this smart church before spending the rest of their lives in Limehouse as shipwrights on the Thames.

Several journeys to Norfolk allowed me to search the extensive Wells registers (then still in the church) and find Francis' baptism there in 1784. His mother died in 1838 and her death entry as an elderly widow gave me his father's occupation, also subsequently confirmed by the helpful eighteenth-century parish clerk who recorded all male occupations at marriage for many decades in the later 1700s, a good example of serendipitous extra information in parish registers. Wells had a local census taken in 1791 which gave me the family street address and a convenient family group with exact ages.

The next generation was based on a William Wright born in the mid-1750s – perhaps at Wells? There are several baptisms in a few years for this name, so sorting them out and ending with a single candidate may take years of further work, with perhaps little hope of any certainty for what is an exceptionally common name in this part of Norfolk.

My Wright grandmother had been born Mabel Gertrude Wakefield in 1894, perhaps at St John's Wood according to the 1911 census which she completed in her own hand at the age of 17, putting her mother as the second house occupant. No birth entry had ever been found, quite in line with the story that she was illegitimate with several half-siblings, but after her death my father handed me, quite unannounced, her baptismal certificate at St Mary Islington, aged 4 in 1898. Her father was Francis Wakefield, a gentleman, whom other family now remembered as having removed himself to Harrow, and indeed the censuses found him there, born in 1837, so 61 (and unmarried) when his daughter was christened. My grandmother had no memory of the date or place of his death (the only photograph of him being a Victorian one) and exhaustive searches threw up just one certificate for a man of 88 dying in a home in Surrey in 1925. I kept the certificate on hold for many years with no proof as to whether it was the right man until the will of his newly found elder brother proved the entry, a good example of confirmation coming from an unexpected source many years later.

What surprised all the family was that the Wakefields were affluent bankers, also originating from Norfolk (one of genealogy's many extraordinary coincidences) who inhabited the better streets of Mayfair in the 1840s and 1850s. The previous generation of Francis and Rose Wakefield were seldom together in any census, and sometimes temporarily far from London. One census revealed Rose as 'Mrs Wakefield' – an entry no index would ever have revealed. No death

43

entry has been found for her, but a chance index find showed her burial at Kensal Green Cemetery in 1849, to be confirmed by the family address.

Back to Charles Elvy Wright, born in 1848, as I was now curious about his middle name, especially as my grandmother told me she used to go and visit Champion Court at Newnham near Faversham where 'relatives' lived. The Wright-Elvy marriage was found at St James Piccadilly (indexed as 'Eloy') in 1843, and now the census told me that the bride was indeed born at Newnham. With trembling anticipation, forty or more years ago, I was seated in the vestry at St Peter and Paul, Newnham, and saw my first ever parish registers. After a long and busy afternoon, I had extracted large numbers of entries for the surname going back three centuries. Sarah Elvy was the daughter of the village butcher but removed herself to Chelsea to be a teacher before marriage.

Elvy is a good example of a generally rare name, but one which is very common in several parts of Kent, namely around Faversham, Dover and the Medway towns. Thirty and more years of a one-name study have produced several enormous trees, the main one covering many villages around Newnham (including Champion Court) and Doddington and secure back to about 1550, but *not* including our family. It never follows that all people of one surname are related, even in a smallish rural location. My grandmother died before I really got going with serious research, so I shall never know whether she actually knew the inhabitants of Champion Court or simply stood at the gates and dreamt about what she had always been told. The moral is that all stories must be rigorously investigated before incorporation into a pedigree.

# Chapter 2

# PRINCIPAL BASIC SOURCES

## A. CIVIL REGISTRATION

England and Wales enjoy perhaps the earliest unified system of civil registration in the world. Unlike Australia, New Zealand and the United States, there is just a single index covering the entire country (plus Wales), introduced just ten days into Queen Victoria's reign on 1 July 1837. The Registration and Marriages Act of 1836 led to the appointment of Thomas Henry Lister as the first Registrar General and the founding of the General Register Office. The nation was divided into 619 registration districts, based on the old Poor Law unions, each sub-divided into various sub-districts, and all overseen by a superintendent registrar whose job was to supervise the efficient recording of births, marriages and deaths occurring within his geographical limits and, every three months, make copies of them to be sent as quarterly returns to Somerset House. In London they would be sorted, briefly checked and entered into national indexes from which copies might be ordered. They are arranged in four quarters, March covering registrations in January, February and March, and so on. Annual computerised indexes replaced quarterly ones in 1984.

The London public searchroom containing the many hundreds of index volumes is now history, as the several hundred million entries are now online from 1837 to 2006, principally at FreeBMD (1837–1983, not yet quite complete), and Findmypast (1837–2006, complete). Note that the last eight or nine years of births, marriages and deaths down to about a year ago are available (in southern England) only on quarterly fiches at the City of Westminster Archives or at the British Library. For these last few years, other than applying to the Kent Certificate Centre (q.v.), you will need to check the fiches and obtain the index details before ordering a certificate at the current price of £9.25 from www.gro.gov.uk/certificates.

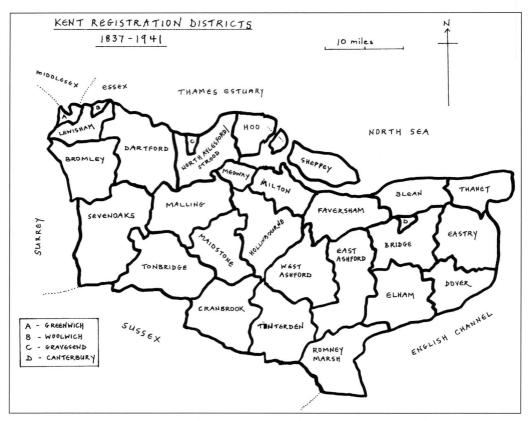

*Kent registration districts: the districts remained essentially unchanged for over a century.*

Kent was initially divided into twenty-eight registration districts which were also used for the recording of the census returns. The system was essentially unchanged until 1941, since when there have been many amalgamations and other changes leading today to the county as a single registration district. Each district included between about eight and thirty parishes, full details and maps of which are in my book *The Kentish census returns 1801–1901*.

In the national indexes the Kentish districts appear as follows:

1837–51: vol. 5 (or V)
1852–1946: vol. 2a (Greenwich, Lewisham and Woolwich volume 1d)
1946 onwards: vol. 5

Finding the correct index entry in order to obtain the certificate is sometimes far easier said than done. In the first full year of registration ending in 1838 nearly 1,000,000 entries of births, marriages and deaths were copied by hand at local level before transmission as paper copies to Somerset House for sorting and indexing. The scope for errors in the form of omissions, misreadings and miscopyings must have been enormous, most of which would have been unnoticed and never corrected. Lateral thinking with regard to surname variants and dropped or added forenames will no doubt rescue some, but others may never be found. Mothers' maiden names are added in the births from 1911 and the age at death from 1866, and a cross-reference given on marriages to identify the spouse's surname from 1912. Deaths from 1969 show the alleged date of birth (not always accurate) rather than the age. Be aware that every event had to be recorded in the district in which it occurred, so births at a distant hospital or deaths in an institution or on a journey may appear to be out of place.

Births before 1911 and deaths before 1866 for common names and in an uncertain location may be very difficult to identify from the very sparse index details, and indeed even full death certificates often contain insufficient information for positive identification of some individuals. Some parents had not decided on a child's name at registration and the entry will therefore appear as male or female at the end of the surname; this applies also to deaths where a dead body had precluded identification. It is acknowledged that there was under-recording until the Births and Deaths Act of 1874 which placed the onus of registration on the parents rather than the registrar.

Marriages before 1912 can be tricky, and the indexes will not positively identify a spouse if you have no prior knowledge of the name. You will probably at least know the spouse's forename, in which case clicking on the FreeBMD page option should solve the problem. Note that any bride and groom must have the same district, volume and page numbers. When applying for a marriage certificate it is often wise to specify just the groom or the bride, but not both, if there is uncertainty about how one or the other is indexed. The useful GRO checking system whereby an applicant could specify parents' or other details before buying was unaccountably abandoned a few years ago, meaning that all purchases today are blind; local registrars may well be more helpful here.

Do not rush too quickly to buy a marriage certificate. Before about

1880 the vast majority of marriages were solemnised in Church of England parish churches rather than at the register office or in a Nonconformist chapel. In the Cranbrook district, for example, there were just six parishes: armed with marriage details and the quarter of registration, it would not take 20 minutes to check the marriage register of each parish and probably locate the entry that would include your ancestors' original signatures, sometimes essential for positive identification of someone with a common name. In much of London this work has already been done for you by Ancestry.co.uk which has digitised and indexed tens of thousands of marriages within the capital.

One final warning: always be mindful that the index entry you seek may be under a different surname altogether for reasons you do not yet understand. Again, the value of digitised national indexes is apparent here in allowing searches under forename only without the necessity of a surname.

On birth certificates note that the address in column 1 may be a hospital or institution (not always apparent), but the informant's address in column 7 will be more certain. Sometimes the actual date of birth is at variance with family details, perhaps because of a late registration where the parents wished to avoid a fine and so simply 'adjusted' the birth date. If no forename is given in column 2, it may be added in column 10, but if not, the entry will be indexed by sex only. Illegitimate births will show no father in column 4 unless the mother actually named him, and from 1875 he will appear only if he consented and was present at the registration. The mother's maiden name in column 5 may be a former married name rather than her maiden name; obtain another child's entry if problems arise. Six weeks or forty-two days were allowed for birth registration so quite commonly a November baby will not appear until the March quarter of the following year.

Large numbers of people married under a name not in exact agreement with that at birth. Many ages (especially women's) are slightly inaccurate, and often adjusted to create a smaller gap between the two parties. Full age in theory meant at least 21, but the party might well have been 17 or even 47. If a marriage was by banns, both bride and groom will frequently share the same (temporary) address: this is commonly not a family one and most certainly no clue whatsoever as to the place of birth. Some fathers are marked as deceased, but as this was not a stipulated question, the evidence must be assessed very carefully; best practice is to obtain the marriages of other siblings before making a final judgement. If the other father is not described as deceased, then there is no evidence either way as to whether he is still alive or not. Never ignore the names of witnesses who are frequently relatives unknown to you, or even future ones.

Death certificates need to be treated with caution as the deceased was not present to verify the information which was subject to the best knowledge of the informant, often not a relative. Thousands of deaths were (and still are) recorded where the given names do not match those at birth or marriage. In column 5 children under 16 should be described as the child of their father, and married women as the wife or widow of their husband. Many adult men's death entries say nothing about marital status (see that for my great-grandfather) and this can be inferred only if the informant is a spouse or child – if you did not know that the author of this book is unmarried, his future death certificate will certainly make you none the wiser as bachelors are never specifically indicated. Sudden or suspicious deaths, especially if followed by a post mortem and inquest, will have that fact listed in column 6 and lead to a newspaper report and other details.

Deaths of stillborn children did not have to be registered until 1874. Although it sounds obvious, no death could be registered without the prior presence of the dead body; there are therefore no death certificates, for example, in the overseas registers for all those who died on the RMS *Titanic*. Some deaths were subject to considerable delay, meaning that registration could be as much as a year after the actual event. Always attempt to kill off your ancestors (nothing is more untidy on a chart than a blank space here) as a death date can lead to probate and funeral records, institutional documents, obituaries, family addresses and perhaps also to unexpected informants.

Experience will teach you that not all certificate details are set in stone, particularly if the informant was not a relative. If you suspect copying errors, it may be worth obtaining a copy from the local registrar who will examine the original entry; remember that certificates from the GRO are at several removes from the original. There may be factual errors of various kinds, accidental or deliberate, in the recorded details, none of which were the registrar's concern at the time of recording: today's modern copy simply guarantees you a faithful reproduction of the recorded entry, irrespective of whether it is wholly truthful or not.

The new Kent Certificate Centre in Tunbridge Wells (which covers the whole of the ancient county less Medway and those north-western parts now in London) has gathered in nearly all original birth, marriage and death registers from 1837 to the present. All marriages, whether in churches, chapels or register offices, are completely indexed down to the present and certificates are supplied at £11. Little indexing has yet been undertaken for births and deaths, but for a fee of £18 you may attend in person and search the original contemporary indexes to find a required entry – a very useful service as these must be at least as full, if not fuller than, the GRO copies. Multiple entries for the same name in the same quarter or district can be checked for known details such as exact date, address or parents' names before the required certificate is issued for £11.

### Bibliography

Annal, D. and Collins, A., *Birth, marriage and death records, a guide for family historians* (2012)

### B. CENSUS RETURNS

By the later eighteenth century it had long been recognised that an accurate estimate of the population was badly needed for all sorts of reasons. The need for a national census had been debated for decades, and those arguments would now soon bear fruit with the taking of the first national census for the whole of England and Wales in 1801 – just a generation before the introduction of civil registration. At that first census Kent's population was 308,667, rising to 548,177 in 1841, 848,294 in 1871, 1,348,841 in 1901, and 1,511,806 in 1911.

The four early censuses of 10 March 1801, 27 May 1811, 28 May 1821 and 30 May 1831 (all Mondays) were compiled for statistical purposes only, giving the number of people in each area by sex and age group (but not by name), the number of houses and other details concerning occupation and the like. Census enumerators sent these details to the central authorities, which were analysed and then mostly destroyed. However, some enumerators listed names and/or family groups, most of which are now held at CCA or KHLC, often in parish registers. A master listing of all Kentish pre-1841 returns, and whether they contain names, was compiled by the late Susan Bourne in her book *Early census returns for Kent, 1801–1831*.

*An early local census: Wootton parish for 1815 showing ninety named inhabitants. The population was 107 in 1801 and 153 in 1851 (CCA: U3/136/28/2). (Reproduced by kind permission of Canterbury Cathedral Archives and Library)*

All the returns from 1841 onwards (always on Sunday nights) are arranged by exactly the same districts used for civil registration. The process was for enumerators to distribute forms or schedules to the head of each household and then return to collect them a few days later. If the head of the household was illiterate or otherwise defaulted, the enumerator would write down the dictated information. People in charge of schools, barracks, prisons and workhouses would have a great deal of work to do in order to make a full return. Once the enumerator had gathered in all the schedules in his district (normally an area that could be completed on foot in a day), he copied all the details into a book and completed tables to show the total population. These books are the ones we view today, the householders' schedules having been destroyed. Like the GRO indexes, it is impossible to know how accurately the fair copies were made.

In rural areas small parishes would have comprised an entire enumerator's district, larger parishes being sub-divided into several parts. In towns and cities the denser population would necessitate many districts, the ancient parishes often broken into later daughter churches and then again by areas, neighbourhoods or even single streets.

Until about a decade ago, a small book could have been written on

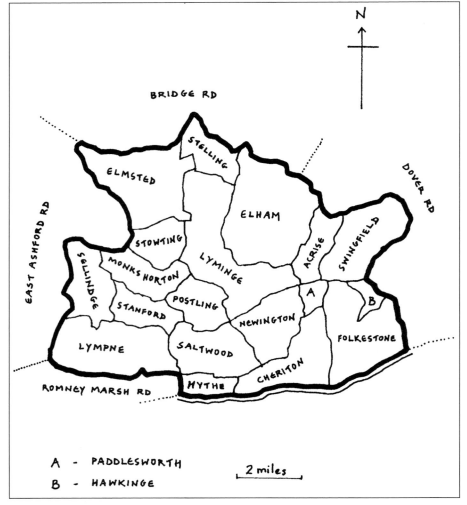

*Elham registration district: note that the large towns of Folkestone and Hythe are subsumed under a village name.*

the various street and name indexes essential to try and find a family in the returns, arranged as they were by parish and not by name. But the almost unimaginable task of completely indexing all the returns from 1841 to 1911 has now been completed (work is in progress on 1921). This is a staggering achievement and has revolutionised genealogy, for previously if a pre-1837 birthplace could not be discovered via the census, then many pedigrees were completely blocked.

Despite these technical marvels, there are downsides as today many people search 'in a vacuum' with little idea of how the returns look in their entirety or how neighbourhoods were covered by the enumerator. By far the best thing is to search at least a whole small parish and also a district within a town or city, looking carefully at the preamble which will gives registrars' and enumerators' names (perhaps your ancestor?), a description of the enumerator's route he took from house to house (often with a sketch) and notes about empty houses and other matters, even sometimes the comments of obstreperous householders who had denied him entry. Be aware that street numbers were highly fluid until the 1870s or so and can be often repeated; do not confuse them with the household schedule numbers in the adjacent column.

It should be stated emphatically that the census returns are concerned with people, not families or other connected groups, and therefore no 'family' is ever guaranteed to be complete. The enumerator went from building to building, delivering and then collecting his schedules. Any empty premises was of no concern; it was simply marked as such ('family absent' or 'gone away') as he progressed. Similarly, whoever was in a house on the night was recorded – absent family members would be enumerated wherever they happened to be. Do not be too hasty in assuming you have a complete batch of children as one may be with an aunt or other relative nearby; conversely, some pedigrees may suddenly be greatly enhanced by an in-law or aged grandparent appearing in the return.

Problems with the 1841 census being written in pencil and much other poor Victorian handwriting have not been wholly overcome, even by modern technology. This as well as the problems of human eyes interpreting millions of unusual surnames (including 'Ditto'!) mean that some people will still be decidedly difficult to find. The general rule is to specify less rather than more in the search boxes, and then whittle down the candidates individually.

Assuming you have found the return you are seeking, there may well be problems of interpretation. The 1841 returns include almost nobody with more than one forename, except perhaps a few tiny children.

Children up to the age of 15 would have their age recorded exactly; all other persons were rounded down to a multiple of five, so 64 or 62 became 60. There are many exceptions to this rule, but it should be borne in mind, as should the fact that no adult in 1841 (or 1851) had a birth certificate, and therefore recorded ages may well be suspect. A man and woman both aged 60 might be a married couple or a brother and sister; a man of 50 and a woman of 30 husband and wife or father and daughter. Many people will find that one great advantage of the 1841 returns is small children; if you are just investigating this generation, strenuous efforts should be made to obtain the post-1837 birth certificate of an infant for the valuable details of the mother's maiden name.

Relationships and marital status are not given in 1841. You will have to exercise great caution in making inferences, even with small children who may be nephews or cousins rather than being with their own parents; the same surname is no guarantee of a particular relationship. The last question to be asked was whether a person had been born in this county of enumeration (Y[es] or N[o]), or in Scotland, Ireland or Foreign Parts (S, I or F). Extraordinarily, the single letters Y and N can often be nearly indistinguishable and this, allied with the fact many declarations are simply wrong, mean that the 1841 census can be of limited value. However, this is no reason to ignore it, even if for the occasional unexpected house occupant.

The later census returns (30 March 1851; 7 April 1861; 2 April 1871; 3 April 1881; 5 April 1891; 31 March 1901; 2 April 1911) are the genealogist's treasure trove and afford wonderful snapshots of Victorian and Edwardian households as well as crucial details for extending a pedigree. Street addresses are now becoming more precise, all household members are described by their relationship to the head of the family (often with full forenames) and exact marital status and age are given, as is the place of birth.

Despite these riches, there are still some important caveats. Step-children are not always indicated as such and may have assumed the present head's surname, to look like children of the full blood. Similarly, the mother may be a second wife and therefore not the mother of any of the children. Be aware that 'visitors' are often actually relatives but with a relationship too complicated to be recorded (in-law, cousin and so on). The eternal problem of age remains, and the wise genealogist will always try to corroborate the census age with some other source.

Birthplaces may require some thought. A proportion will be 'not known' (NK) or county only, and possibly inaccurate. Some people offered only a foreign country without city or town; others like Ash, Boughton or Charlton (all in Kent) admit of two or more similarly named places dozens of miles apart and will require some further work. Many people gave their birthplace as the one of earliest memory, unaware that their parents had moved there at some point after the birth of that child. There was also a noticeable trend for people to state the nearest town or city to the true place of birth, perhaps a hamlet. Be aware that there are places in England called Egypt and Gibraltar before you rush to investigate Continental records. As a general rule you should always find any individual in every possible census to see if there is consistency about age and birthplace, whether parents or grandparents have moved in at the end of their lives, and to investigate visitors, servants and other people whose birthplaces may prove crucial in establishing origins.

All censuses from 1851 noted whether people were blind, deaf, imbecilic or with similar disabilities. The 1891 and 1901 returns additionally recorded details about house rooms and employment details, and the 1911 (actually the householders' original written schedules) includes the immense bonus of how long a couple has been married, how many children the marriage has produced and how many of them are still alive.

## Bibliography

Bourne, S., *Early census returns for Kent, 1801–1831* (1996)

Higgs, E., *Making sense of the census: the manuscript returns for England and Wales* (1989)

——, *A clearer sense of the census: the Victorian censuses and historical research* (1996)

Jolly, E., *Tracing your ancestors using the census* (2013)

Lumas, S., *Making use of the census* (4th edn 2002)

Whiteman, A. (ed.), *The Compton census of 1676: a critical edition* (1986)

Wright, D., *The Kentish census returns 1801–1901: origins, location, registration districts and indexes* (2003)

## C. PARISH REGISTERS AND BISHOP'S TRANSCRIPTS
### Parish Registers

Parish registers are the genealogist's mainstay and may in theory (along with other records) take us back to the later Tudor period. Thomas Cromwell, the Vicar-General of Henry VIII, ordered that they be kept from October 1538, and from that month every one of some 11,000 ancient parishes throughout England and Wales (in Kent, a little over 400) purchased a paper book in which to record baptisms, marriages and burials. The ravages of time have brought losses through neglect, civil unrest, theft and damage by vermin, fire and flood, with the result that many parishes now start considerably later than the original opening year, often having lost the entire first volume; perhaps we should be thankful that in east Kent thirty-five 1538 registers survive.

In 1597 growing concern about the safe-keeping of a priceless national asset as well as the poor quality and illegibility of some registers led to the injunction that entries were now to be kept in parchment volumes rather than paper. At the same time all the previous entries back to 1538 were to be copied into the new book, but some lazy clerks copied only from the beginning of Queen Elizabeth's reign in 1558 rather than from 1538, thus depriving history of the first twenty years' entries. Once copying was complete, the first paper register was discarded as of no importance, although this does in fact survive for a very few parishes. Also at this time it was enacted that annual copies, the so-called Bishop's Transcripts, should be made of every year's entries and transmitted to a central registry (on which see below). The uncertainties of the Civil War, when most ministers were ejected and replaced by a 'Register' or parish official, resulted in poor maintenance of many registers, and later centuries often reveal shortish gaps for various reasons, perhaps a missing page. (For much more detail on the early period, see 'The earliest Parish Registers of the Diocese of Canterbury: some observations, questions and problems', *Archaeologia Cantiana* CXXXV, 2014.)

In 1753 Lord Hardwicke's Marriage Act was passed and came into force the following year. This was an attempt to deal with clandestine marriages, often solemnised by irregular priests in unlicensed buildings, as by now certain venues in London were seeing vast numbers of couples from all over the south-east being married (for example at St James's, Duke's Place, where some 40,000 marriages took place

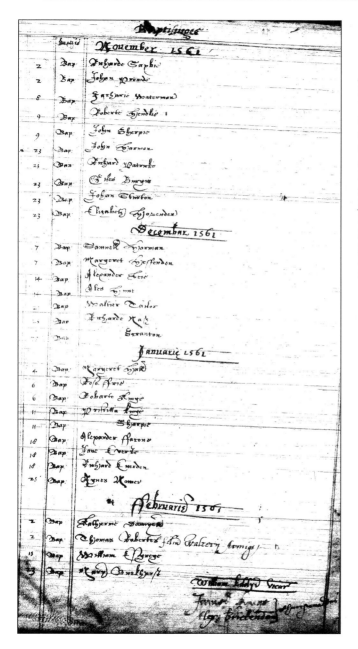

*A Tudor parish register: baptisms in the large Wealden parish of Cranbrook where, typically, the three types of events are listed separately (KHLC: P100/1/5). Note that under the old calendar January is not the beginning of the new year. (Reproduced by kind permission of Kent History and Library Centre)*

Page 25.

BAPTISMS solemnized in the Parish of _Harbledown_
in the County of _Kent_ in the Year 1821

| When Baptized. | Child's Christian Name. | Parents' Name. Christian | Surname. | Abode. | Quality, Trade, Profession. | By whom the Ceremony was performed. |
|---|---|---|---|---|---|---|
| 1821. 11 Nov No. 193. | Edward Son of | Thomas & Sarah | Wood | Harbledown | Labourer | Wm Beckett Officg Minr |
| 23 Nov No. 194. | Edward Son of | Isaac & Mary | Read | Harbledown | Labourer | J B Bunce Curate |
| 22 Dec No. 195. | Thomas Son of | Thomas & Thomazine | Brice | Rough Common Harbledown | Woodman | J B Bunce Curate |
| 1822 1 Jan No. 196. | Hannah Daughter of | William & Hannah | James | Plough-Lane Harbledown | Labourer | J B Bunce Curate |
| 13 Jan No. 197. | Sarah Daughter of | Stephen & Elizabeth | Cork | Bigbury Harbledown | Labourer | J B Bunce Curate |
| 20 Jan No. 198. | Catharine Daughter of | William & Susan | Bassett | Hythe an Adult aged 22 years Servant at Harbledown | Late A Baker | J B Bunce Curate |
| 20 Jan No. 199. | John Son of | Edward & Elizabeth | Sandy | Harbledown | Labourer | Wm Berrett Officg Minr |
| 10 Feb No. 200. | James Son of | Jacob & Mary | Bedwell | Ville of Dunkirk | Labourer | Wm Chafy Officg Minr |

*Left margin notes: "14 Males / 11 Females / 25 Total / born in 1821"*

*A printed baptismal register: printed registers were introduced in 1813 (CCA: U3/194/1/5). Note that only an inspection of the original entry, and not an index, will reveal that Catherine Bassett was aged 22. (Reproduced by kind permission of Canterbury Cathedral Archives and Library)*

between 1664 and 1691). Handwritten marriage entries were now abandoned in favour of a printed register with additional spaces for the names of two witnesses; a marriage must now take place either after the calling of banns or by the purchase of a licence, this fact to be recorded at the time of marrying. Separate printed volumes of banns were now introduced, and can still be valuable for intended weddings which did not take place. Note that between 1754 and 1837, with the sole exception of Jews and Quakers, all marriages by law had to be solemnised in a parish church, and therefore there is no such thing as a Nonconformist marriage during this period.

Marriage licences were issued from mediaeval times allowing people to avoid the more public process of the calling of banns. The practice grew rapidly in the later Tudor period when they were issued by archdeacons, bishops and clergy appointed as their surrogates, but with a single notable absence during the Commonwealth when all bishops had been suspended. The groom would make a sworn statement or allegation concerning the lawfulness of the impending marriage, proof of parents' consent and the parties' ages. Then the marriage bond was entered into when two sureties or bondsmen (one often the groom) would bind themselves in a certain sum. Names, addresses, occupations and the sum involved were recorded, and an undertaking given that both parties would marry lawfully in a specified church (several are often listed). Contrary to popular belief, couples did not marry particularly young: the Canterbury bonds indicate that between 1619 and 1660 the average age was 28 for grooms and 24 for brides.

Before 1858 divorce was well-nigh impossible (there are fewer than 300 recorded) without an Act of Parliament, a process that produced sometimes voluminous proceedings, now to be found at the House of Lords Record Office (HOL). Poorer people might have just separated or eloped, and it was indeed possible for a wife to be sold (as Thomas Hardy's *The Mayor of Casterbridge* proves): quarter sessions records may hold clues, and newspapers, particularly *The Times*, might have recorded the more sensational proceedings. From 1 January 1858 a divorce could be granted by the new civil Court for Divorce and Matrimonial Causes. Men could petition because of a wife's adultery, but until 1925 women had to prove a husband's adultery and also that it had been aggravated by his cruelty or other offences. The numbers of annual divorces rose hugely from about 150 in 1860 to about 800 in 1914 and 8,000 in 1939.

*Commonwealth marriages: for a short period marriages were civil contracts preceded by banns; here at Ash (by Sandwich) extra details were regularly recorded (CCA: U3/274/1/2). (Reproduced by kind permission of Canterbury Cathedral Archives and Library)*

There are indexed registers of decrees nisi and absolute in England and Wales from 1858 to the present, on application to the Family Division of the High Court. TNA: J 77 holds files for divorce actions 1858–1927, and TNA: J 78 comprises indexes to the parties in divorce petitions 1858–1958, in each case whether they were successful or not. Divorce case files 1858–1911 are available at Ancestry.co.uk.

In 1813, following Lord Rose's Act, the format of the printed marriage register was slightly changed and printed volumes of baptisms and burials asking for more detail were introduced. In 1837 the marriage register was again changed to conform with general registration, since when all three types of event continue to be recorded in the same way.

## COPIES OF PARISH REGISTERS

It is now difficult to keep up with these. Those described as 'extracts' are what they say and of dubious value. Parish registers have been transcribed or printed for a century and more by, amongst others, the Parish Register Society, the Harleian Society, and Phillimore & Co. The best collection by far is at the SOG (which includes the Sir Thomas Colyer-Fergusson transcripts for about half of west Kent) and is closely matched by the Kent Family History Society (KFHS) microfiche collection for east Kent. Some of the earlier productions may well include parts of registers now lost or illegible.

The Mormon Church was a pioneer in producing its International Genealogical Index (the IGI) with two slightly different versions in 1988 and 1992. Now renamed Family Search, it is an enormous undertaking, but selective in ignoring burials, taking entries sometimes from transcripts and not originals, and requiring individual permissions, so county coverage varies enormously; Kent is poor but the index remains as a magisterial name finder (http://familysearch.org). The Internet has transformed the situation beyond all recognition with most of Canterbury Archdeaconry (that is, nearly all parishes east of an irregular line running from Teynham to Hythe, 1538–c.1900) available at Findmypast. As I say elsewhere, it is essential to check the coverage of each individual parish, and beyond all this, to return to the original source to check entries. Local libraries often have microfilms of registers for their area, notably Chatham, Dartford, Maidstone, Sevenoaks, Tonbridge and Tunbridge Wells.

A moment's thought may be needed to inspect original parish

registers, as following county boundary re-organisations and the fact that large parts of the north-western historical county are now part of Greater London, this is a tricky subject; see the master parish listing at the end of this book. A good overview is given by the Institute of Genealogical and Heraldic Studies map (in C.R. Humphery-Smith (ed.), *The Phillimore atlas and index of parish registers*) which usefully shows the opening dates of the registers for every parish.

PARISH REGISTER INDEXES

**(1.) Baptisms**
a) Canterbury parishes, 1752–1852 (KFHS)
b) Faversham Registration District, 1780–1840, including Nonconformists; mid-Kent, 1813–40, chiefly East and West Ashford, Hollingbourne and Milton Registration Districts (Raymond Godfrey)
c) Isle of Thanet, 1780–1840 (Gillian Rickard, www.kentgen.com)
d) Kent births from the registers of Dr Williams' library, 1716–1837 (TNA: RG 4/4658-4676) (KFHS)
e) Nonconformist and late baptisms, *c.*1640–1891 (Matthew Copus, www.mcopus.co.uk)
f) Romney Marsh, 1750–1911 (David Hills; www.woodchurch ancestry.org.uk)
g) Weald of Kent, 1538–1600 for eighteen parishes (KFHS fiches)
h) West Kent and north-east Sussex, 1813–70s and beyond, about 100 parishes (Matthew Copus, www.mcopus.co.uk)

**(2.) Marriages**
a) Kent, 1813–37 complete, both parties (Michael Gandy; SOG)
b) East Kent, 1754–1812 complete, both parties (Michael Gandy; SOG)
c) East Kent, 1538–1753, complete, grooms only (Findmypast; CCA)
d) West Kent, 1538–1812, complete, grooms only (Sydney Smith, sydney.smith7@ntlworld.com)
e) Canterbury parishes, 1752–1852 (KFHS fiches)
f) Medway area, 1559–1812 (KFHS; Medway Area Local Studies Centre (MALSC))
g) Mid-Kent (East and West Ashford, Cranbrook, Elham, Holling-bourne, Romney Marsh and Tenterden RDs), 1754–1911 (David Hills, www.woodchurchancestry.org.uk)

East Kent marriage licences, 1568–1837 are fully indexed and in print (J.M. Cowper, *Canterbury marriage licences 1568–1750*; A.J. Willis, *Canterbury marriage licences 1751–1837*) and on KFHS fiches. There is nothing comparable for west Kent, save a manuscript calendar of bonds and allegations in a broken series at KHLC, 1637–1986, but Shoreham Deanery licences, 1684–1859, are abstracted and indexed on the Lambeth Palace website at www.lambethpalacelibrary.org.

CCA also holds East Kent licence records, 1568–1916, bonds, 1664–1882 and allegations, 1694–1882 (CCA: DCb/M/B). Again, west Kent is poor, with bonds in a broken sequence, mostly for 1733–1823, the allegations continuing until 1986 (KHLC: DRb/M) with a manuscript calendar at KHLC, reproduced on KFHS fiches. Shoreham Deanery bonds and allegations, 1684–1859 are indexed in manuscript at KHLC.

### (3.) Burials
a) East Kent, 1813–41 complete, including Nonconformists (David Wright; Findmypast)
b) Canterbury parishes, 1752–1852 (KFHS fiches)

### SEARCHING PARISH REGISTERS
You may wish to start with an indexed transcript, especially if the parish is large, but at some point searches will need to be made in an original volume. Always note the date at which you start searching and whether just for baptisms or all three types of event, as early registers usually combine them. As you proceed you will see a regular succession of handwriting as incumbents and clerks changed. Note carefully any (apparent) gaps and illegible sections, and be aware that the entry you seek may be in the margin, added at the foot or interlined in tiny writing. It is not difficult sometimes to be sidetracked by interesting marginalia and other entries recording the weather, local events and so on. It is also possible for any sequence of events to break off and be continued elsewhere, perhaps upside down or reversed, or even in another book.

It is best practice to record every entry for the surname in question to save duplicated work. However, if you cannot find an entry you think ought to be present, be prepared to search again – we can all make mistakes. Be aware of the extreme value of taking out events chronologically rather than from an index. Some groups of siblings were not all baptised at one church, and this may mean searching all parishes within a 5-mile radius for strays and perhaps also finding another candidate with the same name and parents; this is one of the constant problems in genealogy and it may require great patience and skill to construct the correct pedigree. In the few registers that show dates of both birth and baptism, it is clear that the two rarely coincided, the latter anything up to a fortnight and more later.

It is one of the great genealogical maxims that baptism is not birth: the two events might have occurred at a great distance from each other, even in separate counties. Dangerous also are mass baptisms of a family group, perhaps when the oldest was well into double figures, and also late baptisms generally, even for people aged 50 and more. Some entries record the fact of a private or half-baptism, indicating that a private ceremony had been undertaken by a lay person because it was thought the child might die unbaptised. The baptism of every child to a family should be inspected as it is possible some entries may give more information than others. Failure to find a required baptism in a parish register may commonly be ascribed to various reasons: a late entry, perhaps years after birth; completely different surname because of illegitimacy; Nonconformity; and the event taking place far from the location of birth.

Banns books should not be overlooked. From 1754–1822 banns are usually recorded in the marriage register itself, either alongside the marriage or perhaps in a separate section; thereafter they are in separate volumes. They are valuable for intended weddings that did not take place, and sometimes also for addresses, usually in another parish. For 1822–3 (only) details of residence were required, as well as the ages and status of the parties, and names of parents or guardians if under 21. Copy baptismal entries for each party are often attached.

Marriages by licence are included in the regular and comprehensive Kent indexes and should always be checked for the valuable extra information they may contain (age, occupation, status, parents' or guardians' details), especially in the Tudor and Jacobean periods. Be aware, though, that, as for banns, a licence is not always proof of marriage. Always note carefully the names of the witnesses to a wedding, who often are (or will be) relatives; but, conversely, check that they are not 'professional' witnesses, such as a parish clerk, who attended many weddings, sometimes over long periods.

*Banns of marriage: printed banns registers were introduced in 1754. Here at Margate they are combined with the actual marriages; the entry near the foot proves that the details were written up before the ceremony (CCA: U3/140/1/11). (Reproduced by kind permission of Canterbury Cathedral Archives and Library)*

Burials should be widely searched over many decades as family plots were in use over generations (as evidenced by tombstones) and people could be brought for burial from their latest abode, sometimes many miles away. Often this is indicated and is good evidence for a family having left a parish. A man's elderly parents might have been buried in a parish that he had left many years previously, and so

*Commonwealth burials: entries at Sandwich, St Mary, showing both date of death and date of burial (up to three days apart) as well as some interesting personal details (CCA: U3/11/1/1). (Reproduced by kind permission of Canterbury Cathedral Archives and Library)*

| BURIALS in the Parish of *Ham near Sandwich*<br>in the County of *Kent* | | | | |
|---|---|---|---|---|
| | | in the Years 1815<br>1816. & 1817, 1818, 1819. | | |
| Name. | Abode. | When buried. | Age. | By whom the Ceremony<br>was performed. |
| *Thomas Marsh*<br>No. 1. | *Northbourn* | *March*<br>*19th*<br>*1815* | *74* | *George Shield*<br>*Curate* |
| *Anna Smith*<br>No. 2. | *Worth* | *Augt*<br>*18th*<br>*1816.* | *26* | *W. Perkins*<br>*W. Minister* |
| *Elizabeth Curling*<br>*relict of & in*<br>*Curling Esqre of*<br>*Goldstone near Ash*<br>No. 3. | *Sandwich* | *May*<br>*23.*<br>*1817.* | *64*<br>*years* | *Wm Wadsworth*<br>*Rector Mr Peter*<br>*Sandwich and*<br>*Curate of Ham* |
| *Thomas Turner*<br>No. 4. | *Woodnesborough* | *July 16*<br>*1818* | *75* | *Wm Wadsworth*<br>*Rector of St Peter*<br>*Sandwich and*<br>*Curate of Ham* |
| *Elizabeth Curling*<br>*Daughter of William*<br>*Curling Esq.*<br>No. 5. | *Sandwich* | *Oct. 2*<br>*1818* | *18* | *Wm Wadsworth*<br>*Rector of St Peter*<br>*Sandwich and*<br>*Curate of Ham* |
| *Thomas Curling*<br>*Esqre*<br>No. 6. | *Sandwich*<br>*late of*<br>*Goldstone* | *4*<br>*March*<br>*1819.* | *62* | *Wm Wadsworth*<br>*Rector of St Peter*<br>*Sandwich and*<br>*Curate of Ham* |
| *Mary wife of*<br>*Joseph Smith*<br>No. 7. | *Bettishanger* | *20*<br>*July*<br>*1820* | *55* | *Wm Wadsworth*<br>*Rector of St.*<br>*Peter Sandwich*<br>*Curate of Ham* |
| *Mary Austin*<br>No. 8. | *from*<br>*Bettishanger* | *14*<br>*Jany.*<br>*1821.* | *27* | *W. Wadsworth*<br>*Curate.* |

*A printed burial register, as with baptisms, introduced in 1813. Here at Ham near Sandwich, a tiny parish, all burials for at least eight years are for outdwellers. Were they all born at Ham, but brought back to family graves? (CCA: U3/102/1/7). (Reproduced by kind permission of Canterbury Cathedral Archives and Library)*

prolonging family connections and offering clues to earlier generations. Ages at burial are not regularly given before 1813, but some priests noted them well before that year, perhaps also with a short description of address, occupation or marital status. In theory, babies and infants were described as such, or as the child of their father, but this is not always the case, so caution should be exercised in confusing a parent with his child or vice versa. Nearly all burials were performed within a few days of death, clearly for reasons of sanitation.

## Bishop's Transcripts
At some point you will come across a parish register that starts too late,

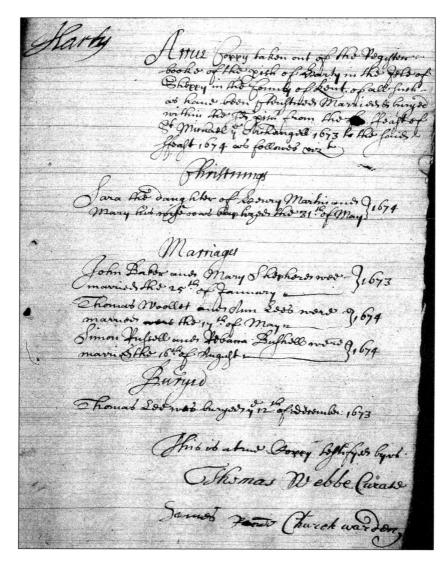

*Bishop's Transcripts: the original registers for Harty on the Isle of Sheppey open in 1679, but the transcripts in 1567, thus giving over a century of unique entries (KHLC: DCa/BT/91/79). (Reproduced by kind permission of Kent History and Library Centre)*

has a missing section or the poor condition of which has rendered illegible what you need to read. However, there is probably no need to despair, especially if you are searching in the eastern portion of the county.

In 1597 orders were given in council for annual copies of parish registers to be made and returned to a bishop's central registry for safe-keeping. Some dioceses had begun the practice considerably earlier, but patchy survival rates mean, for example, that London has nothing before 1800, and west Kent sparse returns from only 1716 onwards (all at KHLC, except Shoreham Deanery pre-1813 at Lambeth Palace). But those for the Diocese of Canterbury are the richest of any collection, for not only does the Archdeaconry series (CCA: DCa/BT), running annually from Michaelmas to Michaelmas, start as early as 1559–63, but there is a second Bishop's or Consistory series (CCA: DCb/BT1) running from Lady Day to Lady Day, opening in either 1565–70 or 1603–11. Both series run down to 1812 (save for a Commonwealth gap of 1642–60), and are then continued by a unified parchment series replicating printed parish registers (CCA: DCb/BT2) and extending often into the later Victorian period. The records fill 1,003 boxes, but all may be seen easily on microfilm at CCA.

A few small caveats are necessary. It is advisable when searching to note odd gaps of a year or two, and also whether an annual return occasionally covers just six instead of twelve months. It is also wise practice always to check both the original register and the two transcripts as there are many discrepancies, partly because the transcript may have been made from rough notes rather than the register itself.

A valuable back-up series covering Lady Day 1640–Lady Day 1641 for some 90 per cent of all parishes is now split between KHLC: U2923 and HOL. A full transcript may be seen at CCA.

## Bibliography

Betjeman, J. (ed.), *Collins guide to parish churches of England and Wales* (1980)

Bettey, H., *Church and parish: a guide for local historians* (1987)

Bourne, S. and Chicken, A., *Records of the Church of England – a practical guide for the family historian* (2nd edn 1991)

Buckland, W.E., *The parish registers and records in the Diocese of Rochester* (1912)

Bullard, J.V., *The English parish and diocese* (1936)

Burn, J.S., *History of parish registers in England* (2nd edn 1962)

Cox, J.C., *The parish registers of England* (1910)

——, *Churchwardens' accounts from the fourteenth century to the close of the seventeenth century* (1913)

Ditchfield, P.H., *The parish clerk* (1913)

Emmison, F.G., *Elizabethan life: morals and the church courts* (1973)

Hill, G., *English dioceses: a history of their limits from the earliest times to the present day* (1900)

Homan, R., *The Victorian churches of Kent* (1984)

Ingram, M., *Church courts, sex and marriage in England, 1570–1640* (1990)

Purvis, J., *Introduction to ecclesiastical records* (1953)

Smith, D.M., *Guide to Bishops' registers of England and Wales* (1981)

Smith, T., *The parish: its powers and obligations at law* (1857)

Tarver, A., *Church court records: an introduction for family and local historians* (1995)

Woodruff, C.E., *Parish registers and records in the Diocese of Canterbury* (1922)

## D. MONUMENTAL INSCRIPTIONS

No genealogist can afford to ignore monumental inscriptions. Do you have an ancestral tomb in a parish church or a family plot in a churchyard or cemetery with an accompanying headstone? Huge amounts of often unique information are literally set in stone on such memorials, now often subject to vandalism, weathering and far too much official clearing, which immediately destroys the historical integrity of adjacent stones and possible relationships. It can never be too late to investigate. In my early days of family history, and on the evidence of a will, I went with great trepidation to the enormous Abney Park Cemetery in Hackney and after many hours did eventually find several family headstones, one of which included children being born and dying between census years, and of whom we naturally had no knowledge. Memorial inscriptions have fascinated people for centuries and many early antiquaries were assiduous in copying those inside churches and elsewhere, much of which is in print and may not still survive on the ground. The Kentish antiquary Bryan Faussett copied a huge number of east Kent church memorials in the 1750s and 1760s, all of which are now at the Society of Antiquaries, London. A great many others have also been published by KFHS, and SOG has an enormous collection covering the whole country. Be sure to note the

*Monumental inscriptions: much unique information is set in stone in church and churchyard memorials. The Bundock brother and sister were buried at Ash (near Sandwich) but then living at Solton in Westcliffe parish near Dover. Robert John Ward at Sutton near Dover is late of Japan. (Copyright Neil Anthony)*

cut-off date and whether the church, churchyard or both are included.

The burials of people living and dying in a large conurbation or city may be extraordinarily difficult to locate, as death certificates offer no information about the disposal of a body. Your best chance is a will, family stories, an obituary or funeral card. The earliest public cemeteries were opened in London in the 1830s, but the age of public burying spaces really got going from the 1850s after an Act of Parliament closed all the massively overcrowded and stinking inner city churchyards. People buried in a cemetery would have been entered into a grave book, so once you have found one individual, the register may well reveal other persons in the same plot, not necessarily mentioned in the inscription, and perhaps with different surnames. Some churches have their own collection of inscriptions with accompanying graveyard map.

Some cemetery records are now transcribed or even indexed. Most are well organised with website and contact details, often at the borough or council offices. Note that many west Kent (now south-east London) inhabitants were buried at the famous Nunhead Cemetery (opened 1840). Nonconformists might have been taken to the Bunhill Fields Burial Ground, City Road, London (open 1665–1854). Cremations after the last war were barely into double-figure percentages, but are now greatly increasing.

As a rule, there are very few churchyard headstones before about 1630, but monuments inside the church have survived more or less intact and in large numbers, and some of the grander ones may well reveal several generations of a pedigree. Mediaeval church brasses, if not hidden under carpets or furniture, are often beautiful works of art but are generally limited to giving a name and date of death only, perhaps with a spouse alongside and pet dog at the foot.

Below is a summary list of Kent cemeteries (not churchyard extensions) founded before about 1900:

Ashford, Canterbury Road, 1859
Beckenham, Elmers End Road, 1876
Bexleyheath, Bank's Lane, Broadway, 1879
Brockley (formerly Deptford and Ladywell), Ladywell Road,
    Deptford, 1858
Bromley, Warner Road, 1877

Bromley, Magpie Hall Lane, 1894
Buckland-in-Dover, St Andrew, before 1857
Canterbury, Westgate Court Avenue, 1877
Charlton, Cemetery Lane, SE7, 1855
Charlton-in-Dover, Old Charlton Road, 1872
Chatham, Maidstone Road, 1859
Dartford, East Hill (formerly The Brent), 1856
Deal, Hamilton Road, 1856 (MIs: KFHS)
Deptford, see Brockley
Dover, Cowgate Hill, 1837
Dover St James, Old Charlton Road, 1855
Dover St Mary, Old Charlton Road, 1870
Erith, Brook Street, 1894
Faversham, Love Lane, 1898
Folkestone, Cheriton Road, 1856
Gillingham, Grange Road, 1860
Gravesend, Old Road West, 1839
Greenwich, Well Hall Road, Eltham, 1856
Herne Bay, Canterbury Road, 1881
Hither Green, Verdant Lane, 1873
Lewisham, Marvels Lane, Grove Park, ?, see also Brockley
Maidstone, Sutton Road, 1858
Minster-in-Thanet, Tothill Street, 1903
Northfleet, Springhead Road, 1893
Plumstead, Wickham Lane, Abbey Wood, 1890
Ramsgate, Cecilia Road, 1871
Rochester, Borstal, 1879
Rochester, St Margaret, 1860
Rochester, St Nicholas, 1873
St Mary Cray, Star Lane, 1881
Sandwich, Boatman's Hill, Woodnesborough, 1856
Sevenoaks, Seal Road, 1906
Sheppey, Western Avenue, Halfway, Sheerness, 1856 (MIs: KFHS)
Sidcup, Foots Cray Lane, 1894
Sittingbourne, Bell Road, 1861
Stone next Dartford, St James' Lane, 1899
Strood, Cuxton Road, 1856
Swanscombe, Swanscombe Street, 1895

Tenterden, Cranbrook Road, 1887

Tonbridge, Shipbourne Road 1855 (indexes/MIs: Tonbridge Castle/Library)

Tunbridge Wells, Benhall Mill Road, 1873

Tunbridge Wells, Woodbury Park, 1849 (indexes/MIs: KHLC, SOG, KFHS)

Whitstable, Millstrood Road, 1857

Willesborough, Church Road, 1882

Woolwich (New), Camdale Road, 1885

Woolwich (Old), King's Highway, 1856

**Bibliography**

Bertram, J., *Lost brasses* (1976)

Bouquet, A.C., *Church brasses* (1956)

Brooks, C., *Mortal remains: the history and present state of the Victorian and Edwardian cemetery* (1989)

Burgess, F., *English churchyard memorials* (1963)

Chapman, L., *Church memorial brasses and brass rubbing* (1987)

Le Strange, R., *A complete descriptive guide to British monumental brasses* (1972)

Macklin, H.W., *Monumental brasses* (7th edn 1953)

Mann, Sir J.G., *Monumental brasses* (1957)

Meller, H., *London cemeteries: an illustrated guide and gazetteer* (2nd edn 1985)

White, H.L., *Monuments and their inscriptions* (1987)

Wolfson, P., *Greater London cemeteries and crematoria* (1985)

## E. PROBATE RECORDS

### Introduction

Never think that your ancestor was too poor to make a will, as thousands of labourers did leave them, even in the higher probate courts. (That said, the experienced searcher may sometimes feel that it often seems the case that those most expected to have left a will did not and those least expected to did!) No other single source of genealogical record can match a will in both intimacy and contents, and therefore strenuous efforts should always be made to locate one. Family details never previously expressed (such as illegitimacy), distant and close relatives, property, burial requests, change of surname and much more may lie within just one or two paragraphs and completely revolutionise

*A will register: the will of Simon Edolph of Hinxhill copied up into a formal register; his gentleman's status is reflected in his coat of arms and magnificent opening letter 'I' (KHLC: PRC/32/40/217). (Reproduced by kind permission of Kent History and Library Centre)*

your knowledge and future research progress (and, conversely, the mention of unexpected relatives may overturn an existing pedigree!).

Other genealogical problems, inexplicable or even unsuspected for many years, may be solved from the evidence of a one-line statement in a will. Many wills were made sometimes decades before death, and so the accompanying probate grant may record the fact that executors or relatives have died in the intervening period. A testator may name children whose births have not been found, describe 'my wife's son' indicating that he has married a widow, or name 'my now wife' implying that he has remarried, perhaps to a woman of the same forename as the first wife. The wish to be buried in a particular churchyard or bequests to the poor of a certain parish may indicate birthplace or at least strong family connections, as may the mention of land in another parish, perhaps leased or purchased from an unknown relative or ancestor.

After the Norman Conquest, interests in real property (that is, land and buildings) descended automatically to the heir of the deceased, usually the eldest surviving son on the principle of primogeniture, but in Kent the unique system of 'gavelkind' or inheritance by all sons in equal shares prevailed, and had to be obeyed by testators. But personal property, such as money, tools and furniture could be freely disposed, even if ecclesiastical law provided that at least one-third should pass to a man's widow and one-third to his children. Testators desirous of avoiding this prohibition on the inheritance of land began to transfer it during their lifetime to trustees who would hold it in accordance with the owner's instructions which were set out by the landowner in a deed or will.

Originally a will covered the disposal of real estate, that is, property and lands and the interests in them (a 'devise'). But the common law courts began to object to the devising of real estate by document and so the testament came to relate to burial and other instructions, and act as an instrument by which the personalty, or personal property (clothing, furniture, stock, tools, sown crops, bonds, credits, debts, leases and money in any form), might be bequeathed as a legacy. The disposal of real estate by will became legal in 1540 by the Statute of Wills, and over the next few decades the will and testament gradually merged into the single document we now know as 'the last will and testament'. The Statute of Frauds of 1678 enacted that there should be three witnesses to a will, all of whom should have heard the testator's wishes during his last illness. Such a will could not cover freehold land or revoke an existing written one. The absence of executors' names immediately converted the entire proceedings into an intestacy.

Even today, not enough people make wills, but in earlier centuries the number was small indeed, perhaps just 10 per cent of the population at best. Until 1837 men aged 14 and above and women aged 12 and above could make a will, but thereafter a testator had to be 21. Also in that year the practice of a nuncupative (or oral) will ceased except for serving soldiers and mariners at sea. Until the Married Women's Property Act of 1882, only men, widows and spinsters could make a will; there are some married women's wills before this date, usually made in special circumstances and with the consent of her husband, but the law was that a husband automatically inherited his wife's estate if she predeceased and, further, that a woman's will made before

In the Name of God, Amen. I Charles Hinde, Vicar of Milton next Sittingbourn in the County of Kent, do make &c this my last Will and Testament in the following Manner. (viz) Imprimis I resign my Soul into the Hands of Almighty God my Creator, hoping to obtain a Remission of my Sins, through the Merits and Mediation of Jesus Christ, our only Mediator and Advocate, our only Saviour and Redeemer: And my Body I commit to the Earth, to be interred in the Church-Yard, (between the Row of Trees at the East End, my Feet pointing towards the Sycomore Tree,) at least half an Hour before Sunset, in a plain Elm Coffin, without any Plates or other Ornaments; and I desire that It may be wrapped in my oldest Cloth Gown, which may soon and easily be converted into a Sheat or Shroud &c; and that a plain black Cloth or Pall, and that only may be laid over my Coffin, when I am carried to my Burying. Thus I desire to be buried, without any Pomp or Expence, save only a Pair of Shammy-gloves, and a silk Hatband to the Minister, two Shillings and six Pence to the Parish Clerk, the customary to the Sexton, and two Shillings each to eight poor Men for carrying me to my Grave: As for the small Portion of worldly Goods, which it hath pleased God to continue unto me, I dispose of them as follows. (viz) Imprimis, I give to my dear Daughter Elizabeth Hinde a Diamond Ring (which hath been some time in her Custody) and a Book, called The new whole Duty of Man; and I intreat her to be kind to her poor Mother, (who has taken great Care of her) and to her poor Brother, and Sister: And, all my other Goods, of what kind soever, I give to my dear and loving Wife Elizabeth Hinde, whom I do also constitute and appoint my sole Executrix, and doubt not her Industry and Care for her poor Children. In witness whereof, I have to this my last Will and Testament set and affixed my Hand and Seal this 30th Day of April in the [...] of the Reign of George the 2 now King of Great Britain France and Ireland, Defender of the Faith, &c And in the Year of our Lord 1750.

Charles Hinde

Signed sealed published and declared by the said Charles Hinde, Testator, as and for his last Will and Testament, in the Presence of Us, who have hereunto subscribed our Names as Witnesses in his Presence. Jno Boykel
J Jonge

*An original will: filed separately from the registered copy, this autograph will is entirely in the testator's own handwriting (KHLC: PRC/16/417). (Reproduced by kind permission of Kent History and Library Centre)*

marriage was nullified by marriage. Those of unsound mind were debarred from making wills, and such was the concern of every testator throughout history to avoid this stigma that he or she would be described as being *compos mentis* – of sound mind and perfect memory. Also excluded were slaves, prisoners, suicides, traitors, heretics and apostates.

An executor needed to determine the correct court for a grant of probate or administration. There were five basic jurisdictions of ecclesiastical authority, the highest being a province (overseen by an archbishop); then diocese (bishop); archdeaconry (archdeacon); rural deanery (rural dean); and parish (vicar or rector). The jurisdictions were based on ecclesiastical boundaries and sometimes overlapped county or civil ones. For a splendid overview of the Kentish ones there are excellent coloured maps available at CCA and KHLC, as well as a series for the whole country in C.R. Humphery-Smith (ed.), *The Phillimore atlas and index of parish registers.*

The general practice was for the will of a testator with *bona notabilia* wholly in one jurisdiction to be proved in the local court; if he had *bona notabilia* in two jurisdictions, probate would be granted in the higher or overriding court. Outside the jurisdiction of these courts there might be single or groups of parishes designated as peculiars which maintained their own series of probate records (on which see below). The wills of most testators above the rank of minor gentry are in the Prerogative Court of Canterbury (PCC) series.

The granting of probate was conditional upon the named executor(s) in the will applying to a court and satisfying the officials that the will was valid. The will would be exhibited, after which a grant was issued empowering them to act in accordance with the will's instructions. Any codicils attached to the will would be included in this process. In the case of an intestacy, a grant would be issued in the same way, usually to a relative within a prescribed degree of consanguinity, and failing that to a creditor or other interested person. For either type of document the act was recorded in a probate act book and the will endorsed to that effect. In early times the original will was retained by the court, which then made and sealed a probate copy to be given to the executors as their authority to proceed. It was at this stage that the clerks might adopt their spelling of the surname and perhaps also miscopy other details. For a fee, a further copy of the will and probate act was made

A true & p[er]fect Inventory of all & singuler the goods, debt[s]
Cattle and Chattell of James Springfeild late
wright the lived of Maydstone in the County of Kent
husbandman, taken & prised by William Barkt
Andrew Turke, Robert Smith & Edmun Gibson the
18 of October 1637.

|  |  | li | s | d |
|---|---|---|---|---|
| Imprimis his purse & girdle & money therein | | 0 | 3 | 4 |
| Item his wearing apparrell | | 0 | 16 | 0 |
| It in the Hall 5 brasse kettell,<br>2 brasse pottes & a chaffing dish | | 1 | 15 | 0 |
| It 15 platters 3 pewter dishes, 2 salt fillers<br>1 bason 3 porrengers & other small pewter | | 1 | 6 | 8 |
| It 3 yron pott; & a chaffing dish | | 0 | 13 | 4 |
| It j spit, j dripping pan, a fire slyce, a fire rake<br>j frying pan, 2 cobyrons, 1 treuet, j pothangers<br>2 paire of sheares | | 0 | 10 | 0 |
| It j table, 3 chayres, 4 cushions, dishes & spoones<br>j little latten panne, j brasse ladle, j sconce<br>j yron cleau | | 0 | 5 | 4 |
| It bookes | | 0 | 2 | 0 |

In y[e] Parlour

|  |  | li | s | d |
|---|---|---|---|---|
| Inprimis one cupboord | | 1 | 0 | 0 |
| It 2 ioynd tables & one forme | | 0 | 10 | 0 |

In y[e] buttery

|  |  | li | s | d |
|---|---|---|---|---|
| Inp[rimis] one meale trough, one noading trough,<br>two baskets, two fines with other old lumber | | 0 | 5 | 6 |

In y[e] malt house

|  |  | li | s | d |
|---|---|---|---|---|
| Inp[rimis] one brewing tub, one bucking tub, one rinsing<br>tub, 3 feeders, one chorne, one old chest | | 0 | 13 | 4 |
| It 3 lynnon wheeles, one basket of wooll, one<br>spade, one shouell, one mattocke, with other<br>small tooles of husbandry, & lumber | | 0 | 10 | 0 |

*A probate inventory: one of Kent's richest collections of documents. Valuers tour a deceased man's house and value his possessions room by room (KHLC: PRC/28/20). (Reproduced by kind permission of Kent History and Library Centre)*

and entered into a bound volume of registered wills for office use and public consultation; if an executor declined to pay for this process the will was still proved but remained unregistered, although its value remained the same as that of a registered will. In many cases both the original will and the registered copy have survived, but the latter will always be the more complete series.

At this stage a bond might be entered into where the executor or administrator promised to carry out certain provisions detailed therein, such as attending to the will or administration or acting as guardian to minors. These testamentary bonds can be important evidence that an act had been granted, especially if the act was omitted from the end of the will or if the act book has not survived. For similar reasons both the original and registered copy wills should be investigated as they may have other documents, such as inventories, deeds and letters attached to them, the existence of which is not recorded elsewhere.

In the case of an administration, the administrator would also enter into and sign a bond, after which an act was entered into an administration act book (sometimes a different volume from a probate act book, or in a separate series within the same book) and also generally endorsed on the administration bond which was then filed. Bonds are important and should always be checked as, like wills, they may have other documents attached to them, sometimes even the will itself which was not copied up into the act book. Occasionally a debtor would apply for the grant, perhaps because relatives saw no point, or because there were none.

From 1529–70 it was mandatory for two disinterested parties to submit an inventory of the goods of the deceased within one year of death, attested by the supervisors or overseers named in the will, in order to allow the executors to expedite matters. Such documents may throw certain light on an ancestor's occupation – a fact that all too often remains a matter of conjecture even after the most exhaustive searches. Probate and intestacy inventories are common down to about 1700 and rare after 1750. In the Canterbury diocese survival rates and numbers are exceptional, probably the best in England, and are of the greatest value in throwing light on social standing and professions, often disclosing multiple business interests by the nature of the itemised goods and chattels. The inventory was usually attached to, and filed with, the administration bond or original will, or sometimes filed separately.

More estates and intestacies than might be imagined were disputed or the subject of a testamentary trust, and if this is the case, or even suspected, strenuous efforts should be made to find the corresponding records which may well be voluminous and reveal genealogical information of the highest interest and importance. Very often, the searcher is alerted to such cases by a marginal note in the act book or register copy alluding to a second or third grant of probate, perhaps many decades after the original one. Some of the TNA smaller PROB classes are now online and may offer clues.

Many wills can be unmanageably long and full of repetitive legal jargon. In all cases an abstract should be made by first skimming the will for a general impression, and then noting as an absolute minimum the following:

The name (and bodily health) of the testator
Parish
Marital status
Court of probate
Dates of the will (and codicils) and probate
Names of the executors, overseers and witnesses

Dates should always be written as 12 October 1746, the month as a word between the date and year (and not as a figure because in this year, for example, the tenth month was not October!). If there is no inventory, write down at the end your estimate of the social and financial standing, such as labourer, poor widow, substantial farmer and so on. As for the contents, there must be absolute consistency with abbreviations (which are generally best avoided) in order not to confuse January and June, Mary and Mercy or Edmund and Edward. Copy the relationships exactly as they appear, always with the surname if given. A separate line for each beneficiary is recommended. You may wish to ignore the bequests or perhaps summarise them as furniture, clothing, silver or money, and concentrate instead on the relationships. Children tend to be listed in order of seniority, but some relationships can be problematical and not what they seem to a modern eye: father can be a natural father, father-in-law or step-father; natural son can be an own son as opposed to illegitimate, son-in-law or step-son; grandchildren can be called nephews and nephews cousins. There was no compulsion

*An act book: grants of wills and administrations are recorded chronologically. The entry for William Usborne refers to a will proved twenty-five years previously and to his now deceased widow (KHLC: PRC/22/25/181). (Reproduced by kind permission of Kent History and Library Centre)*

to list all children as some may have received settlements or been provided for long before a parent's death. Kinsman and cousin are vague terms and may not always even imply a blood relationship.

Esquire originally specifically indicated a man entitled to bear arms, and from the 1500s onwards also a man of a family of this rank. Latterly it was further bestowed upon solicitors, barristers and men holding military or naval commissions from the Crown. Gentleman meant superior by position through birth and breeding, and below an esquire in social precedence, but the title was later debased and assumed by the many who sought social ascendancy, especially in the 1800s. A yeoman lived in his own home as a small landowner or tenant farmer, and the term often has little more significance than householder. A husbandman was a small tenant farmer, one step up from a labourer. A clerk before about 1800 was always a cleric unless he was the parish clerk or held a civic position. A man described as 'Mr' was of some standing, but not a gentleman; a woman described as 'Mrs' until about 1750 could be of any marital status or social rank, but thereafter generally a married woman or widow. Spinsters are sometimes also described as 'Mrs'.

### 1858 Onwards

On 11 January 1858 several hundred ecclesiastical probate courts throughout England and Wales were closed, and on the following day the State took over the business of granting acts of probate and administration. A series of annual calendars, together with the probate records themselves, were housed at the new Principal Probate Registry at Somerset House until very recently when they were transferred to High Holborn. The entire series of calendars of wills and administrations from 1858 to just a few months ago has now been digitised and included in the National Probate Index which covers the whole of England and Wales. All searches are now online and copies of any will and grant, or administration, are priced at £10.

The website requests the date of death, but be aware that many wills took a year or two, sometimes much more, before a grant was made, and so as a general rule you should search for an absolute minimum of three years to find an entry. Some entries have retrospective notes about earlier grants as well as cross-references to further ones, all of which should be examined. The calendars (or annual index volumes) include not only people domiciled in this country but many living or dying abroad with estate in England or Wales.

Up to about 1900 the calendars can be exceptionally informative, as these examples of two wills and an administration show:

RIGDEN, Stephen. Effects under £600.
18 June 1882. The will of Stephen Rigden, an oyster dredger, formerly of the City of Rochester, but late of Albert St, Whitstable, both in the county of Kent, a widower, who died 4 May 1882 at Whitsable aforesaid, was proved by Stephen Rigden junior, oyster dredger of Herne in the county of Kent, and Mary Hadlow, the wife of John Hadlow, carpenter of the City of Canterbury, the son and daughter, two of the executors named in the said will. (Further grant 7 August 1903.)

TOMLINSON, David. Estate under £10.
9 December 1892. Probate under certain conditions of the unadministered portion of the estate of David Tomlinson, late of Hythe in the county of Kent, grocer, who died 8 April 1778 at Hythe aforesaid, was granted to Smith & Sons, solicitors of Deal in the said county of Kent. Former grant 26 September 1802 in the PCC.

BLACK, Thomas. Effects under £20.
10 October 1860. Letters of administration of the personal estate and effects of Thomas Black, labourer, a widower, late of Delf St, Sandwich, in the county of Kent, who died 6 September 1860 at Delf St aforesaid, were granted to John Williams, blacksmith of Margate in the said county, the brother-in-law, Thomas Black, Mary Black and Elizabeth Black, the children of the said deceased being minors in the care and guardianship of the said John Williams. Previous grant 22 April 1859.

It will be seen immediately that in these cases all the entries are highly informative, revealing date of death, marital status, residence and occupation, various relatives as well as previous or further grants, one in another court nearly a century earlier. The full will should of course often reveal a great deal more.

After about 1900 the calendars, alas, give progressively less information, but still enough to identify your candidate (often by the address or executors' names); from about 1960 only the date of death and address are shown, and after 1996 just the date of death and the local registry where probate was granted (not always close to the home address). All of which makes for a good example of increasingly less information the nearer to the present we come.

Every indexed will includes additionally the single-sheet grant of probate, often informative in its own right in containing details not included in the will itself, such as the renunciation or death of an executor, the implied remarriage of a widow or daughter and so on. In the absence of a will, there may be an administration act, that is, a single-sheet grant empowering relatives, creditors or other people to wind up the estate, which is sometimes valuable in mentioning other family members such as in-laws or married daughters, and perhaps a change of address.

**Before 1858**
Wills are almost as old as human history, and English wills certainly exist from the Anglo-Saxon period onwards, with many more or less unbroken series from the late mediaeval period onwards. Kent has several sets of records, but first it is prudent to describe one national series.

The Prerogative Court of Canterbury was housed at Doctors' Commons, St Benet, Paul's Wharf, in the City of London. Its records were transferred to Somerset House and are now at TNA, Kew. It specifically proved the wills of all testators having *bona notabilia* (that is, estate or goods worth £5) in two or more dioceses in the Province of Canterbury, or in both the Provinces of Canterbury and York, as well as those of testators dying in Scotland, Ireland or overseas, but leaving estate in England or Wales. It theoretically claimed overriding jurisdiction in England and Wales but in practice was restricted to the southern province of Canterbury (England south of the Trent plus the whole of Wales). By the earlier 1700s this court was widely used by the rich and many other people desirous of the prestige and security which its name afforded. In consequence, its records are of immense value, no less so than from 1653–60 when all other courts were closed and the PCC exercised a temporary but supreme jurisdiction throughout the

| | Vol. | Folio. | Year. |
|---|---|---|---|
| **Godfrey,** Godfrye, John, Tenterden (Adm.) | A.Act. 14 | 68 | 1561-2 |
| ,, Godfreye, John, Newington next Sittin-bourne | A. 37 | 16 | 1562 |
| ,, Godfrye, John, yeoman, Lydd | C. 32 | 22 | 1573 |
| ,, Peter, yeoman, Lydd | C. 31 | 124 | 1569 |
| ,, Godfrye, Simon, Elham | A. 32 | 46 | 1560 |
| ,, Thomas, Orlestone (Adm.) | A.Act. 13 | 125 | 1559 |
| ,, Thomas, Woodchurch (Adm.) | C.Act. 5 | 31 | 1561 |
| ,, Godfrye, Thomas, senior, Lydd (Adm.) | C.Act. 5 | 72 | 1563 |
| ,, Godfrye, Thomas, Snargate | A. 37 | 183 | 1563-4 |
| ,, Thomas, Snargate (Adm.) | A.Act. 17 | 106 | 1573-4 |
| ,, Godfrye, William, Sutton | A. 39 | 48 | 1565-6 |
| **Godward,** John, Ruckinge | A. 40 | 48 | 1567 |
| **Godwatt,** Isabel, Sellinge | A. 40 | 350 | 1570 |
| ,, Godwat, Thomas, Bobbing | A. 36 | 19 | 1562 |
| **Goffe,** *see* **Gough.** | | | |
| **Golde,** Robert, Pluckley (Adm.) | A.Act. 16 | 105 | 1569 |
| ,, Gold, Silvester, Ash next Sandwich | C. 29 | 146 | 1563 |
| ,, Simon, Sittingbourne | A. 40 | 91 | 1567 |
| ,, William, Kingston (Adm.) | A.Act. 15 | 37 | 1564 |
| **Goldfinche,** Elizabeth, widow, Sellinge | A. 35 | 93 | 1560 |
| ,, Elizabeth, widow, Tunstall | A. 42 | 332 | 1577 |
| ,, Richard, *see* **Gemett,** William | | | |
| ,, Silvester, yeoman, Womenswold | C. 32 | 6 | 1572-3 |
| ,, Stephen, Sellinge | A. 35 | 92 | 1560 |
| ,, Goldfynche, Stephen, Preston next Wingham | A. 39 | 231 | 1565 |
| ,, Goldefynche, Stephen, Waltham (Adm.) | A.Act. 17 | 36 | 1572 |
| ,, Goldfynche, William, Rolvenden | A. 38 | 101 | 1564-5 |
| ,, William, Lyminge | C. 32 | 67 | 1574 |
| **Goldhill,** John, Smarden (Adm.) | A.Act. 16 | 94 | 1569 |
| **Golding,** Goldynge, John, Benenden | A. 40 | 48 | 1567 |
| **Goldocke,** Martin, gent., Elmstead | A. 34 | 105 | 1559 |
| **Goldsmith,** John, Boughton Monchelsea | A.Act. 13 | 221 | 1560 |
| ,, Goldsmithe, John, butcher, Sutton Vallance | A. 35 | 82 | 1560 |
| ,, Goldesmythe, John, yeoman, Boxley | A. 39 | 249 | 1566 |
| **Goldynge,** *see* **Golding.** | | | |
| **Goldwell,** Katherine, widow, Great Chart | A. 42 | 64 | 1574 |
| ,, Goldewell, Stephen, Harrietsham | A. 41 | 62 | 1571 |
| ,, *see also* **Gouldwell.** | | | |
| **Golstede,** Richard, Bethersden (Adm.) | A.Act. 13 | 92 | 1558-9 |
| ,, Richard, Bethersden (Adm.) | A.Act. 13 | 208 | 1560 |
| **Goodale,** Edward, vicar of Elmstead | A. 42 | 273 | 1576 |
| ,, Goodall, Joan, widow, Tenterden | A. 38 | 107 | 1564-5 |
| ,, Ralf, yeoman, Sevington | A. 40 | 270 | 1569 |
| **Goodbarne,** William, Goodnestone-next-Wingham (Adm.) | C.Act. 7 | 61 | 1572 |
| **Goodde,** John, Faversham (Adm.) | A.Act. 18 | 27 | 1576 |
| **Goodhew,** Agnes, widow, Hernehill (Adm.) | C.Act. 7 | 56 | 1572 |
| ,, Goodhewe, Dunstone, clerk, Canterbury | A. 39 | 181 | 1566 |
| **Goodman,** John, Hawkhurst | A. 41 | 147 | 1571 |
| **Goodson,** Agnes, Hastingleigh (Adm.) | A.Act. 15 | 40 | 1564 |
| ,, Edward, Milton next Sittingbourne | A. 36 | 60 | 1562 |
| ,, Goodeson, Joan, Elham (Adm.) | A.Act. 14 | 22 | 1561 |
| **Goodwyn,** Alice, widow of William Goodwyn, Boxley | A. 42 | 59 | 1573 |

*A probate index: Tudor wills and administrations for the two Canterbury courts. (British Record Society, Vol. 65, by permission)*

land. No Kentish pedigree can be considered complete until this court has been searched.

Over 1,000,000 PCC wills (TNA: PROB 11) from 1383–1858 are now digitised and searchable online, and may be downloaded for a small fee or seen freely at Kew or at the SOG. Administrations (TNA: PROB 6), which survive from 1559–1858, are variously indexed in hard-copy forms from 1559–1661, 1663–4, 1700–1800 and 1851–8. The period 1661–99 is currently being indexed by the British Record Society, but the last half-century, 1801–50, an important one, remains unindexed and means that the large annual calendars will have to be searched. Despite these difficulties, if you have found no will, strenuous efforts should be made to find an administration as they may sometimes offer conclusive evidence on various genealogical problems. There is an index of Kent administrations in the PCC from 1559–1660 at drdavidwright.co.uk. The PCC has many other types of probate records, such as bonds and inventories; very full details of these and other probate matters will be found in my book *Kent probate records: a catalogue and practical guide*.

Another important national class must be mentioned. At TNA are also housed the Death (or Estate) Duty Records (TNA: IR 26; indexed by IR 27). Duty was payable on many estates over a certain value from 1796, all administered by the Estate Duty Office down to its closure in 1903. The Death Duty Registers are valuable in looking for (1) a PCC administration after 1800; (2) a will or administration if the date and county are unknown; and (3) additional information if a will has already been found. From 1796–1811 the country courts are in various groupings, but from 1812 there are just the two sequences of PCC and all other courts for England and Wales. After about 1815 the series are ever more complete as the scope of duty was extended, especially after 1853, and from 1858 should include all estates worth £20 or more.

The registers are invaluable in including date of death and occupation, the actual amount left by the deceased after debts and expenses, details of executors and legacies, and the date and place of probate. Additionally, because further information could be added for up to fifty years after the first entry, it is possible to observe sequential annotations recording dates of death, references to law suits, names and (changes of ) address of relatives, changes of surname and so on, as far down as grandchildren. Some diabolical Victorian handwriting will be encountered in the registers, but more difficult are the clerks' complicated abbreviations. Fuller details are on the TNA website, and the indexes are now available on Findmypast.

The SOG holds registers of abstracts of wills from 1717–1845 which were used by the Bank of England in respect of bequests of government stocks (see an article describing them in *Family Tree Magazine* for May 2000), and also the Great Western Railway stockholders' probate registers from 1835–1932 (see the *Genealogists's Magazine* for March 2003).

If you can find no will before 1858, consider the following possibilities:

1. The entry has been misindexed or entered only under an alias unknown to you. Search the act books and original documents.
2. A will might have been made but never taken to the courts after death, and now remains in the family papers or elsewhere.
3. The wealthy might have been in receipt of an income from relatives, but predeceased them, thus necessitating no grant. If children were provided for well before a parent's death, no final grant would be necessary.
4. A will or administration could have been granted many decades after death.
5. The estate might have lain entirely outside the jurisdiction in which the deceased lived and a grant was therefore issued in a distant court. Remember that the place of making a will is not necessarily the permanent parish of abode.
6. For no obvious reasons, most probate courts include stray entries: it sometimes happened that the only person able or willing to wind up an estate lived at a great distance and so took out a grant at his convenience in a local court.
7. As a last resort, if there is nothing for your individual, the standard genealogical practice of examining every entry for the surname, although time-consuming, has revolutionised many pedigrees.

The survival of probate records in east Kent has been remarkable in terms of the covering dates, the different classes of material as well as the sheer quantity; west Kent, in contrast, has far less, and mostly from later starting dates. Summaries of the principal classes and their indexes now follow.

## (1) WEST KENT (DIOCESE OF ROCHESTER)

### a) Archdeaconry Court of Rochester
Act books, 1635–1857 (KHLC: DRa/Pa)
Original wills, 1635–1857 (KHLC: DRa/Pw)
Will registers, 1680–1857 (KHLC: DRa/Pwr)

Index of original and registered wills, 1635–1858 (KHLC)

### b) Consistory Court of Rochester
Act books, 1437–1858 (KHLC: DRb/Pa)
Administration bonds, 1666–1858* (KHLC: DRb/Pb)
Deposition books, 1541–1636 (KHLC: DRb/Jd)
Inventories, 1687–1784* (KHLC: DRb/Pi)
Original wills, 1499–1857 (KHLC: DRb/Pw)
Will registers, 1440–1857 (KHLC: DRb/Pwr)

* Cover both the Rochester courts.

### c) Archbishop's Peculiar of the Deanery of Shoreham
Original wills, 1614–1821
Inventories, 1664–1734 (including some bonds, guardians, c.1664–1816)
Will registers, 1664–1821
Act books, 1629–1821
Caveats, 1664–1831

All of the above Shoreham material is held at Lambeth Palace in class VH, which also includes partial indexes. KFHS has published indexes to wills and administrations 1684–1832 and inventories 1664–1734. Some indexes and films of the originals are available at KHLC.

### d) The Peculiar of the Rector of Cliffe
Probate acts and registered wills, 1671–1702 (KHLC: DR/Cp/Ja1)
Will registers, 1701–95 (KHLC: DR/Cp/Jw1)
Original wills, administrations and bonds, 1675–1843 (KHLC: DR/Cp/Jw2/1-2)
Indexes to this peculiar are at KHLC.

Note that following boundary changes in 1846, the testators of many west and north-west Kent parishes must be sought in the PCC, as nothing has survived locally. The Consistory Court of London records held at the London Metropolitan Archives (LMA) should also be checked. There is also an index of west Kent wills up to 1650 at history@vulpeculox.net.

The *West Kent Probate Index 1750–1858* (drdavidwright.co.uk; searchable at Findmypast) includes probate and administration acts from all the above four courts.

## (2) East Kent (Diocese of Canterbury)
Nearly all the records are housed at KHLC, but there are microfilms of wills and administrations at CCA.

### a) Archdeaconry Court of Canterbury
Accounts, 1568–1728 (KHLC: PRC1-2; indexed in BRS Vol. 112)
Act books, 1487–1858 (KHLC: PRC3)
Bonds, 1660–1858 (KHLC: PRC4)
Caveats, 1625–1858 (KHLC: 5)
Guardians, 1584–1784 (KHLC: PRC8-9)
Inventories, 1564–1842 (KHLC: 10-11; indexed at KHLC)
Original wills, 1450–1858 (KHLC: PRC16)
Will registers, 1449–1858 (KHLC: PRC17)

### b) Consistory Court of Canterbury
Accounts, 1596–1740 (KHLC: PRC19-21; indexed in BRS Vol. 112)
Act books, 1542–1857 (KHLC: PRC22)
Bonds, 1660–1857 (KHLC: PRC23)
Caveats, 1628–1809 (KHLC: PRC25)
Guardians, 1631–1763 (KHLC: PRC26)
Inventories, 1564–1748 (KHLC: PRC27-28)
Original wills, 1450–1857 (KHLC: PRC16; 31)
Will registers, 1393–1857 (KHLC: PRC32)

Divided between KHLC, CCA and various cards and books are numerous partial indexes to the above and other material. But the outstanding new index on the CCA website is the *Canterbury Probate*

*Records Database 1396–1858* which covers the will registers in PRC 17 and 32; well-presented and eminently searchable, all researchers are greatly anticipating its completion. Findmypast have digitised much material including indexes to west Kent wills and east Kent probate inventories.

Not many Tudor records will reveal a man's age and birthplace, but there are two series of deposition papers and registers covering 1555–1755 (KHLC: PRC 38-39) which will. They give a person's answers to a legal interrogation and record his life from birth to the present, showing how long a residence in each parish, and are mostly indexed (Duncan Harrington: www.historyresearch.co.uk).

A miscellaneous class of articles, libels, sentences, inventories, debts, accounts, allegations, illegitimacy etc., in all some 20,000 documents covering years 1581–1799, is indexed to 1639 and transcribed in full (KHLC: PRC18; records at CCA).

## Bibliography

Camp, A.J., *Wills and their whereabouts* (1974)

Gibson, J.S.W., *Wills and where to find them* (1974)

—— and Churchill, E., *Probate jurisdictions: where to look for wills* (5th edn 2002)

Mustoe, N.E., *Executors and administrators* (1952)

Rickard, G., *Kent probate inventories in the PCC* (1998)

Spufford, P., *Index to the probate accounts of England and Wales (BRS vols 112–13, 1998; 1999)*

Wright, D., *Kent probate records: a catalogue and practical guide* (2004)

*Chapter 3*

# MAINLY LOCAL RECORDS

## A. BOROUGH

Boroughs were incorporated by the charter of a king or local magnate from the twelfth century and even earlier, such charters remaining as prized possessions (as at Faversham, which includes a Magna Carta). Once incorporated, these self-governing enclaves were almost independent of county authorities. They were usually of commercial or strategic importance and varied considerably in size and wealth. Their government consisted of mayor and corporation (aldermen and councillors), employing officers like steward and clerk, who exercised administrative, law-making and judicial powers. The borough would jealously guard its records, especially those granting valuable privileges, and keep them secure in a chest. The immense time spans over which their records can stretch indicate the stages by which the town's government developed or decayed. With the establishment of the Kent County Council in 1888, the responsibilities of many institutions were gradually taken away from the boroughs and given to the new organisation.

Other than the highly public charters, there are many equally important and interesting classes of borough records of immense value for the topographical history of a town, its judicial, administrative and financial proceedings, as well as for those individuals connected with them. Some of these collections are prodigious in date range and size. If you are fortunate enough to have an ancestor living in one of them, there is a good chance of finding something about him, with the caveat that voluminous searches may be required, although there are some calendars and indexes within the material. Serious browsing of the archive catalogue is highly recommended; below are listed summaries of those principal collections with good runs of material.

The larger and more ancient boroughs each had several courts with differing judicial and administrative functions, such as Court of Record,

Court of Assembly, Mayor's and Sheriff's Courts, Court of Sessions of the Peace and Gaol Delivery, Court of Requests and Pie-powder Court. The records of Borough Sessions and the Clerk of the Peace are similar to those of County Quarter-Sessions and their clerk; and Borough records of later date usually include those of Guardians of the Poor, Turnpike Trusts, Charity Trusts, School Boards and so on.

The enormous bulk of surviving records may be roughly summarised as accounts, administration, apprentices, assembly books, burgess rolls, businesses, by-laws, charters, committees, coroner, court rolls, deeds, electors, estates, examinations and depositions, finance, freemen, gaols, harbours, health and hospitals, inquests, justices, licences, militia, minutes, property deeds, quarter-sessions, sewers and shipping. From those collections fully catalogued, an idea of some of the best material can be obtained.

## Canterbury City

City charters, c.1155–1836; calendared; Burghmote orders, 1487–1849 and petitions, 1554–1704; calendared; Borough minute books, 1835–1974 (all at CCA: CC-A).

A diverse collection, all of which are calendared, including: House, land and servant taxes, 1750s–90s; Military, 1500s; Plague, 1600s; Poll, 1678; Poor relief, 1600s; Rate books, 1843–1968; Subsidies, 1543–1642; Window tax, 1721–88 (all at CCA: CC-B).

Coroners, 1337–1967; calendared and indexed (CCA: CC-C).

Chamberlain account books, 1393–1892; City tradesmen, 1793–1879; Sheriff's farm of the city, 1635–1833; Expense bills, 1652–1743 (all at CCA: CC-F).

Assizes, 1874–1912; Court of pleas, 1300–1624, 1740–1833; Court of pie powder, c.1460–1604; Court of quarter-sessions, 1461–1972; Jury panels, 1415–c.1503 (all calendared at CCA: CC-J).

Apprentices, 1765–1835; Freemen rolls, 1297–1363 and registers 1753–2003; Statute merchant rolls, 1336–1622 (all at CCA: CC-R).

Leases, indentures, grants and deeds, 1313–1893 (calendared) (CCA: CC-Woodruff).

Maps and correspondence, 1787–1958 (indexed) (CCA: CC-Millens).

### Chatham Borough (MALSC: CBA)
Burial board orders and applications, 1869–1961; Court Leet and Baron, 1756–c.1910.

### Cinque Port Confederation, 1496–1968 (KHLC: CPw)
Further material may be found within the Dover, Hythe, Romney and Sandwich collections (the fifth, Hastings, lying in Sussex).

### Dartford Borough (KHLC: Da)
Mostly twentieth century and financial.

### Deal Borough (KHLC: De)
Burgesses, 1835–1913; Coroner, 1773–1814; Court session books, 1719–1938; Enrolled apprentice indentures, 1765–1833; Freemen,1699–1834; Judicial plaint books, 1707–1836; Juries, 1824–95; Petty sessions, 1749–1850; Quarter-sessions, 1714–1971; Treasurer's accounts, 1747–1962.

### Dover Borough (KHLC: Do)
Chamberlain's accounts, 1547–1835; Charters and grants, 1446–1679; Charities, 1558–1956; Cinque Ports Confederation, c.1285–1936; Court of pleas, 1545–1829; Freemen admissions, 1601–1862; Lord Warden of the Cinque Ports, 1358–1855; Minutes, 1558–1835; Petty sessions, 1852–1974; Quarter-sessions, 1828–1971; Sessions of the peace, 1557–1836; Registration and enrolment, 1601–1974.

### Faversham Borough (KHLC: Fa)
Accounts, 1569–1899; Cinque Ports, 1575–1601; Coroner, 1327–1790; Court rolls, 1510–1704; Lord Warden of the Cinque Ports, 1562–1813; Mercers' company, 1616–1835; Militia musters and lists, 1570–1749; Petty sessions, 1782–1878; Quarter-sessions, and frankpledge papers, 1571–1900s; View of frankpledge, 1569–1694; Wardmote minutes, 1436–1583.

**Folkestone Borough (KHLC: Fo)**
Burgess rolls, 1835–77; Cinque Ports, 1721–1973; Quarter-sessions, 1640–1971.

**Fordwich Borough (CCA: U4)**
Calendared, 1276–1950s.

**Gillingham Borough (MALSC: U398)**
1300s–1600s, including a good collection of early title deeds.

**Gravesend Borough (KHLC: Gr)**
1500s onwards, but mostly nineteenth century, including Quarter-sessions, 1828–78.

**Hythe Borough (KHLC: Hy)**
Later 1200s onwards: Coroners' inquisitions, 1674–1835; Petty sessions, 1843–1941; Quarter-sessions, 1673–1952.

**Lydd Borough (KHLC: Ly)**
Accounts, 1428–1855; Charities, 1553–1984; Cinque Ports, 1390–1690; Coroner, 1434–1857; Quarter-sessions, 1561–1887.

**Maidstone Borough (KHLC: Md)**
Bills and receipts, 1575–1832; Freemen, 1551–1938; Indentures, 1563–1714; Judicial, 1591–1971; Officers, 1710–1834; Victuallers' licences, 1651–1828.

**Margate Borough (KHLC: Ma)**
1777–94.

**New Romney Borough (KHLC: Nr)**
Accounts, 1379–1889; Assembly books, 1577–1835; Cinque Ports, 1300–1931; Court books, 1429–1793; Quarter-sessions, 1496–1873; Taxation, 1489–1894.

**Queenborough Borough (KHLC: Qb)**
Borough of court, 1532–1735; Court papers, 1600–1885; Oath rolls, 1688–1774; Petty sessions, 1814–98; Quarter-sessions, 1719–1828; View of frankpledge, 1496–1885.

### Ramsgate Borough (KHLC: Ra)
1728–1987.

### Rochester City (MALSC: RCA)
Accounts and finance, 1400s–1974; Administration, 1614–1974; Admiralty court, 1565–2003; Charters and customal, 1227–1974; Coroners' inquests, 1621–*c*.1881; Court of portmote, 1530–1835; Freemen and apprenticeships, 1663–1974; Judicial, 1530–1974; Quarter-sessions, 1607–1971; Rochester Oyster and Floating Fishery, 1628–2005; Title deeds, 1564–1973; Voters' lists, 1835–1962.

### Liberty of Romney Marsh Borough (KHLC: Rm)
Coroner, 1745–1853; Quarter-sessions, 1610–1903.

### Sandwich Borough (KHLC: Sa)
Accounts, 1375–1953; Cinque Ports, 1494–1959; Quarter-sessions, 1635–1951; Year books, 1431–1837.

### Tenterden Borough (KHLC: Te)
Cinque Ports, 1598–1695; Minutes, 1538–1839; Quarter-sessions, 1538–1970s; Sessions of the Peace and View of Frankpledge, 1637–1739.

### B. CATHEDRAL AND CHURCH COURTS
The mediaeval Church in England, through its prelates and buildings, owned much property, especially land, which gave rise to great quantities of records. It also controlled a hierarchy of courts the activities of which gave rise to innumerable archives. The Dissolution did not materially affect the routine archives of the archbishops, bishops, archdeacons, and deans and chapters – the great series of registers, rolls and papers of their numerous courts – and indeed these judicial and administrative records continued to grow, in the same way as their title deeds and estate archives multiplied. They are almost entirely in Latin until about 1520, and then an English-Latin mixture to 1733, after which, in common with most other classes, they are in English.

The administration of a cathedral and its endowments was (and still is) under the control of the Dean and Chapter. From ancient times bishops regulated the affairs of the Church – faith, religious practice, behaviour, patronage, wills, property and revenue – and until 1860 thus claimed jurisdiction over both clergy and laymen. The bishop's registers are the most important of the mediaeval records and often the oldest, but after the Reformation their entries relate largely to ordinations and institutions of the clergy and consecrations of churches; other administrative series record a variety of information about benefices and clergy. Very little indeed has been published, let alone calendared or indexed.

There is some overlap between diocesan and archidiaconal records. Unlike bishops, archdeacons did not keep registers of ordinations and so forth, nor did they own estates. The bishop's (or consistory) court for ecclesiastical causes and offences was held usually by his chancellor or commissary and the archdeacon's court by a commissary or 'official'. The records are bulky in the extreme and may require some study to get the best from them (but see below for calendars and indexes).

The later visitation books (usually in English) are often of consuming interest. From the thirteenth century the bishop began regularly to visit certain convenient points in his diocese in order to correct abuses and maintain ecclesiastical authority. The visitation books record under each parish a presentment or return concerning the condition of the church fabric, furniture, ornaments, bells, plate and churchyard walls; delinquencies of clergy, church officers and parishioners, such as schoolmasters teaching without licence, Sunday trading or working, playing football during service-time, drunkenness and recusancy. Bishops' visitations were held, in theory, every three years; those of archdeacons annually. After the Reformation much of the tedious business of hearings and judging was left to diocesan officials.

Deposition or cause cases often contain a mass of information on such varied matters as descriptions of parish boundaries, rural customs, farming practices, prices of commodities, and copies of earlier charters. Registrars would preserve many routine documents about presentations to and resignations from benefices, about licences to incumbents for non-residence, to curates, parish clerks and schoolmasters, and also to surgeons and midwives who could then baptise in case of emergency.

The majority of the offences were concerned with breaches of discipline by clergy or laity (the 'bawdy' courts) for prostitution, drunkenness, adultery and fornication, or were matrimonial, defamation or tithe cases, or related to probate of wills or administration of intestates' property. Even shorter entries can be remarkably informative. The courts were at the height of their powers in the 1500s and 1600s, abolished in 1642 and reinstated in 1661, but rapidly declined with the rise of Nonconformity and the increasing power assumed by the State over people's lives.

Churchwardens could present parishioners to a Church court for offences under ecclesiastical law, such presentments being frequent during a bishop's or archdeacon's annual visitation when prelates would examine parochial administration, dissent, faith and morals. On such occasions, all clergy, churchwardens, church officials and others would be summoned to give evidence. The churchwardens' presentments were noted in detection books (*comperta et detecta*). Sentences varied from light reprimands (monitions and admonitions) to a private or public penance, or even excommunication. Fines levied had to be used for charitable purposes; the guilty had to pay substantial court fees and might have certain privileges temporarily withdrawn, such as attending church.

### (1) Diocese of Rochester

West Kent has suffered enormous destruction or losses and the records are insignificant in comparison with east Kent, particularly after about 1800. What survives is for the rural deaneries of Dartford, Malling and Rochester only:

> Bishop's registers, 1300s–1600s (KHLC: DRb/Ar)
> Induction mandates, 1500s–1800s (KHLC: DRa/Ai)
> Meeting House certificates, earlier 1800s (KHLC: DRa/M; DRb/M)
> Presentments, 1704–1803 (KHLC: DRa/Vp)
> Sequestration papers, 1700s (KHLC: DRb/As)
> Terriers, 1600s–1700s (KHLC: DRb/At)
> Visitation books, *c.*1500–1800 (KHLC: DRa/Vb)

The records of the Dean and Chapter of Rochester are much more extensive. They comprise St Andrew's Priory, Rochester, St Mary and St Nicholas' Priory, Leeds, and Newark Hospital, Strood (1100–1541), and the Dean and Chapter itself (1541–1964).

All the following are at MALSC: DRc:

> Cathedral registers, 1100s–1300s
> Chapter clerks, 1578–1901
> Charity, 1670–1952

Charters, *c*.1100–1539
Choirmaster and organist appointments, 1560–1896
Estate, 1541–1963
Financial, *c*.1080–1959
Legal, 1096–1954
Schoolmaster appointments, 1631–1757; 1863–1935

## (2) Diocese of Canterbury

As for probate, East Kent has a prodigious survival. Here will be found many valuable leads to the clergy, curates and church officials, parish officials, parishioners and property, as well as ordinary people involved in examinations and depositions following disputes or crimes. They may well contain one of the largest bodies of information about the movements of people within England when the inescapable fact is that such records of movement are otherwise almost totally lacking.

Applications and petitions for licences for curates, matrimony, midwives, parish clerks, physicians, schoolmasters, sesses, surgeons and testamentary, 1614–1826 (CCA: DCb/L/B)
Chaplains' licences, 1859–1960 (calendared) (CCA: DCb/F/F)
*Chartae Antiquae* (AD 600s–1900s; about 7,000)
Christ Church Priory officials, *c*.1066–1540 (indexed by name/office).
Christ Church Priory estate farmers and bedels, *c*.1394–1540 (indexed by name)
Churchwardens' presentments on church property, clergy, officials and parishioners, 1565–1700; 1836–1901 (CCA: DCb/V/P)
Citations to appear, 1660–1799 (CCA: DCb/J/C/1-12)
Clergy absence licences, 1804–1927 (calendared) (CCA: DCb/F/L)
Clergy inductions to benefices, *c*.1660–1960 (CCA: DCb/F/A)
Clergy induction books, 1564–1869 (CCA: DCb/F/B/)
Court act books, 1640–1788 (CCA:DCb/J/A/)
Court depositions (*comperta et detecta*):
  a) 1449–1700s (CCA: DCb/J/X)
  b) instance acts, 1372–1710 (CCA: DCb/J/Y)
  c) instance acts and depositions, 1499–1764 (indexed by name and parish) (CCA: DCb/J/Z)
There is a selection of typescript calendars to the X/Y/Z/ series for the 1550s–60s and 1730s–40s

Curates' licences, 1813–95 (CCA: DCb/F/C/)

General licences, 1660–1714 (indexed by subject, name and place) (CCA: DCb/LR)

Ordination lists, 1800s–1900s (calendared) (CCA: DCb/F/O/1)

Ordination papers, 1777–1961 (indexed) (CCA: DCb/F/O/2)

Papers in ecclesiastical causes, 1595–1745 (calendared) (CCA: DCb/J/J)

Penances 1662–1792 (CCA: DCb/J/P/A)

Returns of communicants and householders, 1565, for Appledore, Boughton Malherbe, Lympne, Milsted, New Romney, Paddlesworth, Saltwood and Woodchurch (CCA: DCb/Q/C)

Surrogate appointment bonds, 1755–84 (indexed) (CCA: DCb/J/S)

Visitation call books (parishes listed by deanery with officials, incumbents, churchwardens and sidesmen), 1596–1721; 1743–94; 1811–99 (CCA: DCb/V/V)

Unofficial and other collections:
  Bonds, 1285–1718, calendared, with index of witnesses

Christ Church Priory manors, bedels' rolls, c.1250–c.1450, about forty parishes, Hoo peninsula, Romney Marsh and Sheppey (partly calendared)

Church Commissioners: cathedral estate manorial court rolls (about thirty parishes), 1247–1756 (CCA: U15)

St Augustine's Abbey, 1250–1538 (CCA: U14)

**Bibliography**

Horn, J.M. (ed.), *Fasti Ecclesiae Anglicanae 3: Canterbury, Rochester and Winchester dioceses* (1974)

Houlbrooke, R.A., *Church courts and the people during the English reformation* (1979)

Tarver, A., *Church court records* (1995)

## C. DIRECTORIES

These are fascinating to browse, arranged as they are by counties, towns and parishes. They offer a snapshot of clergy, gentry, tradesmen and principal residents, along with attractions, amenities, transport links, postal services and much more. Earlier ones have far less population coverage, especially as being listed involved payment. By the 1850s listings for cities were enormous and subdivided into commercial, street and court sections. Many were printed every two or three years so are

# SANDWICH,

### WITH THE VILLAGES OF ASH AND EASTRY AND NEIGHBOURHOODS.

SANDWICH is a cinque port, market town, and borough both corporate and parliamentary, with separate jurisdiction, locally in the hundred of Eastry and lathe of St. Augustine—68 miles E. by S. from London, 39 E. from Maidstone, and 13 E. from Canterbury; situated on the navigable river Stour, about two miles from its influx with the sea, and environed by a considerable extent of low ground. It is one of the most ancient towns in the kingdom, and among the cinque ports is ranked as the second—was formerly walled, and had eight gates, only one of which (Fishers' gate, well deserving the inspection of the antiquary and architect,) is now standing. The guildhall, or court, was erected in 1579, and is a handsome building. Sandwich has received various charters; that granted by Charles II remained in force until the operation of the municipal act vested the government in a mayor, four aldermen and twelve councillors, with the usual assistants, under the style of 'the mayor, jurats and commonalty of the town and port of Sandwich, in the county of Kent.' The civil jurisdiction extends to the neighbouring town of Ramsgate, and to Walmer, Sarr and Brightlingsea (the latter in Essex), all of which are members or limbs of Sandwich; and all offences committed in these places are tried before the mayor, recorder and bench, at the sessions, held for the purpose three or four times in the year. The inhabitants have the convenience of a court of record, and also that of a court of requests. Among the many privileges enjoyed by Sandwich as a cinque port is that of appointing three 'Barons' to assist in supporting the canopy over the sovereign at the coronation; and when a queen consort is also crowned, six are deputed, who enjoy the favour of dining at the coronation feast, at a table placed on the right hand of their majesties. Since the 42nd year of Edward III, the borough has uninterruptedly returned two members to parliament, who are styled barons; the mayor is the returning officer, and the present representatives are Sir Edward Thomas Troubridge and Sir Rufane Donkin, Baronets. The foreign trade of Sandwich is principally with Norway, Sweden and Russia, for iron, timber and hemp; and the home trade with Wales and Scotland, comprising the export of flour, seed, hops, malt, fruit, &c. Ship building and rope making are carried on to a limited extent, but not a vestige exists of its once famous woollen trade. There are some excellent inns; the principal are the 'Cinque Port Arms' and the 'Fleur de Lis'— the latter is in high estimation as a commercial house.

The town includes the parishes of St. Clement, St. Mary the Virgin and St. Peter the Apostle. The church of St. Clement is an ancient spacious structure, with a massive tower in the Norman style; St. Mary's also is ancient, and St. Peter's is a specimen of Norman ecclesiastical architecture, but the original south aisles of both have been destroyed by accident. The benefices of St. Clement's and St. Mary's are vicarages, in the presentation of the archdeacon of Canterbury; that of St. Peter's is a discharged rectory, in the patronage alternately of the crown and the corporation. Baptists and Wesleyan methodists have their respective places of worship. The free grammar school, endowed with exhibitions, was founded in 1563; national and charity schools are likewise here. Among the charitable institutions are the hospitals of St. Thomas and St. John, situate within the walls, for the comfortable residence and maintenance of a number of aged persons; and the munificent foundation of Saint Bartholomew's hospital, just without the town, supports sixteen respectable decayed tradesmen, and others of the corporation, in a state of comparative affluence. Wednesday and Saturday are the market days; the Wednesday's market, held at the 'Fleur de Lis' inn, is a considerable one for corn; and on every alternate Monday there is a cattle market, well attended. A large fair is held on the 4th December, which often lasts ten days, and there are several fairs of a minor character. The cinque port and parishes of Sandwich contained, at the census taken in 1831, 3,136 inhabitants.

About three miles west from Sandwich, in the same lathe, and in the hundred of Wingham, is the respectable village of Ash. The church, dedicated to St. Peter and St. Paul, is a handsome stone edifice, with a square tower and clock, conspicuous from the greater part of the village; it was formerly a chapel to the ancient monastery of Wingham. Fairs are held on the 5th April and October 10th. Population of the parish, 2,140.

Eastry, a village and parish, partly in the hundred of Wingham, but chiefly in that of its name, in the same lathe as Sandwich, two miles and a half from that town, was formerly distinguished as the residence of several of the Saxon kings of Kent. The church, dedicated to St. Mary, is a spacious structure, and appears to have been erected partly in the Norman style of architecture. An annual fair, for the sale of cattle, is held here on the 2nd of October. The parish contained, by the last returns (those of 1831), 1,245 inhabitants.

**POST OFFICE,** Market street, SANDWICH, William Pratt, *Post Master.*—Letters from LONDON arrive (by way of Canterbury) every morning at seven, and are despatched every evening at seven.

**POST,** Ash, *Receiving-House* at William Ralphs'.—Letters from LONDON arrive (by foot post from Wingham) every morning at half-past six, and are despatched every evening at seven.

**POST,** Eastry.—Letters arrive (by foot post from Sandwich) every morning at half-past seven, and are despatched every evening at six.

### GENTRY AND CLERGY.

Belsey Mr. Nathaniel, Love lane
Birch Mr. Joseph, Strand st
Bridger William, esq. Eastry Court
Brockman Rev. Thomas, King st
Castle Mrs. Martha, Strand st
Castle Mr. Thomas, Eastry
Chambers Rev. Charles, Eastry
Collard Mr. William, Sandwich
Crane Mr. William, Sandwich
De Bock Mr. Thomas, Lucksboat st
Deane Capt. William, Jail st
Eastry Mr. George, Eastry
Emmerson Charles, esq. Strand st
Farmariss Mr. Robert, Bowling st
Friend Mr. William, Ash
Friend Mr. Wm. jun. Molland
Godfrey John, esq. Ash
Harris Mr. William, High st
Harrison Mrs. Elizabeth, New st
Harrison Mr. George, Delph st
Harrison Mr. Richard, Harnet st
Hatfield Mr. James, Eastry
Hudson Mrs. Sarah, Guilton
Hudson Mr. Zachariah, New st
Joynes Mrs. Frances, Lucksboat st

Keble Mr. Henry, King st
Kelsey Mrs. Elizabeth, Ash
Knight Mr. George, Northbourne
Lawrence Mrs. Elizabeth, Delph st
Layton Rev. James, Canterbury gate
Nethersole Mrs. Mary, Gaol st
Nixon Rev. Francis, Russell Ash
Pemble Rev. Henry, High st
Pott Mr. William, Market st
Rae Mr. James, Walton house, Eastry
Randolph Rev. Geo. Vicarage, Eastry
Richford Mr. Richard, New st
Rolph Mr. William Henry, New st
Sladden the Misses, Ash
Slaughter Mrs. Elizabeth, Delph st
Solly Mr. George, Bowling st
Spencer Mrs. Susan, Ash
Stewart Lieut. Thos. D. R. N. High st
Turner Mr. Thomas, Ash
Waller Miss Mary, Lucksboat st
Wodsworth Miss Elizabeth, High st
Wood John, esq. Delph st
Wood Thomas, esq. Delph st
Woodcock Mrs. Fanny, Strand st
Woodcock Mr. Henry, High st
Wyburn Capt. John, R. N. New st

### ACADEMIES AND SCHOOLS.

Beal Thomas, King st
FREE GRAMMAR SCHOOL, Canterbury gate—Rev. James Layton, master
Jones the Misses, Strand st
Jullion Francis, Eastry
Lass John Lawrence, Strand st
NATIONAL SCHOOL, Harnet st— Henry Hawkins, master; Miss Watts, mistress
NATIONAL SCHOOL, Ash—Samuel Hatchard, master; Mrs. Hatchard, mistress
Powell Esther, Strand st
Smith John, Market st
Stone Sarah, King st
Young Thomas, Eastry

### ATTORNEYS.

Lee William (and clerk to the court of requests), Gaol st
Mourilyan John (& notary public), Strand st [and at Deal
Surrage & Emmerson, Strand st,

### AUCTIONEERS.

Baker John, Market st
Crosoer Francis, Strand st

*A commercial directory (1): Sandwich in 1839.*

101

**KENNINGTON** is a parish and village, on the roads from Ashford to Faversham and Canterbury, 2 miles north from Ashford station on the South Eastern and Chatham section of the Southern railway, and 56 from London, in the Ashford division of the county, hundreds of Chart and Longbridge, lathe of Scray, union of East Ashford, county court district and petty sessional division of Ashford, rural deanery of East Charing, archdeaconry of Maidstone and diocese of Canterbury. The river Stour forms the boundary between this parish and Willesborough. The church of St. Mary is of stone, with some Norman features and other portions in the Early English and Perpendicular styles, and has a tower containing 6 bells: there are some fine stained glass windows, memorials to the Tritton, Burra and Carter families: a tablet commemorates the men connected with this parish who gave their lives in the Great War, 1914-18: the church was restored in 1878, and affords 320 sittings. The register of baptisms and burials dates from the year 1671; marriages, 1673. The living is a vicarage, net yearly value £360, including 7 acres of glebe and residence, in the gift of the Archbishop of Canterbury, and held since 1926 by the Rev. John Alfred Wood M.A. of Emmanuel College, Cambridge. There is a Congregational chapel. The almshouse, with £28 yearly for maintenance, was the gift of George Herbst and Harriet Mary Lake in 1890. Henry Watts left in 1602 1½ acres of land, producing £4 yearly; Mary Marshall left an annuity of 30s. of which 20s. is given to 10 poor persons and 10s. is laid out in repairing the church; William Brett in 1704 left a charge of £1 upon a house and land for clothing; Richard Brett left in 1711 a charge of £1 upon land; William Young left a tithe rent-charge in 1890, now producing £1 7s. 5d.; the above charities are distributed to the poor. Bricks and tiles are made here. Miss Billington, W. J. Jennings esq. and Messrs. the Grosvenor Sanatorium Limited are the principal landowners. The soil is light. The chief crops are wheat, oats, beans, peas and barley. The area is 1,383 acres of land and 8 of water; rateable value, £7,680; the population in 1921 was 1,527.

Post, M. O., T. & T. E. D. Office.—Mrs. Edith Pritchard, sub-postmistress. Letters through Ashford

Public Elementary School (mixed), with master's residence, built in 1872 & enlarged in 1886, for 190 children; William Exton, master

Carriers to Ashford.—John Stayte & A. Smith, daily

Conveyance.—Motor omnibuses pass through at regular intervals

### PRIVATE RESIDENTS.

(For T N's see general list of Private Residents at end of book.)

Ackroyd Sidney J. The Limes
Ackroyd Wm. Lancelot, Vicarage rd
Babington Thomas, Yew Tree house
Bailey Frederick, Maycroft
Baker James William, The Lees
Bentley William, Sunnyside
Benzie Ernest Edwin, Burton road
Billington Miss, Kennington house
Bray Herbert Arthur, Roseash
Broadbent Mrs. Pendennis
Brock Capt. William S. R. Kilara
Byrne Basil Reginald, Windyridge
Burden Miss, West tree
Burrows Alfred John F.S.I. Holmlea
Clark Sidney Hatch, Ellyngg
Clements Sidney Charles, Spearpoint
Collins Frederick, The Cedars
Colver Frank H. Glen Roy
Crispe William H. Meads
Dell Mrs. Lynwood
Eadon Lt.-Col. Frank Henry, Bybrook
Everett Samuel, Eastcombe
Flower Frank, Swiss house
Flower Frank Mainwaring, St. Clair
Foster Samuel, The Nook
Gower Denis, Sterbor
Grace Mrs. Woodbine villa
Griffin Mrs. Fairmont
Hale Leonard Walter, The Lindens
Hail John W. Faversham road
Hamnett Thomas A. Oulton
Headley Lewis Percy, The Cabin
Headley Paul I'Anson, The Croft
Hill John G. St. Margarets
Hunt Harold W. Melrose
Inge Frederick, Elim
Jeffrey Thomas, The Cedars
Jeffrey Wm. Stainton. Meadowside
Jennings William Joseph, Kennington hall
Johnson William, Brents
Judge Raymond, Mendip
King James J. Highview
Kingsland Misses, Brooklyn
Laslett L. W. Orchardway
Leech Mrs. H. W. Penlee point
McKenna Surg-Commander F. V., R.N. Coombe cottage
Mercer Arthur, The Knoll
Millen Mrs. Kennington villa
Morton Edgar, The Studio
Newnham Joseph, Park view

Nightingale John, The Grange
Padgham Mrs. Kildare
Pain William, Seno
Peters W. G. G. The Park
Peters Mrs. The Laurels
Peters William Grice, Abbotsville
Rix Archibald, Ripton
Robertson Miss, Clydesdale house
Rouch Edward Ernest, Ivydene
Scott Major Horace Wm. Temple ho
Scott Alan Winter, The Lawn
Southern George, The Gables
Stanford Fred, Withersdane
Stapley Misses, Forestmere villas
Stickels Elvy, Pinewood villa
Stickels Frederick Cubison, Walnut lo
Strouts Frederick, The Lodge
Strouts Miss, Clyde cottage
Stuart Mrs. Inversnaid
Tomkins John George, Anhurst
Travis John William, The Park
Tym John Samuel, Birtles
Vickers V. R. S. Spearpoint
Warden Miss, Woodbines
Wenborn James, Fair view
West Mrs. Rockholme
Wilson Rev. Frederic D'Arcy M.A The Rosary
Wilson Herbert, Gleniffer brae
Wood Rev. John Alfred M.A. (vicar), The Vicarage
Wood Harry, Albert villa
Wood Misses, Planet view
Wright Joseph, The Hut

### COMMERCIAL.

Early closing day, Wednesday.

Allchin Alfd. Ernest, tea rms
Barnes Wm. farmer, Sunnymead
Blaxland Arthur, grocer
Bockhanger Farm Ltd. farmers (P. H. Jones, director; Jas. Staples, mngr.). T N 9
Burch William, farmer, Vicarage rd
Burton Brick & Gravel Co. (J. M. Poncia, sec)
Chapman Geo. spile mkr
Collins Edith (Miss), dressma. The Cedars
Dew Hy. T. motor engnr T N 8
Everett Arthur E. Golden Ball P.H
File Marshall, farmer, Little Burton
Gilbert Edwd. shopkpr
Gilham John, farm bailiff to W. J. Jennings esq. Home farm
Goodwin Stephen, carpenter

Grosvenor Sanatorium Ltd. (P. H. Jones, governing director). T N 9
Halksworth Samuel, jobbing gardener, Vicarage road
Hamilton Bros. farmers, East Mountain
Harris James, gardener
Headley Henry, grocer
Jeffrey T. & M. motor engnrs. TN 30
Jell Thos. dairy, Tudor ho
Kennington Ex-Service Men's Club (Capt. W. S. R. Brock, sec)
Kennington & District Gardening Society (W. J. Jennings, president; Chas. Skinner, hon. sec)
Kennington Women's Institute (Mrs. Burrows, president)
Kingsland Edward, farmer, Coningbrook farm
Law Arth. W. shopkpr
Mallion Geo. land steward to Miss E. M. G. Billington, The Oaklands
Martin Henry, wheelwright
Miles Francis Adrian, farmer, West Croft
Padgham Wm. & Co. Ltd. thrashing machine & traction engine owners. T N 6
Padgham Ernest C. haulage contrctr, T N 39
Philpott Chas. G. butcher, Marshall ho. T N 38
**Peters William Grice,** builder
Pritchard Edith (Mrs.), statnr. (retail), & post office
Pullen Thomas William, deputy registrar of births, deaths & marriages Wye sub-district, East Ashford union & consulting surveyor of highways to East Ashford Rural District Council & expenditor of sewers, The Hut
Raven James, builder, Burton road
Rogers C. S. grocer. T N 44
Staples Fredk. H. butcher
Tutt Edwin Norbury, bldr

**TUTTS LAUNDRY** (Ernest Edwin Benzie, proprietor) (T N 16); & at Ashford

Ward Alfred John, insurance agent
Watts Ebenzr. Wm. brewers' agt
Webb Frank, assistant overseer & clerk to the Parish Council, Norfolk villa
Woodward Geo. Rose P.H. T N 42

*A commercial directory (2): Kennington in 1927.*

102

useful for following your itinerant ancestor. There are a few Kent directories for the late 1700s, and Finch directories for the main Kent towns from as early as 1803, but the main series get going with *Pigot* in 1822, *Kelly* for the Post Office in 1837 and *Bagshaw* in 1847, all of which are based on a certain amount of original enquiry in the neighbourhood. They have been widely reprinted and fiched, with good collections at KHLC (*Kelly*, 1845–1938), CCA, the SOG and public libraries.

Early telephone directories from about 1900, curiosities in their own right, are useful for ancestors in trade or business and will reveal the commercial address, perhaps far from home. The British Telecom Archives at 268–270 High Holborn WCIV 7EE include an almost complete set of directories from 1880–1984 for London and the provinces. There are many collections of recent volumes held locally if you are looking for living relatives.

**Bibliography**
Bergess, W.F. and Riddell, B.I., *Kent directories located* (2nd edn 1978)
Norton, J.E., *Guide to the national and provincial directories, excluding London, published before 1856* (1950)
Shaw, G. and Tipper, A., *British directories, a bibliography and guide to directories published in England and Wales (1850–1950) and Scotland (1773–1950)* (2nd edn 1997)

## D. HOUSE HISTORIES
To the genealogist, few things are more satisfying than being able to pinpoint the building in which ancestors lived. You may wish to start by photographing known family houses, whether a 1930s semi-detached, Victorian terrace or Georgian town house. All properties were probably named or numbered, and are therefore identifiable with reasonable certainty, with the caveat that house numbers do not regularly appear until about the 1860s and were initially subject to some renumbering.

### a) Printed Secondary Sources
Are you interested in researching the history of the actual building, dating the structure and discovering the ways it has changed over the years? Or perhaps tracing the various owners and occupiers, and then discovering evidence of what stood on the site before the present building? Many domestic buildings in Kent are mentioned in the

standard county histories (Hasted, for example) and countless local societies have written their own town or village histories, to be found in local studies collections. Buildings of above average architectural interest or with unusual features are often noted in J. Newman and N. Pevsner's *The Buildings of England* series. If a building has been scheduled for preservation, its architecture and approximate age will be noted briefly in the *Statutory List of Buildings of Special Architectural or Historic Interest* issued by the Department of the Environment, which is regularly updated. Street and trade directories from about 1850 describe places and list the main buildings and houses, together with the names of private inhabitants and tradesmen. For this purpose, town or area directories are far more detailed than county ones.

The large-scale successive editions of Ordnance Survey maps might reveal an approximate building date and the block-plan at the time of surveying. The best ones are the 1:2,500 (25in to the mile), produced for Kent between 1858 and 1873, and revised for 1893–7 and 1905–10. The best collection is at KHLC, including all of the 1905–10 editions at the 6in and 1:2500 scales. The larger Kent towns were also surveyed in the 1800s on a scale of 1:500 (10ft to the mile), and with their minute topographical detail and annotations these are invaluable for built-up areas. Many libraries have the copies for their own areas, and beyond them the British Library should be consulted.

Tithe maps (q.v.) from about 1839 show numbered plots which can then be traced using the apportionments to reveal owners' names, occupiers (if different from the owners) and the description of the property including field names, state of cultivation, acreage and rent charges. The maps will therefore show immediately whether a particular building existed at this time, whether it had more or less land attached to it and who owned and occupied it.

Estate maps, existing from the 1500s onwards, generally reveal the estate of one landowner, either an individual or corporate body, when the surveyor employed would include all information of interest to the owner. The best collection is at KHLC and fully catalogued.

### b) Original Sources
If you can locate them, title deeds will give you a short description of a house, its position, the size of the plot and the names of one or more of

the previous owners. If the sequence of documents is quite complete then these names and descriptions can easily stretch back over several centuries.

Notices of sale were often nailed up in public, detailed catalogues were produced when estates and larger houses came up for sale, and estate agents' brochures compiled for historical properties. Newspapers would publish notices of house sales, changes of street names and area developments, and images might survive as photographs, postcards or engraved prints, any of which could reveal what formerly stood on the site of a modern building.

When treated with care, the 1841–1911 census returns are extremely valuable, especially the 1911 in which the owner or occupier also stated the number of rooms. Electoral registers from 1832 list voting adults by address and are more valuable after 1867 when the franchise was extended. Rate books list owners and occupiers of properties on which rates were payable; from about 1600 they were collected on a parochial basis, but will now almost certainly be in an archive, and if not then in the parish church.

The various Public Health Acts of the nineteenth century produced bye-laws which increased control over new buildings and alterations to existing ones. Applications for building consents often give the names of owner, builder and architect and retain the plans of proposed works. Surviving consents are usually found in archives as part of local authority collections or are held by existing district councils.

Tax records include the Land Tax, especially valuable from 1780–1832 when payment of this was a necessary qualification to vote, the mid-1660s Hearth Taxes, and the Window Tax of 1696–1851. Probate inventories, especially well preserved and indexed for east Kent (q.v.), list a person's property, often room by room and item by item with individual values.

If a house once formed part of a great estate, then manorial or estate records should be investigated. Buildings that were only partly residential, such as an inn, toll-house, school, almshouse, or devoted to ecclesiastical purposes will have corresponding records.

## Bibliography

Alcock, N.W., *Old title deeds, a guide for local and family historians* (rev. edn 2001)

——, *Documenting the history of houses* (2003)

Barley, M.W., *The English farmhouse and cottage* (1961)

Barratt, N., *Tracing the history of your house: a guide to sources* (2006)

Breckon, B., *Tracing the history of houses* (1991)

Cave, L.F., *The smaller English house* (1981)

Cornwall, J., *An introduction to reading old title deeds* (1993)

Dibben, A.A., *Title deeds* (rev. edn 1990)

Girouard, M., *Life in the English country house* (1980)

Goodenough, R., *Researching the history of a country house – a guide to sources and their use* (2010)

Gravett, K., *Timber and brick building in Kent* (1971)

Guy, J., *Kent castles* (1980)

Harvey, J.H., *Sources for the history of houses* (1974)

Iredale, D., *Discovering your old house* (rev. edn 1991)

*Mediaeval houses in Kent: survey conducted by the Royal Commission on the historical monuments of England between 1986–1992,* 10 vols (n.d.)

Muthesius, S., *The English terraced house* (1982)

Newman, J. and Pevsner, N., *The Buildings of England: Kent: North-east and east* (rev. edn 2013); *Kent: West Kent and the Weald* (rev. edn 2012)

Savidge, A., *The parsonage in England: its history and architecture* (1964)

## E. NEWSPAPERS

There were hardly any newspapers before 1700, and then only in limited circulation as paper was expensive and literacy limited. The first county newspaper was the *Canterbury Kentish Post*, established in 1717. Government taxes on 'knowledge' were designed to limit the circulation of publications and thereby curb unwelcome thoughts about the Establishment. By the 1830s literacy and the demand for reading matter were growing but still hampered by taxation on the production of newspapers; this was removed in the 1850s and allowed the provincial press to expand rapidly. In 1850 there were twenty-one Kentish newspapers, rising to over forty in 1870, mostly priced at 1*d.*, although some even less. Many towns had several titles (in 1865 Gravesend and Tunbridge Wells four, Dover five, Canterbury seven), with strong competition for advertising revenue and the consequent take-overs and closures. The penny post and the railways ensured regular distribution from London, adding to national and international news.

Early reports on such matters as crime (often sensational), marriages and funerals can be fulsome and include many names, although details should be corroborated if possible. Local newspapers are also clearly valuable if your ancestor was involved in a notable event, perhaps a fire, accident, epidemic or mining or shipping disaster. Industry, agriculture and trade fill much space. Business advertisements are frequent and will supply names and addresses. The columnar arrangement featured from the earliest times, small crude drawings in advertisements from the eighteenth century and sketches of people and events from about 1840.

Until very recently the unwieldiness of newsprint and almost complete absence of indexes (Palmer's index to *The Times* being a notable exception) meant that, apart from serendipitous discoveries, most searches were fruitless as news was printed in order of receipt and in no fixed place. However, the modern digital revolution means that vast amounts of historical material is coming online, some of it free to read. The websites of the British Library and British Newspapers Archive are the two main sources, but national papers such as the *Observer* (1791), the *Guardian* (1821), the *New York Times* index (1851–1922) and others are now available.

A list follows of Kent newspapers founded before about 1860 and with reasonable spans of existence. Fuller details can be found in W.G. Bergess and B.I. Riddell's *Biography of British newspapers: Kent.*

*Beckenham Journal*, 1876–date
*Bexleyheath and Welling Observer*, 1867–date
*Canterbury Kentish Post*, 1717–68
*Chatham, Rochester and Gillingham News*, 1859–date
*Chatham Standard*, 1858(?)–date
*Dartford and Swanley Chronicle*, 1869(?)–date
*Dover Chronicle and Cinque Ports and Kent Advertiser*, 1835–1927
*Dover Express and East Kent News*, 1858–date
*Dover Telegraph and Cinque Ports General Advertiser*, 1833–1927
*East Kent Gazette*, 1857–date
*East Kent Mercury, Deal and Sandwich News*, 1865–date
*Faversham Times and Mercury*, 1860–date
*Gravesend and Dartford Reporter*, 1856–date
*Greenwich, Woolwich and Deptford Gazette*, 1833–date
*Isle of Thanet Gazette and East Kent Times*, 1870–date
*Kent and Sussex Courier*, 1872–date
*Kent Coast Times*, 1866–date

*Kent Herald*, 1792–date
*Kent Messenger*, 1859–date
*Kentish Express*, 1855–date
*Kentish Gazette*, 1768–date
*Kentish Independent and County Advertiser*, 1843–date
*Kentish Observer*, 1832–1977
*Kentish Weekly Post or Canterbury Journal*, 1768–1838
*Lewisham and Blackheath Times*, 1870–date
*Maidstone Gazette*, 1815–date
*Maidstone Journal*, 1786–1911
*Rochester Gazette*, 1821–1868
*Sevenoaks Advertiser*, 1840–1943
*Sevenoaks Chronicle*, 1881–date
*Sheerness Guardian and East Kent Advertiser*, 1858–1939
*Tonbridge Telegraph*, 1863–1905
*Tunbridge Wells Weekly Express*, 1863–1902
*Whitstable Times and Tankerton and Swalecliffe Press*, 1864–date
*Woolwich Gazette and Plumstead News*, 1871–1939

Other valuable sources are the *London Gazette*, which has been published since 1665 (partial indexes to 1786; complete thereafter), containing official court and government announcements such as naturalisations, changes of name and bankruptcies. The *Gentleman's Magazine* (indexed) was published monthly from 1731–1868 and is valuable for announcements of births, marriages and deaths, bankrupts and military appointments in the middle and upper classes. The obituaries can be long and include ordinary people if they were in any way remarkable. Sir William Musgrave's *Obituary prior to 1800* (Harleian Society, Vols 44–9) includes many death announcements culled from other sources.

## Bibliography

Bergess, W.G. and Riddell, B.I., *Biography of British newspapers: Kent* (1982)

Crane, R.S. and Kaye, F.B., *A census of British newspapers and periodicals 1620–1800* (1979)

Eagle, S., and Dixon, D., *Report of the Newsplan project in the London and south eastern library region (LASER) January 1992–December 1995* (1996)

## F. NONCONFORMITY

Fear of persecution means that there are no Nonconformist registers nationally before 1644, two of the earliest Kentish Nonconformist registers being the Bessells Green Old Meeting House in Chevening parish (1650) and the Rochester Society of Friends (1674). The first systematic keeping of registers, unique in their thoroughness, was by the Quakers, but until the ejection of Nonconformist ministers in 1662, all the Presbyterians and a few of the Independent clergy were incumbents in the Established Church and did not keep separate registers. Some started in the later 1700s, but many others failed to keep any at all. The Methodist revival made little difference as until the nineteenth century most attended their parish churches; but the revival did see the introduction of the Moravian Church, easily the best record-keepers after the Quakers.

The Compton census of 1676 showed Catholic recusants chiefly at Wrotham, Lynsted and Canterbury, with smaller groups at Benenden, Boughton-under-Blean, East Peckham, Eltham, Lamberhurst, Selling and Sevenoaks. Of other Nonconformists there was almost a county-wide presence, with multiple licences for worship in 1672 at Ash next Sandwich, Ashford, Canterbury, Cranbrook, Deal, Deptford, Dover, Lenham, Maidstone, Nonington, Rochester, Rolvenden, Sandwich, Staplehurst, Swingfield, Tenterden, Wingham and Wye.

Dissenters' marriages are quite often found before 1753 when it was possible to contract a 'common law' wedding by making a declaration before witnesses, accepted, if frowned upon, by both Church and State. In this way the various groups could celebrate marriages in their own meeting houses. All this was swept away by the Hardwicke Marriage Act of 1753, after which all marriages had to be solemnised in parish churches of the Established Church only, until 1837 when civil registration would again free them. The sole exceptions were the Jews and Quakers, together with many Catholics (illegal until 1792) who defied the act and continued to marry before their own priests. After 1837, if a meeting house had been open for at least a year, the superintendent registrar could license it for marriages on the petition of the congregation, but the presence of a registrar was still necessary at each ceremony until 1898.

The national religious census of 1851 attempted to collect denominational data by counting attendance at place of worship on a Sunday in March. Many were shocked to learn that just under half the population now failed to attend a religious service, and of those who did only half of the services were of the Established Church, thus implying a huge growth in Nonconformity since the 1676 survey, particularly in north-west Kent, at Canterbury, in Thanet and the Weald, on Sheppey and in the Medway towns, with Methodism well established throughout the county. Dissenters' churches and chapels were now commonly seen in the landscape, and particularly in the Weald, where the ancient parish churches, often remote and unheated, had lost their former attraction, especially in poor weather.

The wealth, privilege and power of the Church of England were now being challenged, partly fuelled by the Catholic Emancipation Act of 1829, although Catholicism was weak in Kent and its few churches lay mainly in towns. Consolidation of smaller benefices to provide a better income for Established Church ministers, clergy training and the restoration of many church buildings was soon to follow. Anglican finances were reformed following an ecclesiastical commission of 1835, tithes reformed and civil marriage introduced, all within a few years. In the 1840s Tractarianism (otherwise known as Anglo-Catholic ritualism) divided some churches but flourished at Chislehurst, Folkestone and elsewhere.

By 1851 chapels were widespread but mostly in towns, and offered a real alternative to parish churches, often appealing to skilled artisans who could lavish their practical skills on the buildings themselves. Dover and Maidstone had Baptist and Independent unions in 1798 for mutual support and the training of ministers, and along the Thames and its estuary from London to Thanet other sects founded chapels and schools. Whether established or dissenting, such places provided the only means of education for the majority of working people. Relationships between the two were not entirely broken and comfortable co-existence was the norm; many families oscillated between the two, especially as the Established Church had buried many earlier generations and held a prerogative on marriages until 1837. The Jews had an early presence in Kent with synagogues at Canterbury (1760), Chatham (1869) and Ramsgate (1843).

There is still much regrettable uncertainty about the locations and numbers of early Nonconformist churches and chapels, the years over which they were operating and the survival, coverage and location of their registers. Some were founded as early as the 1600s and then closed, only to reopen on a different site (concern with physical buildings was not high) or as a different denomination. Others are known to have existed, but the registers, if any, did not survive or are now lost. A good source of information is *Religious Worship in Kent: the Census of 1851*, containing a full transcript of the 1851 religious census (TNA: HO 129) listing all extant churches and chapels with address, minister, attendance numbers and other information.

In 1840 the Non-Parochial Register Act required all Dissenters except the Jews to surrender their registers to the Registrar General; these are now archived at TNA: RG 4. Quaker registers covering 1656–1837, plus a further general collection made in 1857, are at TNA: RG 6 and RG 8. Microfilms of these are at KHLC and CCA. The SOG has a good collection of copies as well as information on buildings and burial grounds. Very few indeed have been printed: all the baptisms (but not burials) are included on Familysearch.

The Catholics, never prominent in Kent, were the chief group not to deposit many registers and their records for the most part must be sought at the present church. The earliest meetings were in private chapels and registered for public worship from 1791, the first three being Greenwich (1792), Brompton (1795) and Woolwich (1815). Kent was in the London Catholic District from 1688 until the creation of the Catholic Diocese of Southwark in 1850.

Following a visit to Kent by George Fox in 1655, early Quaker meetings started in the following decade at Canterbury, Cranbrook, Folkestone and Rochester, with a later one at Ashford. The next century saw mergings, disbandments and re-formings until by 1874 there was just the one meeting for Rochester and Folkestone, with a short revival of Canterbury and Rochester in 1892. Records for Canterbury (1646–1780), Folkestone (1656–1837) and Kent (1795–1837) are all at TNA: RG 6. Written-up digests of Quaker registers may be seen at the Friends' House Library in Euston Road (films at the SOG).

From early times the Methodists were arranged into large circuits, in no way corresponding to parishes, with a minister travelling widely with his register to record baptisms and burials. This led to such anomalies as the Dover Wesleyan chapel including baptisms for the children of families living as far away as Ashford, Beneden, Ospringe and Ramsgate. Kent included some twenty such circuits, with a few more from the adjacent counties extending into it, especially for that in Rye, Sussex, which stretched well into both west and east Kent and contains entries for 1794–1939. An entry taken from an index may therefore greatly mislead, and in general the archive descriptions and covering dates of individual registers must be most carefully checked against the actual contents.

Many Kent people drifted to or from London, or even settled there. The registers of births (including the mother's maiden name) at Dr Williams' Library, Red Cross, Cripplegate in the City of London (TNA: RG 4/4658-4676; indexes 1716–1837 at the SOG and KFHS fiches) catered specifically for Baptists, Independents and Presbyterians within a 12-mile radius of the capital and originally had been established to counteract increasingly sloppy registration. With the passing of time other denominations and also Anglicans and people abroad came to use it.

Nonconformist baptisms and burials can occasionally be found in Church of England parish registers (and marked as such), and it is to be noted that many families brushed with Nonconformity, particularly in the early 1800s, often moving several times between two or more denominations. A baptism in just the one or the other is therefore no sign of complete adherence, for few families were unswervingly only of one religious denomination.

The best detailed listings of Nonconformist registers by parish are in North West Kent Family History Society's *West Kent sources: a guide to genealogical research in the Diocese of Rochester* and D. Wright's *East Kent Parishes*. KHLC has extensive Methodist records, nearly all after 1900, and there are other earlier local deposits as follows:

Ashford Quaker General Quarterly Meeting, 1648–1775 (KHLC: N/F)
Canterbury proceedings against Quakers, 1741–67 (CCA: CC-J)
Canterbury French Church, 1576–2000 (CCA: U47)
Chatham Memorial Synagogue, 1834–1972 (MALSC: N/J/305)
Gillingham New and Latter House of Israel or Jezreelites, 1858–1960 (MALSC: N/JZ/153)
Medway Methodist Town Circuit, 1768–1986 (MALSC: M5/1)
Milton-next-Gravesend Congregationalist, 1872–1915 (MALSC: N/C252)
Sevenoaks Wesleyan Methodist Circuit Quarterly Meeting, 1841–1965 (KHLC: M2/1)

Declarations against transubstantiation, 1673–1828 (KHLC: Q/RRO1)

Dissenting Ministers' declarations of Christian faith (including Anabaptists), 1689–1779; 1742–83; 1779–1811 (KHLC: Q/RRO 13-15).

Papists' estates, 1717–46 (KHLC: Q/RRP)

Returns of non-Anglican places of worship, 1829, alphabetically by parish, showing denominations and numbers of adherents, east and west Kent (KHLC: Q/CR3 E1-153; Q/CR3 W1-139)

Kent Nonconformist index, *c.*1640–1875 (www.mcopus.co.uk)

**Bibliography**

Barton, D.A., *Discovering chapels and meeting houses* (2nd edn 1990)

Currer-Briggs, N. and Gambier, R., *Huguenot ancestry* (1985)

Gandy, M., *Catholic parishes in England, Wales and Scotland: an atlas* (1993)

——, *Catholic missions and registers 1700–1880*, 6 vols (1998)

——, *Tracing Catholics* (2001)

Green, J.J., *Quaker records, being an index to 'The annual monitor' 1813–1892* (1894)

Kaganoff, B.C., *A dictionary of Jewish names and their history* (1978)

Kirk, J., *Biographies of English Catholics in the eighteenth century* (1909)

Lart, C.E., *Huguenot pedigrees*, 2 vols (1924–8)

Mullett, M., *Sources for the history of English non-conformity 1660–1830* (1991)

Rickard, G., *Dissenting ministers' declarations, 1689–1836* (1995)

Roake, M. (ed.), *Religious worship in Kent – the census of 1851* (1999)

Shorney, D., *Protestant nonconformity and Roman Catholicism: a guide to sources in the Public Record Office* (1996)

Whatmore, L.E., *Recusancy in Kent: studies and documents* (1973)

Worrall, E.S. (ed.), *Return of Papists 1767, Vol. 2: Dioceses of England and Wales, except Chester* (1989)

## G. PARISH CHEST

As the manorial courts declined in importance from the sixteenth century, the ecclesiastical parish became the principal administrative unit, under the responsibility of a parish council (the vestry) and the Justices of the Peace. The parochial minister was frequently its chairman. Centuries of importance was finally eroded in 1834 when responsibility for the poor was transferred to Poor Law Guardians and many other duties to new civil local authorities. All remaining functions and records were taken over by parish councils in 1894.

Information required from parish registers may often be enlarged from many other types of parish records, all originally housed in the parish chest, and can often add interesting details to amplify bare facts in the parochial registers themselves. These are partly detailed below and also elsewhere in this book, but for convenience there now follows the archival classification system for parochial records and descriptions of the more important or interesting items. Survival rates for some categories are quite arbitrary, but the fullest details will be found in the archive catalogues under the individual parishes, some of which have substantial runs of material in several classes.

## a) Ecclesiastical
### Incumbent
1. Parish registers (C, M & B, confirmation, services &c.).
2. Licences (marriage, schoolmasters, midwives, doctors).
3. Property and income (chancel, churchyard, rectory, glebe).

### Churchwardens
4. Rates.
5. Accounts.
6. Property (chancel church, church hall etc.).
7. Personal and miscellaneous.

### Vestry and Parochial Church Council
8. Minutes, accounts, correspondence and papers.

## b) Civil
### Union of Benefices and Team Ministries
9. Minutes etc.

### Constables
10. Minutes, accounts etc.

### Overseers of the Poor
11. Rates (parish, sanitary, window tax, land tax).
12. Accounts.

13. Settlement and Removal (certificates, examinations).
14. Apprenticeship (indentures, registers, accounts).
15. Bastardy (warrants, filiation and maintenance orders).
16. Miscellaneous (law suits, admission to hospital).
17. Militia (conscription papers, orders to pay militia men).
18. Workhouse (parish minutes, accounts, admission and day books).
19. Poor Law union (lists of in and out poor, expenditure statements).

**Surveyors of the Highways**
20. Rates.
21. Accounts.
22. Miscellaneous.

**Statutory Bodies**
23. Quangos, census etc.
24. Special groups and committees.

**Charity and Schools**
25. Minutes, accounts, correspondence.

**Enclosure**
26. Awards, maps etc.

**Tithe**
27. Maps, awards etc.

**Final Miscellaneous**
28. Parish magazines, histories etc.

**c) Apprentices**
A man learnt a trade in order to practise it by being apprenticed. In the earliest times the system was controlled by the guilds, but an act of 1562/3 directed that the term should be fixed at seven years, with fines to be levied on those practising without having served an apprenticeship.

The terms were set out in an indenture, one part signed by the child's parent or guardian and the other by the master who, usually in return for a premium, undertook to house, clothe and feed him during

*Parish officers: a valuable chance find in the Stone-in-Oxney parish registers (KHLC: P353/1/2). (Reproduced by kind permission of Kent History and Library Centre)*

training. The indenture names the apprentice, the master and his trade, the apprentice's father (sometimes also his occupation and residence) and occasionally the date and place of birth of the apprentice. The indenture system lasted until 1757, after which binding by any properly stamped deed was permissible, but a great many poor children were bound by an agreement entered in the vestry minute book or parish register. Poor Law apprenticeships were open to abuse whereby a mean vestry could rid itself of all future liability for maintenance by placing a child with a master at a remote distance, perhaps even a Lancashire mill-owner. Ill-treatment of children was common, especially for those forced upon an unwilling master.

Apart from local holdings, most indentures are registered centrally because stamp deputy was imposed on the master's premium from 1710 to 1804 (TNA: IR 1). Those down to 1774 (about 250,000 entries) have been indexed and published by the SOG, which also has an indexed collection from the 1600s to 1800s called *Crisp's Apprentices' Indentures*.

### d) Bastardy

Illegitimate children were frequently vilified at baptism, perhaps as examples of relatively unusual behaviour in the 1500–1600s. But after the Restoration the event became commoner, so much so that by the Industrial Revolution it was scarcely a matter for comment. Many statutes from 1575 onwards were devoted to the problems of illegitimacy which included inheritance, paternity and settlement, although until about 1750 the parish officers coped without much fuss. Few cases were brought before the quarter-sessions, and the most general method was either that of making the father responsible by bond for the upkeep of the child or allowing him to pay a lump sum in discharge of all responsibility.

In the 1750s the problem grew rapidly and affected the parish in its financial demands. Authorities were faced with the cheaper solution of forcing the putative father to marry the mother before the child's birth and take responsibility for its upkeep, even if the entire family might later become chargeable, or forcing the father to maintain the child under a court order, with the threat of imprisonment if he defaulted. If the father came from a different parish, a speedy wedding would legitimise the infant and ensure its settlement in his parish if the father became chargeable. This is the evidence of those cases that reached legal proceedings, but for the majority there is no entry except in the parish register and we are left wondering whether the father made a payment

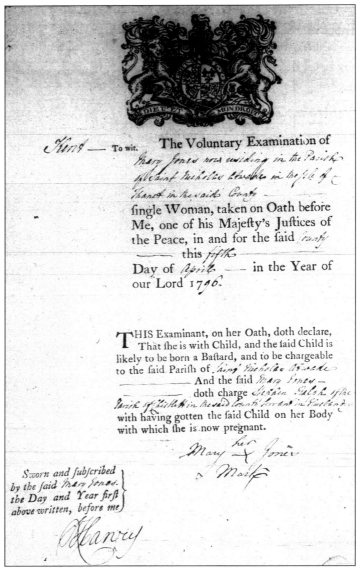

*A bastardy case: Mary Jones reveals the father of her future illegitimate child (CCA: U3/18/15/9). (Reproduced by kind permission of Canterbury Cathedral Archives and Library)*

to the authorities or came to a gentleman's agreement about maintenance.

## e) Charity

England had a wealth of ancient charities. A visit to most old churches will reveal tables of benefactors and their legacies concerning food and clothing for the poor, education and other matters. Such gifts in early times were almost invariably entrusted to the incumbent and churchwardens; after 1894 they were divided into civil and ecclesiastical classes, only the latter then (and still now) in the care of the said officials.

Collections of money, known as 'briefs', may also be found, often in the parish register itself. They were issued for church repairs, the redemption of slaves from piracy and for persons or buildings suffering loss by flood or fire, often at parish churches many counties away. Extraordinary sums of money were sometimes donated on such occasions and the details recorded can make for fascinating reading. The initial appeal was made from the pulpit and the monies collected at the end of the service.

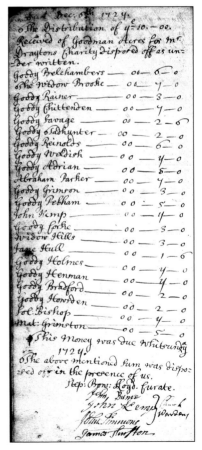

## f) Churchwardens

Churchwardens' accounts are a rich source of information and often survive from before the Reformation. The office of churchwarden was the most substantial of the four chief parochial offices, each of which was usually held by two people for one year, wealthier parishioners sometimes acting in rotation. All were unpaid and some unskilled. The majority of entries deal with routine (but not uninteresting) expenses such as communion wine, cleaning,

*Parochial charity: money is distributed to the deserving poor of Ospringe (CCA: U3/123/25/1). (Reproduced by kind permission of Canterbury Cathedral Archives and Library)*

119

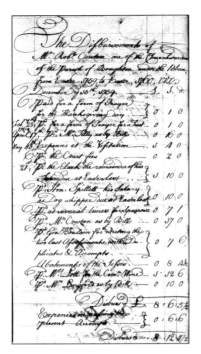

*Spending money: a churchwarden's expenses reflect daily life at Boughton-under-Blean (CCA: U3/221/5/4). (Reproduced by kind permission of Canterbury Cathedral Archives and Library)*

*Collecting money: Boughton-under-Blean raises funds to repair the parish church (CCA: U3/221/5/2). (Reproduced by kind permission of Canterbury Cathedral Archives and Library)*

maintenance and repairs, basic fire-fighting and the destruction of vermin. More important are structural and other alterations to the church, as well as payments to individuals for poor relief. The very existence of the accounts prove the glories of the mediaeval church: exquisite metalwork, jewelled cups and silver plate, carved screens, chests and bells, illuminated service books and much else.

There are many exceptional survivals of the accounts including Folkestone, Herne, Hythe and Sandwich St Mary from the 1400s, and Birchington, Chislet and Wye from the 1500s.

### g) Constables

The office is perhaps the most ancient of all, dating back to the Anglo-Saxon period. From the mediaeval period until 1842 the annual appointment of the petty constable was legally the responsibility of a manorial court, but in some manors there were no annual courts and so the constables (usually two) were elected by the parishioners and then sworn before the justices. On him, as principal executive authority in the parish, were laid many duties, for he had the power of arrest as well as taking in charge any person who had committed a felony or breach of the peace. His primary duty was to keep watch and ward in the parish, but he was also charged with overseeing the militia, collecting rates, paying out reliefs, organising vagrant passes and a great deal else.

Early constables' records may refer to troop movements and the provision of military equipment, but for the most part they relate to rogues and vagabonds and to relieving travellers with an official pass. Account books are few as the constables were usually reimbursed by the overseers whose papers were then placed among the poor relief records.

### h) Enclosure

Enclosure awards, although very few in number for Kent, are important records of commissioners appointed under individual private and local acts or the General Inclosure Acts of 1836 and 1845. They relate to the enclosure and allotment of open fields and common meadows, or commons, heaths, greens or forests, or land of both types, depending partly on whether the parish lay within the open-field region. The great majority belong to the period between about 1760 and 1860, all for the benefit of more efficient and individual farming. Most have accompanying award maps, usually covering the entire parish including the village and old closes, and show boundaries and names of the former open fields.

Until the mid-1700s much of England consisted of open fields farmed on a system of crop rotation. Farmers had strips in each field as well as rights over common pasture, meadows, heath and woodland. This system of open fields, strips and commons was complex and encouraged widely scattered uneconomic smallholdings, which ultimately led to enclosure whereby pieces of land in different ownership were swapped or amalgamated, and also to the division of common land between those who had hitherto enjoyed rights over it. New larger fields were then enclosed with hedges or ditches, resulting in various owners or occupiers having their land divided. This was initially carried out by private agreement between a lord and his tenants, but later by Acts of Parliament, especially after 1760 from when the majority of records survive, often with accompanying maps.

However, enclosure came early to Kent and the landscape was already much dominated by hedged fields by around 1700 so that the great parliamentary enclosure movements had little impact on the county. The enormously expensive parliamentary enclosure system led to much agitation for simplification and the first general enclosure Act of 1801, followed by a more important one in 1836 which permitted enclosure by the consent of a majority of the proprietors without the requirement for any special application to Parliament itself. Most private acts after 1593 will be found in the Parliamentary Archives.

Only about thirty copy awards for the county have survived (KHLC: Q/RDc), but whatever vestry maps and awards survive will be found in parish collections. Both are worth seeking as the awards set out to register the change from open-field ownership and cultivation to the modern system of landownership and cultivation in severalty, and they thus form the best (and only) source of accurate information as to the distribution of landownership in villages, which may include details about endowments, footpaths and rights of way, and the ownership of hedges and fences.

Additionally, the enclosure awards and maps will usually supply the names of the new owners of land which might well cover a large proportion of a parish.

### i) Rates

The commonest types of assessments are the parochial rates – for the church, the poor and the roads – and in later years for the constables and militia (the 'lighting' and 'watching'). Often called the cess (or sess), lists vary considerably in their details but will always give the sum paid alongside each ratepayer's name. The property may be identified with its annual rental value and previous occupier (not necessarily the owner).

### j) Settlement and Removal

From early times parish authorities would be greatly suspicious of the arrival of a man, with or without a family, who looked as if he were incapable of supporting himself and so becoming a charge on the parish.

A Sess made the 24 of June 1734 by W.m Denne
& W.m Loud Overseers of the poore of the parish
of Chilham together with the Churchwardens
and other of the Inhabitants of the said parish-
by Order of a Vestry held the 16 of June att the
Rate of Eighteen pence in y.e pound On Lands
as followeth viz

| Rents | Occupiers | £ | £ | 7 |
|---|---|---|---|---|
| | **Markett Borrough** | | | |
| 82:10 | James Colebrooke Esq.r | 06 | 03 | 9 |
| 75:00 | the Rev.d M.r Bate | 05 | 12 | 6 |
| 51:10 | M.r Jn.o Denne | 03 | 17 | 3 |
| 73:10 | W.m Denne | 05 | 10 | 3 |
| 20:00 | Rob.t Baines | 01 | 10 | 0 |
| 08:00 | More for M.r Whites Land | 00 | 12 | 0 |
| 02:00 | Tho: Holland | 00 | 03 | 0 |
| 02:10 | Rich.d Crow | 00 | 03 | 9 |
| 01:10 | Rich.d Athow | 00 | 02 | 3 |
| 01:10 | W.m Johnson | 00 | 02 | 3 |
| 03:10 | More for Esq.r Colebrooks Land | 00 | 05 | 3 |
| 05:00 | Jn.o Farley | 00 | 07 | 6 |
| 01:10 | Roger Hall | 00 | 02 | 9 |
| 04:00 | Sam: Knowler | 00 | 06 | 0 |
| 01:15 | More for Esq.r Colebrooks Land | 00 | 02 | 7½ |
| 01:10 | W.m Dines | 00 | 02 | 3 |
| 03:00 | Tho: Smith Sen.r | 00 | 04 | 6 |
| 06:00 | More for M.r Lances Land | 00 | 09 | 0 |
| 04:00 | Tho: Smith Jun.r | 00 | 06 | 0 |
| 01:10 | Tho: Topley | 00 | 02 | 3 |
| 01:00 | Tho: Mace | 00 | 01 | 6 |
| 01:00 | Jn.o Wraith | 00 | 01 | 6 |
| 01:10 | W.m Mace | 00 | 02 | 3 |
| 01:00 | Chris.t Triton | 00 | 01 | 6 |
| 01:00 | Aus.t Coleman | 00 | 01 | 6 |
| 01:10 | Jn.o Knock | 00 | 02 | 3 |
| 02:00 | More for Esq.r Colebrookes Land | 00 | 03 | 0 |
| 01:00 | Stephn Mathews | 00 | 01 | 6 |
| 01:00 | Tho: Hobbs | 00 | 01 | 6 |
| 05:10 | Jere: Hatten and Tillman | 00 | 08 | 3 |
| 04:10 | Rob.t Young | 00 | 06 | 9 |
| 01:00 | Mich: Culing | 00 | 01 | 6 |
| 01:00 | James Simpson | 00 | 01 | 6 |
| 01:00 | W.m Thomas | 00 | 01 | 6 |
| 01:00 | W.m Faulkner | 00 | 01 | 6 |
| 01:00 | Jn.o Raynen | 00 | 01 | 6 |
| 09:10 | M.r Cumberland and Esq.r Fagge | 00 | 14 | 3 |
| 02:10 | Dan: Cozins | 00 | 03 | 9 |
| 01:10 | Rich.d Best | 00 | 02 | 3 |
| 01:00 | Jn.o Horn | 00 | 01 | 6 |
| 01:10 | Ken: Carter | 00 | 02 | 3 |

*Ratepayers: Chilham parish overseers raise money for the maintenance of their poor (CCA: U3/191/11/2). (Reproduced by kind permission of Canterbury Cathedral Archives and Library)*

The 1601 Poor Law Act allowed relief to be granted to paupers only in their parish of legal settlement, a restriction intended to prevent influxes of poor labourers into parishes offering temporary work (such as a harvest) which were already overburdened with paupers. As sickness and other misfortunes could occur at any time, often to a breadwinner, it was vital for a family to have a legal settlement in the parish of abode. The 1601 Act allowed for legal settlement after one month's residence in a parish, but still allowed migrants and vagrants to keep moving and repeatedly obtain a new settlement.

The Poor Law Relief Act of 1662, usually called the Settlement Act, provided a newcomer with a legal right to settlement and entitlement to relief in a parish if in one of the following categories: holders of public office or ratepayers; renting a property worth over £10 annually; being of single marital status and having worked in the parish for over a year; apprentices to a master in the parish; resident in the parish for forty days after having given notice of the intention to do so; illegitimate children born in the parish; and legitimate children under 7 whose father was resident in the parish.

The rules were strictly enforced. People were commonly ejected from a parish if not legally settled and likely to become a charge to it; conversely, immigrants could stay in their new home as long as no relief was claimed. Newcomers were examined under oath as to their legal place of settlement, such examination records amounting to a virtual biography and including details of age, place of birth and marriage, employment or apprenticeship and the last several parishes of abode. The survival of these records has been haphazard, but some parishes have very rich collections, usually handwritten on small pieces of paper until about 1740; thereafter, printed forms were the norm. Frequent disputes arose and the records of these should be sought in the quarter sessions, which include cases relating to both the poor and the affluent.

Removal orders were issued if a person or family needed or were likely to need relief, but had no right to settlement in the parish. Such people were then directed to their parish of legal settlement, and escorted by the constable to the parish boundary, having been issued with passes detailing the parish of legal settlement which would be shown to various constables along the route.

The system made a search for work difficult and uncertain, and so a further Act of 1697 allowed overseers to issue certificates to people on the move, guaranteeing their being accepted back in the event of needing relief later on. Thus a receiving parish could now allow migrants with a settlement certificate to stay, in the sure knowledge that they could be returned to their old parish if they required relief.

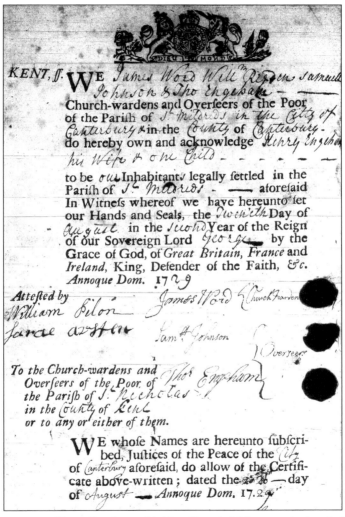

*A settlement case: Henry Engeham with his wife and child are received at St Mildred, Canterbury, from St Nicholas at Wade in Thanet (CCA: U3/18/13/12). (Reproduced by kind permission of Canterbury Cathedral Archives and Library)*

Settlement acts remained in force until 1834, after which paupers in need of relief generally had to enter a workhouse; but migrant paupers could still be denied entry to a workhouse and removed to the union legally responsible for them, even well into the twentieth century. Records after 1834 should therefore be sought in the appropriate union.

There is a parish list of surviving east Kent material at CCA, the following having good collections: Canterbury St Dunstan, Chartham, Chilham, Faversham, Hernhill, Luddenham, Petham, Preston next Faversham, Reculver, St Nicholas at Wade, Sandwich St Mary, Sturry and Woodnesborough.

Index to county settlements and removals, 1500s–1800s (Gillian Rickard, www.kentgen.com)

### k) Surveyors

The Highways Act of 1555 obliged every parish to elect annually two surveyors of highways, or waywardens, and to assess every adult according to his station to provide cartage or labour ('statute labour'). A surveyor was appointed by warrant sent to him by the constable, upon which he interviewed his predecessor, took over any cash balances and learnt something of how the accounts were kept. Three times a year he had to view the roads and present their condition to the nearest justice. One main duty was to fix the days of statute labour and supervise his fellow parishioners in this unpleasant task which in later years was often commuted to fines in lieu out of which payments for gravel-digging, stone-picking, filling in ruts and so on were made. The whole system was inefficient and standards very low, but it survived until the General Highway Act of 1835, latterly by the enforced use of pauper labour. Kent has good survival rates of material, and there are particularly fine ranges of accounts for Birchington, Kenardington, Kingsnorth, Stelling, Tenterden, Wingham and Woodchurch, some from the earlier 1600s.

### l) Vestry Minutes

The ancient meeting of the parishioners which levied the church rate and regulated parish affairs was named after the church vestry where they assembled. The Tudor legislation that imposed on the parish the responsibility for the poor and the roads gradually gave the vestry increasing importance, giving rise to surviving records from the mid-

1500s. By the Georgian period the collecting of various small rates was abandoned in favour of a single larger poor rate. A 'parish book' or 'town book' may give just brief summaries of annual accounts, or perhaps a vivid picture with illuminating details of the affairs of a parish and its inhabitants. The period between 1689 and 1834 was the only one in English history when central government took little trouble over local affairs, leaving each parish as an individual story.

There are excellent collections of vestry minutes, many parishes having good or complete runs from the earlier 1800s onwards. Some have much earlier material, often indexed, including most Canterbury parishes from the early 1700s: Ash near Sandwich, 1704–1870; Chislet, 1770–1840; Deal, 1792–1852; Dover St Mary, 1611–1832; Elham, 1729–1834; Faversham, 1732–1906; Hernhill, 1693–1925; Hougham, 1731–1861; Lyminge, 1735–1855; Northbourne, 1708–1877; Petham, 1793–1919; Postling, 1780–1912; Sandwich St Clement, 1772–1928; Sandwich St Peter, 1601–1752; Sturry, 1737–1917; Teynham, 1585–1726; Thanet St Lawrence, 1739–1954; and Whitstable, 1705–1948.

After 1834, when the Boards of Guardians took over the chief duties of the parish overseers, the vestry business generally shrank unless the parish was an urban or industrial one. Henceforth new problems created other business to record, such as public transport and health, often under new committees with separate registers.

**Bibliography**
Davey, H., *Poor law settlement and removal* (3rd edn 1925)

Gonner, E.C.K., *Common land and inclosure* (1912; 2nd edn 1966)

Hollowell, S., *Enclosure records for historians* (2000)

Kain, R.J.P., Chapman, J. and Oliver, R., *The enclosure maps of England and Wales, 1595–1918* (2004)

Rickard, G., *Kent settlement (poor law) records: a guide and catalogue: Part One East Kent (Diocese of Canterbury)* (1993); *Part Two West Kent (Diocese of Rochester)* (1994)

Slater, G., *The English peasantry and the enclosure of the common fields* (1907)

Tate, W.E., *The parish chest* (3rd edn 1969)

——, *The English village community and the enclosure movements* (1976)

——, *Domesday of English enclosure acts and awards* (1978)

## H. POOR LAW AND HOSPITALS
### Poor Law
From the reign of Elizabeth I every parish had a duty to look after its own poor and supply them with the bare minimum of shelter, food, clothing and medical attention. These precepts were first enacted in 1597 and 1601 when a parish poor rate and two annually elected overseers to care for the 'idle poor' were created. Consequently, few records exist before this date because the two Acts called for the provision of stocks of raw material for setting the able-bodied to work, but not for a workhouse. Poverty was the daughter of unemployment and so parishes were now empowered to put the poor to work in workhouses. Little seems to have been acted upon or even steps taken by parishes before 1660, the Act hitherto regarded as machinery to be adopted in a time of crisis on the assumption that in normal times poverty could be successfully coped with by private charity. Indeed it is estimated that over 90 per cent of the money spent on public welfare before the Restoration came from private pockets in the founding of almshouses, hospitals, schools, scholarships and libraries, and in providing sums for prisoners, apprentices and newly married couples.

Initially, direct relief of the poor lay in monthly or weekly payments to the aged, impotent, sick and orphans or to goodwives for looking after them, but new methods were now tried. An Act of 1723 allowed churchwardens and overseers (with the consent of the parishioners) to establish workhouses, and, importantly, also to deny relief to paupers who refused to enter the institution, a regulation that became crucial by the 1830s. The Act further permitted parishes to combine in order to establish workhouses, the cost shared by all, if they were too small to support their own. By 1776 a basic system was operating in Kent with some 132 workhouses providing accommodation for nearly 6,000 sick, aged and orphaned poor, thereby taking the burden off the parish which would otherwise be bound to pay for their rent and food. Large towns and cities with numerous parishes (Canterbury had seventeen) found it easier if they built a single workhouse rather than allow people to keep moving from one parish to the next. Such buildings varied from small cottages to substantial premises holding several hundred paupers, with a noticeable preponderance in the north-west and south-west of the county. Gilbert's Act of 1782 provided common workhouses for unions of parishes, twelve of which were built, mostly in east Kent. By

1813 two-thirds of all parishes kept their poor in workhouses which were often squalid and inefficiently run, a higher proportion than any county except Middlesex, and one that reflected the extent of the county's Poor Law problems. Such records as survive will be found in archive parish listings.

Despite Gilbert's Act, most parishes continued to cope independently with the alarming problem and appalling burden of poor relief – today it is perhaps difficult to comprehend how the then government acted so slackly. By the 1830s the system was much abused as the burden of poor relief mounted rapidly. Many people also believed that the system encouraged the avoidance of work and allowed employers to pay low wages since the parish ensured that workers and their families did not starve. At Lenham, for example, the population was 2,197 of whom no fewer than 1,200 received relief: the parish expenditure on poor relief had increased from about £1,000 to £4,300 in three decades, agriculture being the only industry and one that offered fewer jobs than there were men available. In 1831 fifty people were paid to emigrate to Quebec, but the letters coming back were so downhearted that few others wished to follow. Meanwhile, the poor rate continued to rise and one farmer surrendered his estate, unable to afford the annual £300 rates on it: his farm became redundant and its workers unemployed. Overseers tried to solve unemployment, often by public work schemes such as road-building and parochial farms. A crisis point was all but upon everyone.

Parliament had to act, and did so in 1834 because individual parishes were now too small a unit for the relief of the poor, unable as they were to afford full-time parish officers or have their own efficient workhouse. Parishes were now grouped into the now familiar unions by the Poor Law Commission under Sir Edmund Walker Head, each of broadly the same population and centred on a town or large village where the union workhouse was usually erected. Each union was divided into sub-districts with a relieving officer who considered the circumstances of anyone applying for relief. Many unions now erected new buildings and by 1841 nineteen out of twenty-seven had done so, with later ones at Canterbury, Chatham, Gravesend, Sevenoaks and Tenterden. A Board of Guardians oversaw its running, its members elected by men occupying property of a certain rateable value. Some of the abuses of the old system now disappeared and outdoor relief was curtailed to some degree, so much so that the county expenditure dropped from £345,000 in 1834 to £185,000 in 1837. The boards were abolished in 1930 and their responsibilities transferred to the county council. The old union buildings survive today in many rural districts, usually converted for different purposes.

A birth or death certificate will note if the event occurred in a workhouse, and the census returns will list all inmates on that night. Otherwise, it is easy to establish which union any parish was in from the census enumerators' books or from D. Wright's *The Kentish Census Returns 1801–1901*.

Below are listed the main classes of union records that should be examined first; there are also vagrants' admissions, creed registers, relief order books, minutes, correspondence, expenditure and rate books, punishment registers, lists of apprentices, vaccination lists and other material which may add much background detail to your individual. Some have variable closure periods of approximately sixty-five to eighty years from the date of the last entry in each volume.

Except where stated, all records are at KHLC: G.

**Blean Union** (Workhouse at Herne)
Births, 1836–66; Deaths, 1848–1957; Admissions and Discharges, 1836–1929.
**Bridge Union** (Workhouse at Bridge)
Births, 1836–1912, 1915–20 (BTs for Baptisms 1885–96 at CCA); Deaths, 1835–1914; Admissions and Discharges, 1835–1934.
**Bromley Union** (Workhouse at Locks Bottom, Farnborough)
Births, 1879–1936; Deaths, 1907–1932; Admissions and Discharges, 1882–1930. Records held at Bromley Local Studies Library and Archives.
**Canterbury Union** (Workhouse at Nunnery Fields, St Mary Bredin parish). No surviving records.
Canterbury City Workhouse (est. 1728) at Poor Priests' Hospital, St Margaret's parish: Admissions and Discharges, 1827–8; 1832–3 at CCA. Canterbury City Union, 1792–1848 at CCA: CC-Q/GB.
**Cranbrook Union** (Workhouse at Hartley, Cranbrook)
Births and Deaths, 1836–70; Admissions and Discharges, 1913–30.
**Dartford Union** (Workhouse at Lurchin's Hole, Dartford)
Births, 1898–1929; Deaths, 1914–30; Admissions and Discharges, 1836–1930.

**Dover Union** (Workhouse at Coombe Valley Road, Buckland)
Births, 1878–1914 (Baptisms 1885–1928 in Buckland parish registers);
   Deaths, 1878–1935; Admissions and Discharges, 1835–95.

**East Ashford Union** (Workhouse at Willesborough)
No Births; Deaths, 1836–1906; Admissions and Discharges, 1836–99.

**Eastry Union** (Workhouse at Mill Lane, Eastry)
Births, 1837–1914; Deaths, 1835–1914; Admissions and Discharges,
   1835–1929.

**Elham Union** (Workhouse at Etchinghill, Lyminge)
Births, 1867–1942; Baptisms, 1872–1966; Deaths, 1836–1952, 1898–
   1914; Admissions and Discharges, 1836–1931.

**Faversham Union** (Workhouse at Faversham)
Births, 1891–1914; Deaths, 1835–66; Admissions and Discharges, 1835–
   1929.

**Gravesend Union** (Workhouse at Trafalgar Road, Gravesend)
Births, 1848–1913; Deaths, 1871–1914; Admissions and Discharges,
   1832–1933.

**Greenwich Union** (Workhouse at Vanbrugh Hill, Greenwich)
Births, 1863–90; Deaths, 1848–1941; Admissions and Discharges, 1854–
   1936. Hospital and Infirmary: Births, 1874–1941; Deaths, 1892–1942;
   Admissions and Discharges, 1876–1935. Records held at LMA.

**Hollingbourne Union** (Workhouse at Hollingbourne)
Births, 1866–1920; Baptisms, 1837–1920 (BTs 1837–76 at CCA); Deaths,
   1866–1921; Admissions and Discharges, 1897–1914, 1920–1.

**Hoo Union** (Workhouse at Hoo St Werburgh)
Births, 1838–1922; Deaths, 1837–1922; Admissions and Discharges,
   1904–23. Records held at MALSC.

**Lewisham Union** (Workhouse in Lewisham High Street)
Births, 1866–1909; Deaths, 1883–1915; Admissions and Discharges,
   1837–1920. Records held at Lewisham Local History and Archive
   Centre (other material at LMA).

**Maidstone Union** (Workhouse at Coxheath, Linton)
Births, 1836–42, 1866–1941; Baptisms, 1841–70; Deaths, 1866–1939;
   Burials, 1840–1941; Admissions and Discharges, 1915–30. Baptism
   and Burial BTs, 1840–52 at CCA.

**Malling Union** (Workhouse at West Malling)
Births and Baptisms, 1870–1936; Deaths, 1870–1940; Admissions and
   Discharges, 1883–1933.

**Medway Union** (Workhouse at Magpie Hall Lane, Luton)
Births, 1878–1914; Deaths, 1877–1930; Admissions and Discharges, 1867–1931. Records held at MALSC.

**Milton Union** (Workhouse at North Street, Milton)
Births, 1866–1939; Deaths, 1893–1936; Admissions and Discharges, 1835–1928.

**North Aylesford Union** (renamed Strood from 1885; Workhouse at Gun Lane, Strood)
Births, 1884–1902, 1914–30; Deaths, 1871–1937; Admissions and Discharges, 1901–37. Records held at MALSC.

**Romney Marsh Union** (Workhouse at Church Road, New Romney)
Births, 1836–1930; Deaths, 1836–1931; Admissions and Discharges, 1911–26.

**Sevenoaks Union** (Workhouse at Sundridge)
Births and Baptisms, 1846–1932; Deaths, 1866–99, 1914–51; Burials, 1887–1947; Admissions and Discharges, 1912–33. Records held at Sevenoaks Library.

**Sheppey Union** (Workhouse at Minster)
Births, 1835–1930; Deaths, 1866–1930; Admissions and Discharges, 1853–1929.

**Tenterden Union** (Workhouse at Tenterden)
Births, 1866–1929; Deaths, 1866–1939; Admissions and Discharges, 1912–33.

**Thanet Union** (Workhouse at Minster)
Births, 1848–66, 1898–1914; Baptisms, 1905–29 (BTs, 1906–9 at CCA); Chapel Baptisms, 1848–1930; Deaths, 1866–1931; Admissions and Discharges, 1872–1930.

**Tonbridge Union** (Workhouse at Pembury)
Births, 1835–1934 (Baptisms, 1836–47 at Holy Trinity, Tunbridge Wells); Deaths, 1835–1932; Admissions and Discharges, 1835–1931.

**West Ashford Union** (Workhouse at Hothfield Common)
Births, 1838–1913; Deaths, 1847–1914; Admissions and Discharges, 1863–1932.

**Woolwich Union** (Created 1868 from parts of Greenwich and Lewisham districts) (Workhouse at Tewson Road, Plumstead)
Baptisms, 1877–1936; Deaths, 1932–39; Admissions and Discharges, 1931–44. Additional Workhouse at Plumstead: Admissions and Discharges, 1896–1931. Records held at LMA.

These parishes have good local collections at CCA: Chartham, Chilham, Canterbury Christ Church, Doddington, Dover St Mary, Hernhill, Northbourne, Ospringe, River and Sturry.

**Other Poor Law records:**
Chatham Local Board of Guardians, 1792–1855 (MALSC: LBG)
Gilbert Act Unions of 1781–2 (KHLC: GA):
    Dover and Folkestone Union (thirteen original parishes), 1824–35;
    Eastry Union (nine original parishes), 1792–1834; Faversham Union
    (Preston, Selling and Sheldwich), 1790–1835
Strood Parish Trustees, 1812–1936 (MALSC: SPT)
Vagrant passes, 1707–10, 1814–18, 1837–1843 (KHLC: Q/RSp3)
Workhouse agreements between parishes, 1789–1829 (KHLC: Q/RSp1)

If your ancestor was a workhouse employee, the guardians' and commmmissioners' records contain registers from about 1834–1921 of paid officers including masters, clerks and nurses, noting salaries and dates of appointment, resignation or dismissal (TNA: MH 9). There are also appointment registers for Boards of Guardian staff from 1834–50 (THA: MH 19) and Poor Law Commissions, *c.*1834–1900 with such matters as staff appointments, pauper examinations, guardians' accounts and financial assistance for emigration (TNA: MH 12).

**Bibliography**
Digby, A., *The poor law in nineteenth-century England and Wales* (1982)

**Hospitals**
Many early hospitals were monastic or charitable foundations of which there were some 500 nationally by about 1300. Private individuals often founded hospitals by their wills or founded charities to establish hospitals for the poor. Many more were set up in the eighteenth century, some still surviving, as at Canterbury. Some parishes also founded hospitals, usually in the same building as the workhouse. Until the earlier 1800s hospitals for the mentally ill were either private establishments or charitable hospitals.

    Like all other counties, Kent was subject to the great epidemics of the plague, smallpox, measles, whooping cough, influenza and cholera (the last highly prevalent in the lower Medway Valley), some of which regularly killed many thousands of people annually until well into the twentieth century. Only with the provision of clean water and the removal of sewage would things gradually improve from about 1850. Wealthy subscribers supported the opening of the Kent and Canterbury hospital in 1793, while others such as the West Kent in Maidstone developed from dispensaries. The County Asylum was built at Barming in 1830, but many of the poor had to rely on medical care offered by the workhouses, a service that was so important that many extended their facilities and became hospitals when the welfare system was changed in the 1920s.

Medical care and assistance had been available for many centuries from mediaeval infirmaries, almshouses and other establishments, so much so that even before the advent of the National Health Service in 1948, Kent was well supplied with a wide variety of hospitals, sanatoria, nursing and convalescent homes, and lunatic asylums. Major earlier deposited collections include the following, but there are many later, and smaller, ones. Patients' records are generally closed for 100 years, and administrative ones for 30.

Ashford Hospital, 1878–1974 (KHLC: MH/SEK4)
Barming Heath Lunatic Asylum, 1833–1970s (KHLC: MH/Md2); returns of pauper lunatics, 1842–90 (KHLC: Q/GLr)
Canterbury, Eastbridge Hospital, c.1200–1978 (CCA: U24)
Canterbury, Jesus Hospital, 1596–1971 (CCA: U32; U38; U204)
Canterbury, Kent and Canterbury Hospital, 1790–1984 (KHLC: MH/T4)
Canterbury, St John's Hospital, 1538–1962 (CCA: U13)
Chartham, St Augustine's County Asylum, 1854–1993 (KHLC: MH/T3)
Dover and New Romney Hospital returns, 1666 (CCA: DCb/Q/H1-2)
Folkestone, Royal Victoria Hospital, 1846–1990 (KHLC: MH/SEK6)
Maidstone, Kent Ophthalmic Hospital, 1846–1973 (KHLC: MH/Md3)
Margate Royal Sea Bathing Hospital, 1791–1991 (KHLC: MH/T1)
Ramsgate, Haine & Northwood Hospital, 1876–1985 (KHLC: MH/T2)

Rochester, St Bartholomew's Hospital, 1627–1855 (MALSC: Ch2)
Sandwich, St Bartholomew's Hospital, 1370s–1894 (KHLC: EK/CH)
Sandwich, St John's House/Hospital, 1287–1920 (KHLC: EK/CH)
Sandwich, St Thomas's Hospital, 1725–1903 (KHLC: EK/CH)
West Kent General Hospital, 1881–1964 (KHLC: MH/Md1)

## I. QUARTER-SESSIONS

The county records proper, that is, those of the justices in quarter-sessions and of their officer, the clerk of the peace, yield information on an extremely wide variety of subjects, namely crimes, offences and punishments, police, gaols and houses of correction, roads and bridges, poor relief and vagrancy, markets and fairs, weights and measures, rates of wages, inns and alehouses, agriculture, enclosure of open fields and commons, Dissenters and Roman Catholics, charities, friendly societies and savings banks, canals, railways and other public schemes. It can therefore readily be seen that not only events in your ancestor's life may be traced, but perhaps also considerable background detail in the form of local history as well.

Justices of the Peace (also known as magistrates) were appointed from the fourteenth century by commissions of the peace from the king. Their power and jurisdiction gradually increased from dealing with less serious cases on behalf of the Crown to inheriting the jurisdiction of the Church and manorial courts and being given new duties by central government. From 1361 until 1971 they met four times a year at Easter, Trinity, Michaelmas and Epiphany. As the workload increased various statutes empowered the justices to meet between quarter-sessions to deal with minor matters at a meeting that came to be known as the petty sessions. All the work of the justices was kept by a lawyer known as the Clerk of the Peace. At MALSC there is a west Kent quarter-sessions typescript index giving name, parish, status, date, type of document and folio, covering QSB 7-15 for 1657–84.

The Test Act of 1673 obliged everyone holding civil or military office to deliver to quarter-sessions a certificate of his having received the Lord's Supper, signed by the minister, churchwardens and two witnesses. Many thousands of names are recorded in these so-called sacrament certificates, which become fewer after 1750. Registers of papists' estates, from 1716, give detailed descriptions of their properties. Protestant Dissenters' meeting house certificates or applications for registration may have been preserved from the date of the 1688 Toleration Act, and cease in 1852. They give brief but valuable particulars of the owner or occupier of the property, and usually his denomination; they are often signed by several prominent Dissenters.

Among the assorted documents that the Clerk of the Peace had to file, copy or register were numerous lists of persons. Almost the earliest are the hearth tax assessments for 1662–68 (q.v.) which give extremely valuable lists of householders in every parish and the numbers of hearths in each house, although some lists exclude poor persons.

Much bulkier series of land tax assessments, one for every parish or township each year, are preserved, generally from the mid-1700s. They were transmitted as evidence of one basis of a claim for a vote at parliamentary elections, and were superseded in 1832 by registers of electors. These lists give for each property the owner but not his abode or occupation; the occupier, if different (from 1786); the sum payable; and the rental, but this bears little or no relation to the actual rent as it was based on the original county assessments of 1692. Redemption of the tax was permissible in 1798. From 1826–32, however, there is an additional column for brief description of the property, such as land, farm, windmill or inn.

The names of men aged between 21 and 70 in each parish qualified to serve on juries are recorded in freeholders' (or jurors') lists. Men are listed in their home parish, but that in which the qualifying estate lies, if different, may be given, along with age, annual value of property and sometimes rank or occupation.

Registers of electors survive fairly complete from 1832 when the county franchise was widened now to include copyholders of £10, leaseholders of £50 and long leaseholders of £10 a year. Each entry shows abode (larger houses with names and, later, streets and numbers), nature of qualification and the situation of the qualifying property in parish, hamlet or street, or its farm or inn name. Poll books exist from the later 1600s, either as bare names under the parish in which the qualifying property lay, although the elector's abode (parish), if different, may be given and later on occupations.

The annual licensed victuallers' registers, 1753–1828, give the inns and alehouses and publicans' names in each parish with their signs, but no other details, and the frequency with which some names of inns changed should be borne in mind.

Courts of quarter-sessions were empowered in 1828 to create within each county districts or divisions for petty sessions, thus regularising earlier informal divisions. They appear gradually and sporadically, often differing in origin and purpose. Formal minute books are extant for the 1700s, and occasionally the relevant papers from about 1800.

Petty sessions meetings of the local JPs at monthly or petty sessions were established early in Kent, and include adoptions, bail registers, bastardy, case papers, convictions, correspondence, examinations, juvenile court, licences, militia, minute books, orders and sessions volumes.

There now follows a list of the county's principal deposits. Note that further and separate collections will be found within the borough collections (qq.v.). At KHLC in the search room are three useful printed volumes of quarter-session calendars (1574–1672 and 1690–1714), affording a good overview of the material.

### Constables' Presentments
1684–1734 (KHLC: Q/SBp).

### Constable Rolls
Lists of coroners, stewards, bailiffs and high constables, 1650–1800 (KHLC: Q/SRo); after 1801 in sessions papers (KHLC: Q/SBe and Q/SBw).

### Freeholders' books
Names by hundred, parish and borough of residence, 1701–1824 (KHLC: Q/RJf2).

### Freemasons
Lists of names, status and abode, 1799–1889 (KHLC: Q/RSm2).

### Gamekeepers
Register of deputation: manors and lords, gamekeepers and status, 1711–86 (indexed), 1784–1807 (KHLC: Q/RSg; Q/RTg).

**General Sessions**
Order Books, 1814–89, indexed (KHLC: Q/GO).
Minute Books, 1814–45 (KHLC: Q/GMa).

**Indictment Rolls**
East Kent, 1639–1944 (KHLC: Q/SIE).
West Kent, 1650–1944 (KHLC:Q/SIW).

**Inhabited House Tax**
East Kent rates and duties on houses and windows, showing names
and payments, *c*.1778–85, about 120 parishes, St Augustine's Lathe
(KHLC: Q/CTi).

**Insolvent Debtors**
1737–1855 (indexed), mostly tradesmen (KHLC: Q/CI).

**Jurors**
Returns of freeholders by hundreds, names and place of residence,
1696–1803; some to 1824 (KHLC: Q/RJf1).

**Justice lists**
1705–77, and oaths 1761–1971 (KHLC: Q/JL; Q/JO).

**Land Tax**
Thirteen Wealden parishes, *c*.1780–1899; Lower Scray Division, 1795,
Maidstone, Malling and Tonbridge areas, 1790–1887 and beyond;
Faversham, Milton and Sheppey areas, 1856–1949 (KHLC: Ta).

**Land Tax**
Kent, most years 1780–1832 (KHLC: Q/RPI) (digitised at Kent History
Source).

**Land Tax duplicates**
East Kent, about 250 parishes, *c*.1698–1779 in short runs of years, with
landlords, tenants, rents and payments (KHLC: Q/CT1).

**Minute Books**
Kent, 1677–1704; east Kent, 1705–1835; west Kent, 1684–1735 (KHLC:
Q/SMa).

## Oath Rolls
Association Rolls for office holders, 1696–1702 (KHLC: Q/RRO4).
Oath rolls for the Protestant succession, 1702–13 (KHLC: Q/RRO5).
Oath rolls of royal allegiance and supremacy, 1715–1874 (KHLC: RRO6).
Oaths of allegiance against the Popish pretender, 1723, about forty-five larger villages and towns (KHLC: Q/RRO7).

## Order books
East Kent, 1653–1962; west Kent, 1625–1962, both partly indexed (KHLC: Q/SO).

## Petty Sessions
The whole county is well covered in about twenty-five divisions from the mid-1800s down to the twentieth century (KHLC: PS). Starting dates for early collections include: Ashford (1773), Bearsted (1748), Blackheath (1743), Bromley (1747; at Bromley Library); Dover (1792), Faversham or Upper Scray (1722), Malling (1747), Sevenoaks (1709), Wingham (1705). There are also minute books for the North Aylesford Division, 1754–67, 1813–72 (MALSC: PS/Na).

## Prisoners
Calendars of prisoners (name, parish, status, crime), 1626–74, 1702–6, 1836–78 (KHLC: Q/SMc1).
Printed calendars of prisoners, 1891–1971 (KHLC: Q/SMcE).

## Process Records
Discharge certificates, petitions, lists of creditors and debts, 1691–1844 (KHLC: Q/SPd1).
Gaolers' schedules of debtors, 1728–1814 (KHLC: Q/SPd2).
Indictment books, Canterbury and Maidstone, 1700–19; whole county 1649–1792 (KHLC: Q/SPi).

## Recognisance rolls
East Kent, 1650–1730; west Kent, 1651–1732 (KHLC: Q/SRc).

## Sessions Papers (Assizes)
1640–1800, calendared (KHLC: Q/SB).
East/west Kent, 1801–83, partly calendared (KHLC: Q/SBe; Q/SBw).

East Kent, 1862, full calendar and index (KHLC: Q/SD/E1).
West Kent, 1861–98, full calendar and index (KHLC: Q/SD/W1).
Ancestry.com has criminal registers for the whole country, 1791–1892 from which may be found the court in which a trial took place.

**Servant Tax**
East Kent, 1778–80 (KHLC: Q/CTs).

**Subscription rolls**
1714, Doddington, Minster-in-Sheppey and Warden, names and occupations (KHLC: Q/RRO 18).

**Tithe**
Awards made under private acts, about forty parishes, c.1805–80 (KHLC: Q/RDc).

**Turnpike**
Mostly late 1800s–1900s (KHLC: T).

**Victuallers and Alehouse Keepers**
Original recognisances and licences (including inn signs from c.1700), 1595–1752, 1753–1828 (KHLC: Q/RLv1-2).
Registers of alehouse keepers, whole county (including some inn names until 1782), 1753–1827 (KHLC: Q/RLv4).

**Window Tax**
East Kent, 1705–86, about 100 parishes (KHLC: Q/CTw).

## J. SCHOOLS AND EDUCATION

As is still the case today, Kent was well endowed with grammar schools, having twenty-one by 1700, although at this date few children attended school regularly. Three were pre-Reformation foundations: Canterbury (731), Sevenoaks (1432) and Wye (1448). The others, mostly founded between about 1520 and 1670, were spread widely, including Dartford, Greenwich, Lewisham and Rochester in the north-west, Tonbridge in the south-west, Maidstone, Milton Regis, Sutton Valence and Yalding in the middle of the county, Biddenden, Cranbrook, Goudhurst and Tenterden in the Weald, and Ashford, Faversham,

Dover, Folkestone and Sandwich in the east. All took boys only, for Latin and Greek instruction was a preparation for the male-dominated world of Oxford and Cambridge. Teachers were licensed from 1662 in order to control those teaching the young, and in that year thirty-nine parishes had such a man, probably in addition to many more unlicensed ones.

The main beneficiaries of teaching were the wealthy, but the later foundations were part of the national trend to a greater secularisation of education, even if close links with the Church predominated. Later privately endowed schools, such as those at Leybourne, Rochester, Staplehurst and Yalding, recognised the need for more practical subjects, for example, mathematics and casting accounts. New growth came in the 1780s with the Sunday school movement with pupils learning reading, writing and the Bible in buildings widely spread across the county. The general success of Sunday schools is reflected in the attendance numbers, which approached 60,000 in 1851, and the consequent and significant contribution to rises in literacy before 1870.

In about 1800 there were roughly a dozen Kentish grammar schools, 4 times as many permanent endowed elementary schools, a few dozen charity and ragged schools, and probably hundreds of little 'dame' schools, in all catering for no more than 10,000 (perhaps far fewer) children, of whom well under half attended a school for no more than 3 or 4 years, and with little if any regularity. Victorian expansion was enormous but initially slow, the local church or chapel usually in charge of the early institutions, which included Beckenham, Bromley, Chatham, Deal, Molash, Newchurch, New Romney, Nonington, Sheldwich, Smarden, Ulcombe, Waldershare, Westerham and Westwell, a good mixture of both town and village, and entirely dependent upon the enthusiasm of local people.

In 1833 a government national grant of £20,000 allowed for the erection of many more schools. The initial impetus was still local, but there were twenty-four new schools before 1840, widely spread across the county and noticeably far more rural than urban. Lower costs in Kentish paper mills contributed to the availability of cheap books and reading material in the first few decades of Victoria's reign. Between 1840 and 1870, the year of the Elementary Education Act, 159 further new schools were built, and a decade later most parishes except the tiny ones had at least one elementary school, the larger urban areas having several. These earlier changes were gradually taken over by the principles of a free, State-provided system, which came to dominate education by the end of the century. The Registrar General reported that male literacy rates had risen from 67 per cent in 1841 to 80 per cent in 1871, reinforcing the conclusion that Kentish improvements were well advanced before the 1870 Education Act.

CCA has a list of holdings by parish, mostly for the 1800s–1900s, and this is usefully augmented by a North West Kent Family History Society publication, *School records: a guide to the location of school records in the Diocese of Rochester* for the other side of the county. At KHLC and MALSC are extensive county-wide collections of school records in class C/ES. For the most part they start around the 1860s and consist of account books, admission registers, log books and minutes. Many admission registers may be found on Findmypast. There is a general closure date of eighty years on the material. The following are the notable early ones, broadly including administration, finance, legal, school management and title deeds, all at KHLC in class CH except where stated. There are many later, and smaller, ones.

> Aylesford, Holy Trinity and other charities, 1600–1952
> Benenden, Gibbon's Charity School, 1602–1877
> Biddenden, John Mayne Charity, 1566–1934
> Canterbury city charities, 1584–1894 (CCA: CC-S)
> Canterbury, King's School, 1546–1977 (CCA: DCc/King's)
> Chatham, Sir John Hawkins' Hospital, 1594–1987 (MALSC: CH 108)
> Cranbrook School, 1563–1883
> Dartford Grammar School, 1700s–1800s
> Edenbridge, Great Store Bridge, 1560–1924
> Faversham Institute, 1815–1955
> Folkestone, Sir Eliab's Charity (Harvey Grammar School), 1596–
>     1964 (KHLC: Fo/QH)
> Northfleet, Huggens College, 1759–1970
> Maidstone Bluecoat School, 1818–1910
> Maidstone British School, 1758–1953
> Rochester, Guardians and Trustees of the Parish of St Nicholas,
>     1819–50 (MALSC: GTNR)

Rochester, Gunsley's Charity, 1824–1993; Sir Haywards' Charity,
    1776–1861; Watts' Charity, 1500s–1700s (all at MALSC: RCA)
Rochester, King's School, 1660–1964 (MALSC: DRc/KS)
Rochester, Sir Joseph Williamson's Mathematical School, 1707–
    2010 (MALSC: C/ES/306/4)
Sevenoaks, Lady Boswell's Charity, 1616–1973
Tenterden, Lady Maynard Charity, 1693–1878

## K. MAPS

It was only after the revival of learning in the sixteenth century that
interest in the techniques of surveying land was revived and led to the
production of detailed maps. Those after about 1700 are often works of
art in their own right and have never been surpassed. From then on
many other early maps exist and may throw great light on family
properties; a single map for a whole parish is often more valuable than
hundreds of title deeds and other documents.

A little familiarity with old land measurements will help you in
getting the most from these records. An acre was 4,840 sq yd; a rod,
pole or perch 5½yd; a furlong 220yd; a mile 1,760yd; a rood 40 square
rods; a square mile 640 acres; a chain 22yd, and a yard 3ft or 36in.

### a) County Maps

County maps started to be made in about 1570 and show towns,
villages, forests and old place names. They are notable for the absence
of roads for the very good reason that were none: people moved along
tracks and lanes in good weather, but in winter any lengthy journey was
unimaginable as main thoroughfares would have been rutted and full
of water or mud. The work of famous early map-makers Christopher
Saxton (1574–9) and John Speed (1611) has been widely reproduced,
although it is of limited use because so many other types of document
provide a clearer picture of the countryside. More detailed county maps
appeared from the later 1700s onwards, adding roads, canals, factories,
monuments and parish boundaries; they are almost as informative as
Ordnance Survey maps, even if the scale is still small.

### b) Estate Maps

Maps of landowners' estates normally survive with the other records
of their property. From the Tudor period onwards many landowners

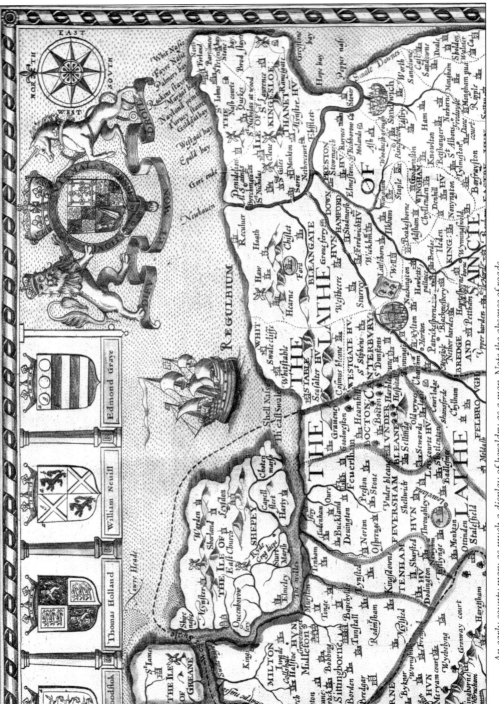

*An early county map: as much a display of heraldry as a map. Note the absence of roads.*

commissioned surveys and maps, particularly to value their property or establish rents, and these are an important source (particularly for place names), especially if used in conjunction with tithe or enclosure maps. Details may include each (named) field, gardens, trees, hedges, woods, roads and lanes, paths, marshes, streams and ponds, greens and wasteland, as well as acreages, land use and buildings. Physical features may include cliffs, marshes, ferries, fortifications, beacons, seawalls, mines, windmills, schools and parks. They may also record a farmer's fields and buildings throughout a parish and the names of adjoining landowners and occupiers, and perhaps survive in various dated editions. Attached to them sometimes are rentals or rent rolls listing tenants, the rent paid or due and their land and cottages; a sequence of them might necessarily describe several generations of a family.

The survival of such material is haphazard as many remain in private hands or solicitors' offices with leases, rent registers and correspondence. However, many thousands of items dating to before 1850 have been deposited, and there is a good chance one will exist for any parish. Beware that they are usually catalogued under the name of the family or the depositing solicitor, and that therefore establishing the name of the landowner at the time your ancestors worked on, or rented land from, an estate or the names of subsequent landowners will be your first priority. A landowner holding land in several counties may have deposited all his papers at one county record office: check the website of the National Register of Archives in the first instance. The KHLC collection of estate maps, nearly all of which are filmed, may be investigated in Kent County Council's *Catalogue of estate maps 1590– 1840 in the Kent County Archives Office* which includes indexes of surveyors, places and people.

### c) Surveys

In the absence of an early map, the next best thing is a survey, or written description of an estate (some run to a thousand and more pages), commonly produced between about 1550 and 1700. Most relate to a manor rather than a whole parish, and then describe the lord's demesne (park, home farm and similar) only, but the majority cover freeholds, copyholds and leaseholds. The best ones name fields with their acreages, and pinpoint their position by naming adjacent fields, while dwellings are related to roads and lanes, with tenants' names always given. Terriers and rentals are briefer, perhaps giving only fields, cottages and the manorial tenant, some modern ones naming the actual occupier if different from the tenant or owner.

### d) Tithe Maps
Tithe maps are amongst the most important of diocesan records, and were prepared for nearly all parishes between 1838 and 1850 following the Tithe Act of 1836 which finally commuted tithes in kind to fixed rent charges on each plot. This was long overdue for the tithing system was nothing but a nuisance and burden to agriculture, and led to frequent disputes between farmers and the Church. From Anglo-Saxon times people had paid tithes (or tenths) on the main produce of their land as well as on stock and labour to the rector or vicar, the former receiving the great tithe of crops and timber, and the latter the small tithe of, for example, newly born animals and wool. The value of the tithes was agreed at a village meeting and assessed on the average price of corn over the preceding seven years. After the Dissolution of the Monasteries the rights to receive tithes were often obtained by laymen to whom the monastery had been granted or sold. Later on the Church's rights were also bought and sold, so that by the Victorian period many tithes were paid to landowners and not to the clergy. Quite frequent by now was the agreement to pay in cash, but as inflation reduced its real value the tithe owner tried to revert to the one-tenth payment in kind. Many court actions arose as a result of this and can be valuable for information about land in a parish. The tithe rent charge was finally abandoned in 1936 in favour of annuities payable by landowners to the government for sixty years.

In what amounted to the most detailed examination of land occupation since Domesday, parishes were surveyed by a professional valuer and resulted in an apportionment or award and a large-scale map. The maps show every field and dwelling that have numbers relating to the apportionment or schedule, which has columns for owner, occupier, description of the property, its use (arable, wood, pasture, house, shop etc.), exact acreage and sum payable. Owners' names are arranged alphabetically in the apportionment which means that some searching will be necessary to find a given house or field. As a general rule, commons, greens and heaths are marked and named, and so too are some farms.

The process was begun by the commissioners who directed enquiries to all parishes as to what extent commutation had already taken place, and such files, if they have survived, will be found at TNA: IR 18. Three copies of the maps and awards were made, the earliest for each parish being listed in the North West Kent Family History Society's *West Kent Sources* and D. Wright's *East Kent Parishes*. For some parishes there may be one or more altered apportionments, each with a map and covering a few acres to the entire parish, dealing with amendments made necessary by the construction of a railway or major building developments.

1. Parochial, retained by the incumbent and now mostly deposited at KHLC
2. Diocesan (CCA: DCb/T/O/A; B) (KHLC: CTR; CTS)
3. Tithe Redemption Commission, deposited at TNA; apportionments in class IR 29 and maps in IR 30 (films at CCA and KHLC)

The entire county's parish maps (but not the awards) are digitised and may be seen at CCA, KHLC and at some larger libraries (for their own areas). They may also be purchased (www.kentarchaeology.org.uk).

## e) Town Maps
Town maps can be fascinating as the early street patterns of many urban centres have hardly changed for centuries. Many add famous buildings and other points of interest in the margins. Ordnance Survey 1in maps start with Kent in 1801 and include many highly detailed town plans at about 5 to 10ft feet to the mile; the 6in series followed in 1840 and the 25in in 1853. The British Library holds the best collection, but many have been reproduced and are available at modest cost. Fire-insurance companies commissioned the production of town plans in the eighteenth century, the most important series being made by Charles Goad between 1885 and 1896.

## Bibliography
Bartholomew's *Survey gazetteer of the British Isles* (1932)
Beech, G. and Mitchell, R., *Maps for local family history; the records of the tithe valuation office and national farm surveys of England and Wales* (2nd edn 2004)

Bergess, W., *Kent maps and plans* (1992)

Evans, E.J., *The contentious tithe* (1976)

Harley, J.B., *The historian's guide to Ordnance Survey maps* (1964)

——, *Maps for the local historian; a guide to the British sources* (1972)

——, *Ordnance Survey maps: a descriptive manual* (1975)

Hindle, B.P., *Maps for local history* (1988)

Hull, F., *Catalogue of estate maps 1590–1840* (1973)

Kain, R.J.P., *An atlas and index of the tithe files of mid-nineteenth century England and Wales* (1986)

—— *Tithe surveys for historians* (2000)

—— and Oliver, R.R., *The tithe maps of England and Wales – a cartographic analysis and county-by-county catalogue* (1995)

——, and Prince, H.C., *Tithe Surveys* (2000)

Kent County Council, *Catalogue of estate maps 1590–1840 in the Kent County Archives Office* (1973)

Lynam, E., *British maps and map makers 1250–1935* (1944)

Moule, T., *The English counties delineated*, 2 vols (1837)

Tooley, R.V., *Maps and map-makers* (1949)

Wallis, H., *Historians' guide to early British maps* (1994)

## L. TRADES AND INDUSTRY

Thousands of business archives remain in private hands at workshops or factories, but even a modest self-employed craftsman would have created some records like correspondence or accounts, although such records do not long survive the owner's death and may therefore be recovered only by chance. Larger enterprises were by no means uncommon even in the earlier mediaeval period, and by Tudor times people began to contribute to joint-stock groups which traded as companies using the services of paid officials.

Guilds of craftsmen developed in the Middle Ages for commercial, religious and social reasons and dominated the life of many English towns. The craft guilds regulated such trades as tailors or weavers and were originally voluntary associations of craftsmen. They recognised three grades of skill: master craftsman, the journeyman who hired himself on a daily basis and the apprentice or trainee. In London the guilds were known as the livery companies because of the distinctive dress worn by senior members, and included such famous groups as the cutlers, glaziers and goldsmiths. Through royal grants and charters they obtained monopolies to restrict business practice to members only, mostly in the City but sometimes also far out of the capital. Many of their records are printed and indexed at the Guildhall Library and elsewhere, and include apprenticeships and freedom admissions from the 1500s. Men from well outside London, including Kent, can be found here from the later 1700s, especially watermen and lightermen from parishes along the Thames.

Stamp duty was levied on premiums for apprentices (q.v.) from 1710–1804 for the whole country, but unfortunately no premium was payable if an apprentice was bound to his father or other relative, and stamp duty was not payable on the premiums of parish and charity apprentices. The whole process was a private contract, and apprentices outside this period are largely unrecorded, although indentures may sometimes be found in family or employer records.

In cities and boroughs the corporation often controlled and enrolled apprenticeships which usually led to freedom of the borough and gave trading and voting rights. Freedom might be obtained by inheritance (patrimony), by apprenticeship to a freeman (servitude), by purchase (redemption) and occasionally by marriage to a freeman's widow or daughter. Entries give father's name and place of residence. Those for Canterbury are indexed, 1392–1835 (CCA; KFHS; SOG).

Kent trade and industry always benefited from the proximity of the Continent and its own many harbours, creeks, estuaries and rivers, notably the Cray, Darenth, Dour, Ebbsfleet and Ravensbourne. In his *Itinerary* John Leland noted the commodities of Kent as general fertility, wood, pasture, cattle, fish, fowl, rivers and havens with ships.

Burgeoning trade soon attracted immigrants and Kent became something of a magnet for many disparate groups of people. Manufacturing in Kent now comprised serge cloth, paper and linen thread, all introduced by foreigners. The Wealden textile and iron industries had enjoyed two centuries of production but were now dying and so allowed economic and religious migrants, chiefly Dutch and Walloons from Flanders, later Huguenots from France as well as many more from the southern Netherlands, to arrive in considerable numbers. The three main original centres were Sandwich in the 1560s and 1570s, Canterbury in the 1570s and 1680s and Maidstone from the late 1560s. Dover too had many immigrants and there were also Flemish drainage engineers on Romney Marsh in the 1400s. By the post-Restoration period there are references to immigrant surnames at Boughton Malherbe, Chatham, Dartford, Denton by Elham, Faversham, Greenwich, Hollingbourne, Hythe, Little Mongeham and Worth, perhaps refugees or skilled artisans or farmers. Many of these peoples in the cloth and related trades had close kinship ties with London immigrant settlements and onward migration to the capital continued throughout the sixteenth and seventeenth centuries.

Urban growth proceeded at an unprecedented rate after 1700. In the two centuries down to 1900 the county population multiplied nearly sevenfold, the urban one by nearly twice as much. The long coastline and many rivers, important for the traffic in heavy goods, had made Kent towns bigger than corresponding ones in the other Home Counties. The proximity of London offered a huge market for farm produce, raw materials and manufactures, a source of summer visitors and, in the north-west, residents in need of military and naval defence in the county nearest to the Continent. In 1801 the four largest towns were Canterbury, Deptford, Greenwich and Rochester, closely followed by Deal, Dover, Maidstone, Sheerness and Woolwich. They were for the most part country towns, often on the coast or a navigable river, with markets and shops trading with neighbouring towns or with London. A few, such as Lydd and Westerham, had stagnated and been squeezed by better connected neighbours or competing markets. However, Maidstone, for example, benefited enormously from its central position on the navigable River Medway, and as a county town holding sessions and assizes attended by the gentry soon overshadowed much of central and western Kent, and enjoyed the profits from brewing, distilling and paper-making.

Along with urban growth, agriculture expanded and diversified after 1700, chiefly through population growth and better land and water communications. The economy flourished on farming and all the while stimulated related activities such as brewing, milling and engineering. Over a million London inhabitants in 1801 provided a ready market for its produce. Enclosures had come early to Kent and resulted in little land being held in common; by 1700 hedged fields dominated the landscape and so the parliamentary enclosure movement of the 1700s and 1800s had little impact and left farmers at liberty to grow what they pleased. From about 1650 Kent accounted for one-third of the nation's hop acreage, chiefly around Canterbury, Faversham and Maidstone, the fields of which attracted annually thousands of hop-pickers from London and elsewhere.

Many early writers praised the county's apples, cherries and hops, which were superlatively good in the areas around Teynham and Faversham. Domesday Book mentions vineyards at Chart Sutton, Godinton, Halling, Leeds and Teynham, and Hasted recorded them at Hall Place, Barming, and Tonbridge Castle. The proximity of London always guaranteed permanent markets for the county's bountiful produce.

Dutch immigration influenced market gardening, and a vegetable and seed industry was established early at Sandwich, where in 1768 the carrots were rated as sweet and large as any in England. At this time there was also much market gardening around Blackheath and Lewisham.

At the close of the Victorian age almost all industries were concentrated in the west of the county: paper-making from Darenth as far south as Tonbridge; printing at Bromley and Sidcup; cement-making at Northfleet and Swanscombe; engineering and munitions at Crayford and Erith; engineering and ship-building at Chatham, Rochester and Sheerness; and brick-making along the north coast from Rainham to Faversham. The county town of Maidstone retained many industries including brick-making, cement, engineering, food-processing, paper-making and printing.

**a) Banks and Bankruptcy**
Trades and industries need banks, and by the time of the Regency there were no fewer than thirty-nine in Kent, all in towns and all private businesses, widely and regularly distributed in the north from Woolwich to Margate and in the south from Westerham to Dover. (Savings banks came a little later; the records of the one at Dover, 1817–99, are at KHLC: CH.) Their function was to finance trade, agriculture and industrial projects, and to provide deposit and lending facilities to both individuals and corporate bodies. Those situated in ports were more involved in overseas transactions and often became important beyond the local area. The mark of a successful man turned banker was his ability to issue banknotes, no special licence being necessary until 1808 when the Stamp Office issued licences (both easy and cheap to obtain) to 30 Kentish banks out of a national total of 552. All survived on the reputation of the founder of the bank and by the

goodwill engendered and maintained between him and his customers and note-holders.

Such founders generally ran a bank in tandem with a main trade or profession, such as law, medicine, brewing or shipping. The bank's capital was a partner's personal capital and not separable from his capital in his other businesses, perhaps around £10,000 being the minimum requirement. The absence of limited liability until 1862 meant that the lure of profits was balanced against great personal risk. In the early 1800s, fourteen Kent banks failed, sometimes because of London agents, local mismanagement or even fraud. Tonbridge lost all its banks between 1813 and 1816, a massive blow to the town, and that at Faversham failed in 1813 when the partners over-extended themselves in funding Welsh ironworks. Most country banks were ultimately too small with just a few hundred customers, and those that survived until the mid-Victorian period were generally subsumed into the modern nationals.

Anyone in trade or business could fall into debt and be imprisoned, and also face court proceedings and be declared bankrupt. A court could suspend a debtor's business, call meetings of his creditors and divide remaining assets among them. This was overseen by the Lord Chancellor from 1571 until the Court of Bankruptcy was established in 1831. Their records from 1710 (TNA: B 1–B 12, B 39–B 40) include order and minute books, cause and order books, and petitions. Appeals against bankruptcy after 1864 are in TNA: B 7, J 15, J 56, J 60, J 69, J 70, J 74 and J 95. The SOG has a register of all bankrupts, 1820–43. Notices about debtors and bankrupts appeared in the *London Gazette* in order that creditors could call in the debtor's goods and value his estate. Debtors often remained incarcerated for many years until their family could clear their debts, in a county gaol or debtors' prison or perhaps a famous one such as the Fleet or Marshalsea in London, records of which are at TNA: PRIS 1–PRIS 11.

### b) Bell-founding

Bell-founding was a noted and ancient Kent speciality and probably originally undertaken by monks. The first recorded maker is William le Billiter (*fl.*1325), and a bell at Stodmarsh is dated 1300. There are nearly 2,000 examples, 98 being pre-Reformation, 38 Elizabethan and many hundreds from the 1600s, at which time the Hatch family of Ulcombe was pre-eminent. Other foundries were at Canterbury, Hythe, Maidstone and St Mary Cray.

### c) Brewing
In the twelfth century Kent ale was considered the best in England. Brewing was strongly connected with farmers, grain and hop merchants, and maltsters. Some successful brewers also became bankers, such as the Brenchleys of Maidstone, the Cobbs of Margate and the Rigdens of Faversham. Water quality was essential and the chalk streams of the North Downs supplied early breweries at Ashford, Hythe, Maidstone, Sevenoaks, Wateringbury, Westerham and Wrotham. Best's Brewery at Chatham flourished as a result of its proximity to the naval dockyards, the Lower Brewery at Maidstone operated from about 1650 and the Phoenix Brewery at Dover from 1740. The difficulties of transporting heavy barrels over poor roads were the reasons for limited markets and numerous independent breweries until the mid-1800s, after which better roads and the railways ensured the consolidation of the industry. Such names as Fremlins, Mackeson and Shepherd Neame were extremely well known over a long time.

### d) Brick-making
Millions of bricks were shipped annually from Crayford, the lower Medway and Sittingbourne with Milton Regis, the latter the largest of all the manufacturing areas which in the 1700s followed the line of the clay districts of the Weald. The famous yellow stock bricks were sun-dried, so made only between April and September. Tiles were produced at Naccolt, Wye and at Boxley in the fourteenth century, and mediaeval designs are known from Tyler Hill at Blean.

### e) Cement-making
An important modern industry began at Northfleet in the early 1830s after William Aspdin had found a way of making cement, which he called Portland after its resemblance to Portland stone. The North Downs provided sufficient quantities of the requisite chalk and clay and this together with the proximity of river transport soon ensured a rapid development of production along the Thames from Gravesend to Dartford, in the Medway Valley between Burham and Rochester, and at Sittingbourne. Many of the villages involved grew quickly and lost their

rural nature, but nearly all the cement-works in the Medway Valley closed in the 1920s slump, although some still remain now as overgrown ruins.

### f) Cloth-making

The woollen cloth industry was of enormous county and national significance for centuries, and indeed Sandwich was exporting wool and cloth in the 1200s. Edward III considered that the English were as wholly ignorant of what to do with wool as sheep were, and in 1331 invited John Kemp, a Flemish clothworker, to settle in England. It was at Cranbrook that the indigenous population first learnt the art of weaving broadcloth in a variety of colours, and Canterbury then became the first mart for the staple of wool with Sarre as its chief port. The Flemish soon developed the art of fulling or milling and dyeing the cloth, leading in 1338 to a prohibition on the exporting of raw wool and the wearing of only English wool. Cranbrook grew greatly as the centre of the Kent weaving industry between 1350 and 1500, but it was the incoming 'strangers' who dominated, producing bays and says at Sandwich (where the workers numbered 500 in about 1645), silk at Canterbury (900) and thread at Maidstone (20). Soon after internal disputes and other causes led to the rapid decay of the industry by the 1670s, later worsened by the migration of its weavers to London's Spitalfields and to the woollen industries of Yorkshire and the west of England.

Intimately connected with cloth-making was fuller's earth, of which a famous vein was situated at Boxley, with others at Gillingham, Maidstone and in the Sandwich district. It was much exported to other counties, being easy to produce as all that was necessary was to clear away rust particles before drying it and grinding it to a fine powder.

### g) Coal-mining

Coal-mining enjoyed a relatively busy but short life. All the mines were in the extreme east and by the 1920s four had emerged as viable prospects (despite constant threats of floods and the coal lying at great depths) at Betteshanger, Chislet, Snowdown and Tilmanstone. Large numbers of unemployed miners in Wales and northern England flocked to seek work, but by the peak in 1935 high expectations had not been realised and the expected population growth had not occurred despite the building of small townships at Aylesham, Elvington, Hersden and

Woolage. All the mines were closed between 1969 and 1989, and the modern records are now available at KHLC: NCB.

## h) Copperas
Kent was noted for the production of copperas, used in dyeing, tanning and making ink, and flourished at Whitstable (and also at Deptford and Queenborough) as a small-scale industry from the Elizabethan period.

## i) Dockyards
Extraordinarily large numbers of men worked at the royal dockyards of Chatham, Deptford, Sheerness and Woolwich, which in total employed over 7,000 men in 1814, as well as at Smallhythe, then on the course of the River Rother. The dockyards were originally based on the Wealden forests and iron industry which could supply the vast quantities of raw materials needed. By 1700 their influence was waning in favour of Plymouth and Portsmouth, fuelled by lack of government funding. However, ship-building was still the busiest Kentish industry by around 1800, especially at Chatham, which was supplied with many fine buildings and saw the construction of Nelson's *Victory*, and also at Sheerness. A natural consequence was rope-making, which developed at Chatham, Deptford, Dover, Gravesend, Greenwich, Sandwich, Sheerness and Woolwich.

Increasing difficulty of access and constant silting reduced the efficiency of the Kent shipyards to the extent that the Admiralty began to look for an entirely new yard. However, the invention of the steam dredger suddenly resolved the problem by allowing a thousand tons of mud to be dredged daily from the Thames and Medway. At the same time the future of Chatham was secured by the development of the paddle-steamer which allowed large sailing warships no longer to be at the mercy of windless conditions, and henceforth to be dragged from dockyard to river mouth by steam-tugs. Merchant ships and fishing boats were later built at Deal, Dover, Faversham, Gravesend, Rochester, Sandgate and Sandwich, and there were boatyards at Ramsgate and Whitstable building small wooden sailing vessels, barges and hoys.

## j) Fishing
In 1431 Whitstable fishermen claimed the rights to sell their catches in Canterbury. By its nature, the industry was based in coastal towns, and

in the eighteenth century Kent fisheries operated on a small scale at Dover, Faversham, Folkestone, Gravesend, Herne, Queenborough and Whitstable (still famous for its oysters), where the local waters were fished, and also around Thanet where the North Sea was worked for herring and cod. Fishing slumped during the Napoleonic Wars and did not recover until the 1850s when catches could be taken quickly to London by train.

### k) Gunpowder

Faversham's famous gunpowder works (which supplied the royal armouries) date from Elizabethan times and covered 160 acres in five parishes. From 1732 it was also produced at Dartford, where the firm of Hall's began from 1785 to make engines, boilers and machinery for the gunpowder and paper industries.

### l) Iron-making

There were many furnaces in the Weald, notably at Cowden and Lamberhurst. Their chief products were nails, horseshoes and irons, fire-backs and the distinctive church tomb ledger slabs. A gradual decline led to there being just four county furnaces by 1740, the industry now subject to competition in other parts of the country, better ore imported from overseas and soon to be taken over by the new iron-smelting and gun-founding technologies elsewhere in Britain. The founding of the Royal Brass Foundry in 1717 at Woolwich and the subsequent development of the Royal Arsenal dominated employment in the north-west.

### m) Paper-making

The industry started around 1589 at Dartford and was famous enough to merit a visit by James I in 1605. Following a vast influx of Flemish papermakers after 1685, a superior quality paper industry was established by the mid-1700s with some twenty paper mills in the Medway Valley (notably the Turkey and Lower Tovil mills at Maidstone), and on the Cray, Darent, Dour and Stour rivers, but the product remained expensive until cheaper machine-made papers arrived in about 1830. Demand increased following the abolition of duty in 1861, and newspapers contributed enormously to later production, accompanied by three printing centres at Canterbury, Maidstone and

Tunbridge Wells. All of these industries, although some were quite famous, employed in total just a few thousand men, only a fraction of those working in agriculture.

### n) Quarrying
Chalk-quarrying and lime-burning took place at Dover, Chislehurst, Gravesend and Northfleet. Kent produced the best chalk in England and there were pits in the north-west at Charlton, Deptford, Gravesend, Greenhithe, Lewisham and Northfleet, some producing 100,000 tons annually. Potting clay was utilised at Aylesford and Greenwich, and sand and lime dug at Aylesford, Bearsted and Hollingbourne.

A stone-quarrying industry operated at Folkestone from 1263, and quarries at Maidstone were noted by Lambarde. Other important products were the famous Kentish ragstone, heavily used for buildings and roads, quarried at Allington, Barming, Boughton Monchelsea, Hythe, Ightham and Offham. The eponymous Bethersden marble (a shelly limestone) was very widely used in buildings, especially the major churches.

### o) Silk-weaving
Canterbury saw the Huguenots introduce silk-weaving, after which it soon became the first chief seat of manufacture, equalling London in the seventeenth century. The reign of Charles II was Canterbury's golden age when thousands of looms were producing silks and sumptuous striped brocades which sold for between 10s. and 20s. a yard. The industry collapsed suddenly when the East India Company began importing woven silks from the Far East, and by 1799 there were just ten master weavers remaining. Records of the Canterbury woollendrapers' and tailors' company, 1529–2002, are deposited at CCA: U12. Linen-weaving was practised over a considerably wider area and survived longer. Maidstone was its centre and linen thread from that town was exported all over the world in the seventeenth century.

### Bibliography
Clark, P., *The English alehouse; a social history 1200–1830* (1983)
Cleere, H. and Crossley, D., *The iron industry of the Weald* (2nd edn 1995)
Coleman, D.C., *The British paper industry 1495–1860: a study in industrial growth* (1958)

Davis, A.C., *A hundred years of Portland cement 1824–1924* (1924)

Feltwell, J., *The story of silk* (1990)

Fowler, S., *Researching brewery and publican ancestors* (2009)

Francis, A.J., *The cement industry 1796–1914, a history* (1977)

Gourvish, T.H. and Wilson, R.G., *The British brewing industry 1830–1980* (1994)

Hills, R.L., *Papermaking in Britain 1488–1988: a short history* (1988)

Hodgkinson, J., *The Wealden iron industry* (2008)

Kenyon, G.H., *The glass industry of the Weald* (1967)

Morris, R., *The royal dockyards during the revolutionary and Napoleonic wars* (1983)

Parsons, D. (ed.), *Stone-quarrying and building in England AD 43–1525* (1990)

Pearson, M., *Kent clocks and clockmakers* (1997)

Probert, E.D., *Company and business records for family historians* (1994)

Richmond, L. and Turton, A. (eds), *The brewing industry: a guide to historical records* (1990)

Shorter, A.H., *Paper making in the British Isles: an historical and geographical study* (1971)

Straker, E., *Wealden iron: a monograph on the former ironworks in the counties of Sussex, Surrey and Kent* (1931; new edn 1969)

## M. VOTERS

When Charles I declared war in August 1642, control of Kent was seen as essential to the cause of Parliament, and by the end of that year a parliamentarian administration had been set up, which formed the basis of local government throughout the 1640s and 1650s. The strongest areas of support for Parliament were Ashford, Canterbury, Cranbrook, Deal, Dover, Hythe, Maidstone and Sandwich. From the Middle Ages an MP represented not a body of people but rather a borough (as a burgess) or county (as a knight of the shire), each division usually returning two members. Until 1832 the old established boroughs were all represented, even if the population had greatly declined in importance or size, to the exclusion of larger and newer towns. Eight boroughs (only) returned members, all but one in east Kent, an antiquated and absurd system that perpetuated the nonsenses of rotten boroughs, such as the notorious 'pocket borough' of New Romney, which had just eight voters, all in the pocket of the Dering family and liable to expulsion if not bribed to toe the party line. Even then, every (male) voter had to own freehold property worth 40s. and to travel to Penenden Heath in order to cast his vote – a representation of about 3 per cent of all adult males. It goes without saying that most elections at this time were uncontested and subject to bribery and other subterfuges. Until the early 1800s east Kent was primarily Tory and west Kent Whiggish, the county being for the most part rural and strongly Anglican and therefore devoid of those who supported the great radical and moral issues of the day: slavery, Chartism, the Corn Laws, Catholic emancipation and parliamentary reform.

In 1832 Kent had 18 MPs, 2 of which were elected for county seats by 7,000 freeholders, in great contrast to the other 16 who were elected by a mere 4,000 voters in 8 parliamentary boroughs. From 1429 the qualification to vote was given only to men over 21 who owned freehold land with an annual (leasable) value of 40s. or more. Five Acts of Parliament, starting with the Great Reform Act of 1832 and ending in 1928, gradually extended the franchise to small landowners, tenant farmers and shopkeepers (as well as disenfranchising fifty-six rotten boroughs) and reduced the total to sixteen when the county was for the first time split into the West and East Kent divisions. A further Reform Act of 1867 enfranchised smaller agricultural owners, artisans and urban labourers, but still generally benefited those in the towns, kept some boroughs under government influence and allowed the gentry to retain the upper hand. Now some 30,000 county electors returned 6 MPs, while in the boroughs 23,000 elected 15. One consequence of this would be the 'Swing' riots and the agricultural rising at Canterbury and Blean, leading to the Battle of Bossenden Wood in 1838, the last battle to be fought on English soil.

Poll books exist from the late 1600s, usually privately printed, and show names and votes cast, sometimes adding abode, occupation and property qualification. Publication ceased in 1868, soon to be succeeded by the secret ballot in 1872. At KHLC are county wide poll books for various years, 1713–1837 (the ones to 1796 at KHLC: Q/RPe1) and west Kent, 1835–68. The SOG has a good collection, and there are smaller ranges at CCA and at many libraries, which often cover their own borough.

Electoral registers date from 1832 as the Great Reform Act stipulated that all voters should be registered, and their names, addresses and property qualification put on a public register. In 1918 all men over 21 normally resident in the constituency were enfranchised; women over 30 who were householders or the wife of one were granted it in 1918, the age being reduced to 21 in 1928. Earlier volumes are in a single alphabetical sequence, but increasing population led to compilation by wards, streets and houses, often tiresome to search if the ward is not known, and indeed success is unlikely without a known address. There are smaller collections at the SOG and CCA. Libraries will have recent editions, often down to the present; for example, LMA has Deptford, Greenwich, Lewisham and Woolwich boroughs, 1890–1999 (LMA: LCC/PER/B).

Records held locally:

Kent, 1832–3 by hundred, parish, name, abode, qualification and
   property or tenant (CCA: U83)
Kent, 1832–65+, manuscript (KHLC: Q/RPr2)
Kent, 1855–89, printed (KHLC: Q/RPr3).

# Chapter 4

# MAINLY NATIONAL RECORDS

## A. CRIME AND PUNISHMENT

Litigation, like genealogy, is almost as old as civilisation. For centuries people sued or were sued for a host of major and minor crimes and disputes, leading to actions in secular or ecclesiastical courts. From the 1300s hundreds of thousands of disputes were heard by the Lord Chancellor or his deputies. The very earliest are likely to be found in manorial records, whilst records of the Church courts and justices are described elsewhere (q.v.). Civil and criminal court records for the most part are at TNA and for other classes of material it is wise to check first the printed calendars at Kew as well as TNA's online catalogue for what may be already calendared/indexed, and its expanding Equity pleadings database within the Discovery website.

Most courts sat for four slightly variable terms annually, starting with Michaelmas around October, Hilary in January, Easter in March and Trinity in June, and the various classes of records will generally be thus sub-divided. In civil proceedings a plaintiff instigated an action with a writ of summons or bill of complaint setting out the cause and basic facts and the amount sought. The defendant responded with a defence or answer, after which either or both might serve further material, all of which are known as pleadings. Then followed evidences, questions and witness statements, affidavits and depositions (usually looking like written speech), perhaps over a protracted period of time and amounting to a great number of parchment sheets containing huge amounts of genealogical and other information. Be aware that chancery clerks had complicated filing systems, and that in many disputes the various bills and answers of a single case may be filed in different series. If the dispute was settled out of court, there will be no further record, but if no prior settlement was reached, a trial ensued and the result was known as a judgement, order or decree; if challenged, the case might be taken by way of appeal to a higher court. All such cases were undertaken by the Courts of Equity, and included the Court of Requests, the Court of Star Chamber, the Court of Exchequer and the Court of Chancery.

The Court of Chancery exercised jurisdiction over civil disputes usually worth more than £10 in England and Wales or where common law could provide no remedy; it became the Chancery Division of the High Court of Justice in 1875. Its proceedings, all in English, from 1386–1875 (TNA: C1-C16, C21, C22, C24, C25, C31, C33, C36-C39) are calendared or indexed and form a supremely valuable corpus of information about family disputes over trusts, marriages, wills and much else, containing in all perhaps 750,000 actions between 1600 and 1800. Classes C1-C12 (1386–1800) are now searchable online. A valuable secondary finding-aid is the Bernau Index at the SOG and LDS family history centres, containing over 4,000,000 parties and witnesses to about 1800 from the Chancery, Star Chamber, Requests and Exchequer courts.

The Court of Exchequer supervised the collection of tax as well as having some jurisdiction over individual disputes, and later over matters of equity, trusts, wills, mortgages, land disputes and so on. In 1875 it became the Exchequer Division of the High Court of Justice. Its records are mostly in English and start around 1558; check the TNA website for what has been indexed (particularly at TNA: E 134 down to 1773), and then the pleadings bill books, 1558–1841, at TNA: IND1/16820-53.

The Court of Star Chamber was formed in 1487 as a series of separate judicial meetings of the King's Council, and was abolished by Charles I. From the 1550s it dealt only with criminal cases, especially those connected with official corruption and abuse of legal procedure, forgery, fraud, trespass, assault and riot. Its records from 1485–1649 (TNA: STAC 1-STAC 9) are mostly indexed by names or places.

The Court of Requests existed from about 1493–1642, principally for poorer litigants, dealing with civil disputes as well as some criminal cases, and its records include bills, answers, depositions, affidavits and exhibits. The records (TNA: REQ 1- REQ 4) are calendared or indexed for at least 1485–1625.

The Supreme Court of Judicature, otherwise known as the High Court of Justice and Court of Appeal, was established in 1875, and its records constitute a major resource for social and economic history. It was divided, amongst others, into Chancery, Common Pleas,

Exchequer, Divorce and Probate, and later into Queen's Bench, Chancery and Family. Most records after 1945 have been destroyed, but from 1876 to the 1920s–40s there are full series of affidavits, depositions, orders, pleadings and writs of summons, some with indexes (TNA: J 4–J 7, J 15–J 17, J 54–J 55, J 59).

**Assize Records**

From the fourteenth century a system of visitations to the counties was undertaken by court judges from Westminster and their hearings known as the assizes. Their powers were gradually extended from property disputes to criminal cases, and they became the principal English criminal courts until they were replaced by the Crown Courts in 1971. The assize justices, usually in pairs, worked on circuits (in Kent the 'Home' circuit), moving between towns on royal commissions of the peace or of gaol delivery to try prisoners, or to hear and determine those cases, such as murder, rape, burglary and treason, that were not heard by the local courts.

The assizes took place two or three times a year in the county town or perhaps in another one supplied with a prison. The circuit lasted some number of weeks depending on the volume of business and if considerable, then trials might be very short indeed as up to two-dozen or so cases might constitute a day's proceedings. The judges would inform the county sheriffs of the intended dates and places of the assizes, upon which calendars of prisoners, alleged crimes and the names of jurors and officials would be drawn up, plus outstanding matters from the previous session. Some minute books list the defendants' names and personal details, but the most important records are the indictments which record the name and description of the accused, the offence and its date, and the name of any victim.

From the 1200s onwards most counties had at least one prison or gaol to hold people awaiting trial, which was far more common than inmates being punished because so many crimes at an early date carried the death penalty. Many parishes also had a village lock-up for temporary imprisonment of offenders. Prison building began on a wider scale during the Victorian period, a dozen or so gaols existing in the 1850s, together with others for male convicts (those sentenced to hard labour or transportation) including one at Chatham.

Until 1782 transportation was chiefly to the British colonies in

America and the West Indies, but after the American War of Independence that destination was no longer a possibility and the courts were then empowered to sentence convicts to hard labour on prison hulks anchored in the Thames, including Chatham and Sheerness (TNA: HO 8; 1824-54 at Findmypast). The names and parishes of those transported between 1654 and 1717 are at TNA: C 66, and for the period 1661–1782 at TNA: SP 35–SP 37 and SP 44. Transportation to Australia took place between 1787 and 1868, and there are convict transportation registers for the entire period (TNA: HO 11). A valuable list of convicts in New South Wales and Tasmania and an 1828 census of 35,000 persons is at TNA: HO 11.

Nearly all prisoners' records to 1559 are at TNA: JUST 3. Kent is fortunate in that indictment books for the Home circuit survive from the 1500s onwards and are published (J.S. Cockburn, *Calendar of assize records, Kent indictments, Elizabeth I–Charles II* (1559–1675)). Lists of prisoners who were tried at the assizes between 1758 and 1832 may be found in the assize vouchers (TNA: E 389/241)], and those tried between 1868 and 1971 in TNA: HO 140. Kent criminal trials in the assize courts, 1559–1971 are at TNA: ASSI 31, ASSI 32, ASSI 34, ASSI 39, ASSI 90, ASSI 94 and ASSI 95. The criminal registers for England and Wales list all those charged with indictable offences, the date and place of trial, verdict and sentence, 1791–1892 (TNA: HO 26, 27). These are online at Ancestry.co.uk, along with other records including calendars of prisoners held for trial at quarter-sessions and assizes, 1774–1882 (TNA: PCOM 2).

Trials at the Old Bailey were generally confined to London and Middlesex, but the proceedings, 1674–1913, are searchable online; thereafter newspaper reports are the best alternative. State Papers Domestic from 1547 (TNA: SP), now mostly with online indexes, also contain much information about crime and legal disputes; see also www.gale.cengage.co.uk/statepapers.

## Coroners

The office of coroner dates from 1194. Its purpose was to hold inquests into suspicious or sudden deaths, the jury usually consisting of between twelve and twenty-three people (between seven and eleven after 1926) who were elected by freeholders to hold jurisdiction over a county, but many boroughs also held the right to have their own coroner. From 1888 counties were divided into districts, each with a coroner appointed by local authorities. The survival of records has been patchy (but see also Borough Records), and they are generally closed for seventy-five years. To some degree this may be compensated for by newspaper reports which often described the proceedings in great detail and are sometimes unique records of the event. The results of coroners' inquests from the sixteenth to eighteenth centuries were forwarded to the Court of King's Bench (TNA: KB 9–KB 12).

## Bibliography

Bryson, W.H., *The equity side of the Exchequer, its jurisdiction, administration, procedures and records* (1975)

Cockburn, J.S., *A history of English assizes 1558–1714* (1972)

——, *Calendar of assize records, Kent indictments, Elizabeth I–Charles II (1559–1675)*, 5 vols (1979–95)

Coldham, P.W., 'Genealogical resources in Chancery Records', *Genealogists' Magazine*, XIX, 345–7 and XX, 257–60

Fowler, D.B., *The practice of the Court of Exchequer* (1795)

Garrett, R.E.F., *Chancery and other legal proceedings* (1968)

Gerhold, D., *Courts of Equity . . . A guide to Chancery and other legal records* (1994)

Hawkings, D., *Criminal ancestors* (2009)

Horwitz, H., *Chancery equity records and proceedings 1600–1800* (1998)

——, *Exchequer equity records and proceedings, 1649–1841* (2001)

Knafla, L., *Kent at Law 1602* (1994)

Melling, E. (ed.), *Kentish sources VI. Crime and punishment* (1969)

Moore, S.T., *Family feuds: an introduction to Chancery proceedings* (2003)

Sharp, H., *How to use the Bernau index* (1996)

## B. DOMESDAY BOOK

Domesday Book (formerly the Book of Winchester) had its origin in William the Conqueror's decision in 1085 to send his commissioners across England to make a personal enquiry into those holding land in chief of the king and the annual dues payable on it. In 1086 it was conducted on a minute scale 'so that there was not even one ox, nor cow, nor one pig which escaped notice'. Its findings were considered definitive, and from which no appeal would be heard – hence its famous name. The king's men assembled juries in each place consisting of a sheriff, priest, lord of the manor, reeve and six villagers, who on oath answered the following questions:

1. What is the name of this manor?
2. Who was tenant in 1065 when King Edward died?
3. Who is now tenant?
4. How many hides [about 120 acres] in the manor?
5. How many ploughteams are working in the lord's demesne and villagers' lands?
6. How many family units specified by social class (serf, villain, cottar, priest &c.)?
7. How much pasture, meadow and woodland?
8. How many mills, fishponds and other assets like salt-pans? What is their value?
9. How much has been added or taken away?
10. What was the total value of the manor in 1065?
11. What is the value in 1086?

In all, Domesday describes the country at the end of 500 years of English settlement when woodland had been cleared and most present-day settlements had been founded. Be aware that it did not set out to record churches; there are enough famous Anglo-Saxon churches still extant but not included to prove this point. The answers, somewhat condensed, were despatched to the king and written up in clear abbreviated Latin in the now familiar two large volumes ('Great' and 'Little' Domesdays), often on display at TNA. The four northern counties are absent, as are Winchester and the City of London, and Lancashire and Yorkshire are hastily sketched; in addition, lands held by religious prelates or houses were exempt and so do not generally appear.

The text was first set in print in 1783 in 'record type' which imitated the Latin marks of abbreviation; this was repeated in county volumes by Phillimore with a facing translation, and there are further indexes of persons and places for every county. Editions Alecto has produced colour facsimiles which are downloadable from the TNA catalogue.

Domesday shows the extent of Norman penetration and English survival two decades after the Conquest, frequently by the many distinctive personal names. On this point alone it is commonly consulted by genealogists and place-name historians, although of course at this date there are hardly any formal surnames. The likelihood of a *proven* descent from one of the Conqueror's men-at-arms is infinitesimal (there were just three such families in England in 1986!). Of far greater and lasting value are what are often the earliest spellings of countless place names which offer reasonable certainty in some cases for an accepted etymology.

Domesday Book has produced an enormous literature which discusses the many problems still concerning this extraordinary work, unique in Western Europe, if not the world.

**Bibliography**
Ballard, A., *The Domesday inquest* (1906)
Bates, D., *Domesday Bibliography* (1986)
Camp, A.J., *My Ancestors came with the Conqueror* (1990)
Darby, H.C., *Domesday England* (1977, 1986)
*Domesday Re-bound*, Public Record Office Handbook (1954)
Flight, C., *The survey of Kent: documents relating to the survey of the county conducted in 1086*, BAR British Series 506, 2010
Galbraith, V.H., *The making of Domesday Book* (1961)
Hallam, E.M., *Domesday Book through nine centuries* (1986)
Lennard, R., *Rural England 1086–1135* (1959)
Morris, J. (ed.), *Domesday Book*, Phillimore county vols (1975–92)
Roffe, D., *Decoding Domesday* (2007)

## C. HERALDRY

To some people, heraldry in the twenty-first century might seem a highly coloured and trivial anachronism, but the evidence of coats of arms (and flags bearing them) is all around us and great importance still set by them. The obscure origins of heraldry lie in the twelfth century when the adoption of colourful devices served as a ready means of identification for knights in battle, the first recorded bearer being Geoffrey Plantagenet, Count of Anjou, in 1127. As time passed the early and simple designs inevitably became more complex and led to the beginnings of codification and regulation, put on a formal footing with the founding of the College of Arms in 1484. Its county surveys, begun in 1530, continued until 1688, and involved nationwide tours of inspection which invited the gentry to register their arms. The process

## Harward.

[*D. 18, 166.*]

Thomas Harward of Ashford⊤Eliz: da. of . . . .
in Com. Kent. | White.

Vincent Harward⊤Dorothy da. of Thomas Brewer of
of Ashford. | West Farley in Com. Kent.

Richard Harward of Mayd-⊤Barbara, da. of Will:
stone in Com. Kent, gᵗ. Anᵒ | Codd of Wateringbury
1663. | in Com. Kent, Ar.

Vincent, sonne & h:
æt. 6 Anᵒ 1663.

*RI: HARWARD.*

## Hawkins.

[*D. 18, 27.*]

Vid. C. 16, 114.

Sʳ Thomas Hawkins of Nash Court in⊤Anne da. of
yᵉ pˢʰ of Boughton vnder yᵉ Bleane in | Ciriack Petit
Com. Kent, Knᵗ. | ofColkin, Ar.

Richard Hawkins of Nash⊤Mary da. of . . . . Long-
Court, 3 sonne. | worth, Dʳ in Divinity.

John Hawkins of Nash⊤Mary da. of . . . . Wollascot
Court, Ar. 1663. | of . . . . in Com. Berks.

| Thomas s. & | Mary vx. | 2. Susan. | 4. Bridgett. |
|---|---|---|---|
| h. æt. 14 Anᵒ | Jacobi | — | |
| 1663. | Bryan. | 3. Anne. | |

*JAMES BRYAN for Mᴿ HAWKINS.*

1. HAWKINS.    2. HAMES.

[For the earlier part of this pedigree see Visitation of 1619, Harl. Soc. Pub. XLII., 204.]

*The heralds' visitation: seventeenth-century pedigrees compiled after the heralds had visited individual houses and families (Harleian Society, Vol. 54, 1906).*

was fraught with difficulty as not too many gentlemen had precise details about parents and grandparents at their fingertips. This resulted in some sketchy early visitations, but the heralds were soon accustomed to accepting arms not actually granted by them if they had been borne for a sufficient period and if the users were persons of gentility – that is, the right to arms by prescription. Those whose right to arms could not be established had to sign a form of disclaimer and lists of these were publicised as far as possible locally, forbidding them to be styled 'gentlemen'. A man entitled to bear arms was armigerous, and commonly described as *armiger* (or knight) in parish registers and elsewhere.

The right to bear a coat of arms (strictly, an achievement, and consisting of shield, helmet, crest and supporters) descended from the original grantee to the eldest son, and so on. During the lifetime of the present holder, the eldest son displayed the same coat, but added a 'label' as a mark of difference, removing it when he succeeded in his own right. Younger sons made permanent small alterations or marks of cadency, called 'differences' (a crescent, a star and so on in a prescribed order). The right to bear arms passed to a daughter only if there were no sons to inherit, and then to her children in the normal way. If you have no coat of arms and do not believe you are entitled to one (the arms must relate to the correct family, not just your surname), that is probably the end of the story, although today the College of Arms will search their tremendous library for possible proof of your entitlement if you supply them with a thoroughly researched pedigree, and still makes new grants to many kinds of persons and organisations.

Heraldry is highly important to genealogists as the descent of arms is proof positive of relationships, and indeed heraldic glass and pedigrees in about 150 east Kent churches were recorded in the 1750s by the antiquary Bryan Faussett, whose papers are now at the Society of Antiquaries. The language of heraldry is Norman French and will require some little effort to gain a basic proficiency. (Let it just be recorded here that the right side of the shield as the wearer would view it is *dexter*, and the left side *sinister* – Latin terms, not French!) Coats are described (the blazon) in a highly precise sequence, using two metals, five colours and various furs including ermine and vair. Of more importance to the genealogist are the assumption of another family's arms: if a bearer married an heraldic heiress, his wife's coat of arms would be incorporated into his (an impalement), four or more subsequently being called quarterings, and often leading to a much sub-divided and highly colourful display over the centuries. The motto beneath the shield, often in Latin, French or English, formed no part of the formal grant, was changeable at will and frequently used by various families at the same time.

The great majority of arms granted between 1687 and1898, together with many earlier ones, can be found in J. Foster's *Grantees of Arms*. As with other subjects, heraldry was subject to much vanity and pretension, and in Victorian times a man might assume a simplified coat of arms or crest on his stationery, cutlery or silver, essentially for display but in no way proof of being armigerous. You can check Burke's *The general armory of England, Scotland, Ireland and Wales* and the later period in A.C. Fox-Davies' *Armorial families* to see if a particular family had a coat of arms, and if you come across a coat of arms with no indication of the family name attached to it, refer to J.W. Papworth and A.W. Morant's *An alphabetical dictionary of coats of arms belonging to families in Great Britain and Ireland* which lists British coats of arms in alphabetical order of the various charges on the shields, enabling you quickly to locate a shield bearing, for example, three lozenges or a leopard's head.

**Bibliography**

Armytage, G. (ed.), *Visitation of Kent 1663–1668*, Harleian Society, Vol. 54, 1906

Bannerman, W.B. (ed.), *Visitations of Kent 1530, 1574, 1592*, Harleian Society, vols 74–5, 1923, 1925

Boutell, C., *English heraldry* (rev. edn 1965)

Brooke-Little, J.P., *An heraldic alphabet* (2nd edn 1975)

Burke, B., *The general armory of England, Scotland, Ireland and Wales comprising a registry of armorial bearings from the earliest to the present time* (1884, repr. 1961)

Butters, L., *Fairbairn's crests of the families of Great Britain and Ireland* (4th edn 1905, repr. 1996)

Councer, C.R., *Lost glass from Kent churches* (1980)

Foster, J., *Grantees of arms* (1915–17)

Fox-Davies, A.C., *Armorial families, a directory of gentlemen of coat-armour* (repr. 1970)

——, *A complete guide to heraldry* (rev. edn 1969)

Friar, S., *A new dictionary of heraldry* (1987)

——, *Heraldry for the local historian and genealogist* (1992)

Hovenden, R. (ed.), *Visitation of Kent 1619–1621*, Harleian Society, Vol. 42, 1878

Humphery-Smith, C.R., *Armigerous ancestors and those who weren't; a catalogue of visitation records together with an index of pedigrees, arms and disclaimers* (1997)

Lynch-Robinson, C. and A., *Intelligible heraldry* (1948)

Moncreiffe, I. and Pottinger, D., *Simple heraldry* (1953)

Papworth, J.W. and Morant, A.W., *An alphabetical dictionary of coats of arms belonging to families in Great Britain and Ireland forming an extensive ordinary of British armorials* (1874, rev. edn 1961)

Pine, L.G., *The story of heraldry* (rev. edn 1963)

——, *Heraldry and genealogy* (4th edn 1974)

Sims, R., *An index to the pedigrees and arms contained in the heralds' visitations and other genealogical manuscripts in the British Museum* (1849)

Squibb, G.D., *Visitation pedigrees and the genealogist* (1978)

Summers, P. (ed.), *Hatchments in Britain, 5: Kent, Surrey and Sussex* (1985)

——, *How to read a coat of arms* (1986)

Wagner, A., *Heraldry in England* (1946)

——, *The records and collections of the College of Arms* (1952)

——, *Heralds and ancestors* (1978)

## D. LAND AND ITS POSSESSION
### a) The Early Mediaeval Period
Saxon charters were beginning to be superseded in the tenth century by much simpler sealed writs or letters addressed to the shire courts. Early mediaeval deeds (or charters) also survive in large numbers and, if calendared or indexed, offer valuable references to place names and individuals, especially if the seals are still attached. They record that on a certain date a person had given and delivered seisin (the handing over of a physical part of the property, such as a turf) to another person in the presence of named witnesses.

*An early charter: a grant to the barons of Faversham, 1252. It is typically written in small, neat and abbreviated Latin and, with a little practice, not too difficult to read. (Reproduced by kind permission of Faversham Town Council)*

### b) Final Agreements

Later on the place of charters was taken by fines, and then recoveries, used to record the transfer of property. Vendor and purchaser co-operated in legal proceedings about a fictitious dispute over possession of land to obtain a court judgement recording the purchaser's right to a property, the vendor now bound by a 'final agreement' (*finalis concordia*) after which the court permitted the settlement to be effected and the land was passed to the purchaser. The final concord recorded the court's judgement in triplicate on the same piece of parchment, one copy going to each party, the third at the foot retained by the court to be enrolled on the feet of fines of the Court of Common Pleas (TNA: CP 25/1-2). These survive in an almost unbroken series of seven centuries from 1195–1834 with calendars and indexes (TNA: IND 1/ 7178-7232), many also having been published. Typically they give a date, personal details of vendors and purchasers, and descriptions of the land in question, perhaps also naming heirs. Uniformity of handwriting and format makes searches fairly easy.

## c) The Four Rolls Series

The ownership of land could be registered in other ways. There are four other prime sources of substantial longevity. The Close Rolls (TNA: C 54) survive for 1227–1903 and are named from the fact of not being readable until the seal was broken. They were used to enrol documents for preservation, such as grants of land by the Crown and deeds recording the sale of private property. Such material includes deeds of bargain and sale, deeds poll, deeds of conveyance, patents, the estates of bankrupts and the deeds and wills of papists.

Patent Rolls date from 1201–1946 (TNA: C 66) and were a record made in Chancery of such matters as correspondence, treaties, grants of land, offices and pardons and are another rich source of personal and place names. Both the Close and Patent series are available at TNA and CCA, are mostly calendared and indexed, and coming online.

Charter Rolls (TNA: C 53; calendared) record the granting by royal charter, 1199–1537, of land, honours and privileges to individuals and

| 3 April. | Whereas Thomas Fane, late of Tunbridge, gentleman, Leonard Dygges, late of Barham, esquire, and John Neyler, late of Maydston, 'yoman,' all in the county of Kent, are indicted for that they and other false traitors and rebels did with force and arms on 7 Feb., 1 Mary, with a great multitude of rebels and public enemies of the queen to the number of 3000 men, rise in insurrection at Braynforde, co. Middlesex, and so arrayed marched to the city of London, the queen being then in her palace in Westminster, and made war at Charyngcrosse in the parish of St. Martin in the Fields against their due allegiance ; |
|  | Pardon to the said Fane, otherwise Vane, otherwise late of London, gentleman, of the said rebellion and of all treasons, felonies, etc., heretofore committed by him, so that he stand to right if anyone imparl him. By Q. |
| [m. 9.] |  |
| 3 April. | The like pardon to John Naler, late of Maydston, 'yoman,' otherwise John Nayler of Aldington, otherwise of Allington, co. Kent, otherwise late of London, of the like offences, so that he stand to right, etc. By Q. |
| 5 April. [m. 10.] | The like pardon to Thomas Culpeper, late of Aylesforthe, co. Kent, gentleman, otherwise esquire, for his participation in the above described rebellion, and of all treasons, felonies, etc., heretofore committed by him, so that he stand to right, etc. By Q. |

*The Patent Rolls: Kentish traitors and rebels are pardoned. (Patent Rolls, Philip and Mary, 1553–4, HMSO, 1937)*

corporations. The Pipe Rolls survive almost in their entirety from 1155–1832 (TNA: E 372; duplicates in E 352). Their purpose was to record money that a sheriff had collected, how much money was outstanding and his expenses. The rolls include the names of landowners and other debtors, the location of the property and perhaps also the names of wives, heirs and other relatives. Various years have been published by the Pipe Roll Society and county record societies.

**d) Inquisitions Post Mortem**
Inquisitions Post Mortem (IPMs), also known as escheats, were held by chancery writ after the death of tenants-in-chief of the Crown to ensure that all the monarch's rights as overlord were respected. This was a reliable source of royal income from 1066 until the abolition of feudal tenures in 1660. A tenant-in-chief held directly of the king for rent or service, and even if he possessed very little land his heir would succeed only by paying a relief and then taking possession (livery of seisin). Failing an heir, the land would revert or escheat to the king; if a heir were a minor, the king claimed wardship, administered the estate and took its profits until the heir was disposed of in marriage.

On the tenant's death a writ was issued to an official and a jury summoned to which the family steward supplied answers: the name of the tenant; date of death; description of lands; names of various lords of whom property was held; value of individual properties; services due; and the heir's name and age (if over 21, often an estimate), perhaps here reciting a family history. If proof of age was needed before succeeding to the lands (*de probatione aetatis*) the sheriff would summon a jury and members would recall events in their own lives as corroboration. In passing, details of local customs, the growth of industries, the existence of mills and jobs of town dwellers may be found, and also the names of townships, fields, lanes and estates.

The IPMs for 1236–1447 are in print with detailed summaries and indexes; these lead to the original documents in TNA: C 132–9 and E 149. From 1447–85 original documents must be examined in TNA: C 139–41 and E 149. From 1485–1509 the IPMs are published in English and lead to the originals in TNA: C 139 and E 149. From 1509–*c*.1640 the original documents must be examined in classes C 142, E 150 and WARD 7, all of which have indexes. All IPM records may now be searched online.

---

## Robert atte Wode

*Writ:* 8 October, 6 Richard II

666. KENT. *Inq.* taken at Badelesmere, Monday after St. Luke, 6 Richard II. He held the under-mentioned manor in his demesne as of fee.

Attewode in Badelesmere. The manor, whereof the site and 50 *a.* land, pasture and wood are held of the king in chief, as of his castle of Dover, by a rent of 5*s.* for ward of the said castle to be paid from year to year at the end of every 20 weeks, and the residue is held of divers lords, services not known.

He died on 18 December last. William atte Wode, his uncle, aged 40 years and more, is his heir.

*Writ* of *Devenerunt,* 12 October, 6 Richard II

667. KENT. *Inq.* taken at Batelysmere, . . . . . . . St. Luke, 6 Richard II. The under-mentioned manor came to the hands of Edward III by the death of Robert, the deceased's father, and by reason of the minority of the deceased, and is still in the present king's hand by reason of the said minority.

Attewode in Batelysmere. The manor, tenure as above.

He died on 18 September last. William atte Wode, brother of Robert his father, aged 40 years and more, is his uncle and heir.

*Writ* to the escheator to enquire whether William atte Wode, the deceased's heir, is his uncle on the father's side or on the mother's. 15 October, 6 Richard II.
668. KENT. *Inq.* taken at Batelysmere, Monday after All Saints, 6 Richard II. The said William is brother of Robert, the deceased's father.

*C. Ric. II. File* 24 (1)

*Inquisitions Post Mortem: a manor at Badlesmere is inherited by a 40-year-old uncle.*
*(Inquisitions Post Mortem, Vol. XV, 1–7 Richard II, HMSO, 1970)*

### e) Bargain and Sale

From 1536, following the Statute of Uses, property might also be transferred by a bargain and sale which opens with details of the parties and the date before stating the consideration (or cash paid) and extent of the property involved. The particular formula employed is 'doth grant bargain and sell', after which the document was signed and sealed by both parties. The bargain and sale was a contract to convey interests in real estate following payment of an agreed price. The vendor bargained and sold his land to the purchaser, but remained seised to the use of the purchaser as implied in the terms of the agreement. Such a deed had to be enrolled with the clerk of the peace and written out in duplicate on one piece of parchment which was then divided between the two parties.

## f) Lease and Release

By about 1630 lawyers had become irritated by the publicity and inconvenience of both delivery of seisin and the enrolment of a bargain and sale, a situation that saw the introduction of a system that would last until 1845, that of lease and release: on one day the lessor (Smith) bargained and sold a release to the lessee (Jones) who normally paid 5s. Smith was seised of his property to the use of Jones for six months or a year, depending on the terms. However, the Statute of Uses caused the lease immediately to vest in Jones, and on the second day Smith released the freehold reversion to Jones who was already in possession. Jones then paid the full price of the property under the terms of the release. The lease is a short document folded inside the more substantial release, which is distinguished by the words 'granted bargained sold remised released quitclaimed and confirmed'. This system swiftly had immediate effect wherever English law operated because no public livery of seisin or enrolment was involved; it was replaced in 1841 by a simple release and in 1845 by a deed of grant.

## g) Title Deeds

Title deeds prove ownership to property by recording transfer from one owner to another. Legally necessary from 1677, they survive in large numbers, but suffer greatly from underuse because of imperfect cataloguing, dirt and folding, lack of indexes and complex Latin legal terms, in all making the effort of investigation sometimes out of proportion to the anticipated rewards. If your ancestor owned or leased a property, however, the search may well be worth it. A seller's title to land that was not registered, or any land before registration was introduced, is evidenced by title deeds that will show whether the interest in it was freehold, leasehold or copyhold, describe its location and area, and record the dates and names of new owners, landlords and tenants. Archived title deeds are normally in bundles which reflect the need to prove title, to hand them to the new owner and lawyers' filing systems. Once split, the deed bundles lose meaning and cannot reveal the sequential history of land or buildings.

Material should be deposited at KHLC or perhaps in the hands of the family that owned the land. It is possible that the deeds have been retained not by your family but by that of the landlord, in which case it is important to ascertain the names of the owners of any land that your ancestors occupied, perhaps from the evidence of land and hearth tax records, parish registers or directories. Some great landowners have deposited title deeds in their tens of thousands; municipal corporations, the Church, businesses and charities also held large amounts of property.

Even a humble farmhouse with a few cottages would have had title deeds including conveyances, mortgages, leases, admissions and surrenders of copyhold, and so on, often surviving from the 1600s, and sometimes considerably earlier. Abstracts of title will recite still older deeds. Such documents have survived in their millions, covering the smallest properties to enormous estates, and may include specific references to such things as advowsons, almshouses, deer parks, ferries, inns, markets, mills, shops and warrens. The information may be concise, giving only manors and parishes, or much fuller, itemizing farms and chief properties, with or without acreages and occupiers, and even with details of every building and field. Some will be located by 'abuttals' or 'bounds' where the adjoining property and its owner are given, making for a valuable source of names of lanes and roads, bridges, commons and greens, islands, marshes, streams and other landscape features. The state of cultivation of parcels of land may be shown, and detailed plans are sometimes found, generally after about 1840. Such material is occasionally catalogued in a highly summary way, and a single archive reference may actually include dozens of items with just a covering date.

### h) Other Material
Deeds of the Exchequer (TNA: E 40–E44; E 210–E 214) comprise thousands of deeds from the mediaeval period to the nineteenth century, and records of the Court of Chancery include ancient deeds to 1603 (TNA: C 146–C 148), modern deeds to the 1800s (TNA: C 149) and deeds produced as court exhibits, 1200s–1800s (TNA: C 116). Many of these are calendared and published by HMSO.

State Papers Domestic, 1547–1665 (TNA: SP 10–SP 17) deal generally with the peace and prosperity of most localities, and are a vast collection of the papers of secretaries of state relating to home affairs, social and economic matters, law and order, religious policy, private correspondence and much else. Again, much is calendared and published, some are online and others searchable at British History Online.

## E. MANORIAL RECORDS

Manorial organisation was in place before the Conquest when communities had already been divided into estates of varying size, developing yet further from a fusion of Anglo-Saxon agricultural estates and a feudal system of military tenures introduced by the Normans. The courts regulated the responsibilities and interrelationships of the lord, his steward, bailiff, reeve, hayward and constable with the village people. Courts were held as often as fortnightly and dealt with every aspect of agriculture, industry and social life; changes of tenure and tenancy; and with services, dues and rights, tying many people to lives of semi-servitude by the imposition of labour and carefully regulated series of payments and fines. As a rule, judicial cases were heard before the shire, royal or hundred courts, but the Saxon views of frankpledge at which people presented cases of breach of law and order among their own community are regularly found. The court was attended by all those free tenants whose attendance was a condition of their tenure, and also by customary tenants, often copyholders, who held their land by an agreement made at the court and entered on its roll, a copy of which was regarded as proof of title. From the fourteenth century the work of manorial courts was gradually transferred to the Church or secular courts and to the ecclesiastical parishes.

These records are frequently the only way to take a pedigree back before the parish register period. Material survives commonly from the thirteenth century, usually in the form of rolls or books, and includes court proceedings and verdicts, accounts, rentals, surveys, extents and much else, and is crammed with references to ordinary people. The courts survived nominally until 1922 when the Law of Property Act abolished the form of land tenure known as copyhold, but as proof of title to former copyhold was very often contained within manorial books and rolls, it was essential that they be preserved. The documents were placed under the charge of the Master of the Rolls and saw the establishment of the Manorial Documents Register, now housed at TNA.

The register records the whereabouts of all deposited material, whether at TNA, KHLC, Lambeth Palace, the British or Oxbridge libraries and elsewhere, and includes indexes of parishes and manors for which material has survived (Kent is soon to come online). The *Victoria County History* is sometimes also useful for manorial references. But it should be noted that much else still remains in private hands, and therefore the holdings vary enormously from parish to parish and manor to manor, some having nothing and others considerable collections, initially in Latin, and requiring considerable skills to read and interpret. Records after about 1660 are for the most part far easier to tackle, and are increasingly written in English.

There were perhaps double or triple the numbers of manors as there were parishes, one manor consisting of a farm and cottages, but often far larger and incorporating villages, farmlands and forests and covering perhaps several dozen square miles. Manorial boundaries were rarely contiguous with parochial ones, and large parishes would commonly include portions of several; some manors existed separately from the main body of the manor in different parishes or counties. For east Kent there is a copious index of manorial names by parish in D. Wright's *East Kent Parishes*.

It is well worth familiarising yourself with life on the manor, how people's lives were circumscribed, how land was apportioned and farmed, how the lord's officials went about their duties, the development of tenancies, the workings of the courts and how people were charged or fined for everyday activities and misdemeanours. Deaths of tenants and the succession of heirs, occupations of lands, descriptions of boundaries, unproved wills, elections of local officials, the obstruction of highways and watercourses, and the name of the lord are some of the many fascinating subjects that may be found here, as is the presence of ordinary people at the court over periods of years.

Manorial tenants were not free and so could not transfer their lands to heirs or anyone else without the lord's consent, dealt with by a surrender or admission in the manorial court. At a tenant's death his heir would attend court to seek admission as the new tenant upon payment of a fine to the lord, at which point this was noted on the court roll and a copy given as proof to the new tenant, such customary tenancies becoming known as copyhold. The rolls normally note the relationship between old and new tenants, and sometimes their ages; surviving court rolls (or the tenants' copies) may therefore reveal several generations of a family holding property, whether just a small plot or a large farm.

A typical manorial court roll records the date and type of court, and the names of the lord and his steward. Then follow tenants excused from attendance (essoins) and those fined (amercements) for non-excuses. Various men are then sworn as a jury to adjudicate on disputes and to act as accusers about offenders and disputes. Next, the court filled vacant manorial positions, after which disputes and offences were considered, a good description of which may be found in 'Manorial Documents', *Genealogists' Magazine* (March 1983), and reveals fascinating insights into ordinary people's lives, such transgressions usually being punished by fines or the stocks. Finally, the court dealt with property transactions, the deaths of tenants and the admission of heirs. Anyone's ancestors may be found in these records, which frequently come well within the parish register period.

The 1922 Act did not abolish manorial lordships, and these may still be bought and sold, although a new lord is not automatically entitled to documents relating to the manor unless they have been specifically conveyed to him. It was established definitively in 1925 that the lord of the manor could sell the lordship whilst retaining ownership of any documents in his possession relating to the manor; and, conversely, dispose of any documents while retaining the lordship.

Many misconceptions surround the title 'Lord of the Manor of X' after the owner's name. He is not automatically entitled to a coat of arms; he may apply to the College of Arms but cannot demand a grant simply on the basis of ownership of the title, which is quite unconnected to a peerage, and nor may he style himself 'Lord X' or sit in the House of Lords. The Land Registry keeps an index of registered lordship titles, and a guide to searching it may be found on their website.

Searches for Kentish manorial documents should start with the Manorial Documents Register at TNA. Many are held at KHLC, and just one at Canterbury, that of the Canterbury Barton manor estate, 1575–1963 (CCA: CC-P).

### Bibliography

Bailey, M., *The English manor c.1200–c.1500* (2002)

Bennett, H.S., *Life on the English manor: a study of peasant conditions 1150–1400* (1937)

Coredon, C. and Williams, A., *A dictionary of mediaeval terms and phrases* (2004)
Ellis, M., *Using manorial records* (1997)
Harvey, P.D.A., *Manorial records* (1999)
Hone, N.J., *The manor and manorial records* (1925)
Humphery-Smith, C.R., *Mediaeval genealogy* (1974)
Jessel, C., *The law of the manor* (1998)
Overton, E., *A guide to the mediaeval manor* (1994)
Palgrave-Moore, P., *How to locate and use manorial records* (1985)
Park, P.B., *My ancestors were manorial tenants* (1990)
Pollock, E.M., *Manors, their history and their records* (1933)
Stuart, D., *Manorial records: an introduction to their transcription and translation* (1992)
Vinogradoff, P., *The growth of the manor* (1932)
Wrottesley, G., *Pedigrees from the Plea Rolls, 1200–1500* (1905)

## F. THE PROFESSIONS

A great many men who aspired to a formal career would first have gone to university. In England before 1829 there were just the two foundations of Oxford and Cambridge, the alumni of which are all in print (J. Foster, *Alumni Oxonienses 1500–1886* and J. and J.A. Venn, *Alumni Cantabrigienses to 1900*) and will supply home parish, age and date of matriculation, and father's name and occupation, sometimes leading to several generations as fathers and sons are cross-referenced.

### a) Church

Clerical ancestors are perhaps some of the easiest to trace, especially as they were nearly all graduates and usually left wills. Start with *Crockford's Clerical Directory* which from 1858 lists all Anglican clergy and was preceded by the *Clerical Guide* in 1817 and the *Clergy List* in 1841. Senior clergy and Oxbridge officials from 1066–1857 are listed with biographical details in *Fasti Ecclesiae Anglicanae*, which includes about 41,000 indexed clergy. The valuable Clergy of the Church of England Database 1540–1835 website aims to record biographical details of all ordained men from the Reformation to the Regency.

**FISHER, Henry,** *Leamington, Warwickshire.*—Literate; Deac. 1850 Pr. 1851, both by Bp of Chest; P.C. of St Luke's, Leamington, Dio. Worc. 1856 Patrons, Rev Edmund Clay and the present P.C; P.C.'s Gross Inc. 320.) [1]

**FISHER, James,** *The Rectory, Dorchester.*—Worc. Coll. Oxon. B.A. 1847, M.A. 1851; Deac. 1847, Pr. 1848, both by Bp of G. and B; R. of Holy Trinity, Dorchester, w Frome Whitfield R. Dio. Salis. 1855 (Patrons, Trustees of the Free School Almshouses; R.'s Gross Inc. 500l and Ho; Pop. 1549.) [2]

**FISHER, John,** *Heapey parsonage, Chorley, Lancashire.*—Literate; Deac. 1822, Pr. 1823, both by Archbp. of York; P.C. of Heapey, Par. of Leyland, Dio. Manch. 1832 (Patron, V. of Leyland; Tithe—App. 63l; Imp. 32l; P.C. 50l; Glebe, 13 acres; P.C.'s Gross Inc. 135l and Ho; Pop. 1853); Author, *The Wisdom of Winning Souls* (a Visitation Sermon, preached at Blackburn); *The Blessedness of having God for our Father and the Guide of our Youth* (a Sermon addressed to Young Persons who have been Confirmed), 3rd edit; single *Sermons.* [3]

**FISHER, John,** *Higham-on-the-Hill rectory, Hinckley, Leicestershire.*—Sid.-Suss. Coll. Camb. B.A. 1819, M.A. 1820; Deac. 1821, Pr. 1822; R. of Higham-on-the-Hill, Dio. Peterb, 1832 (Patron, the present R.; Glebe, 368 acres; R.'s Gross Inc. 586l and Ho; Pop. 544.) [4]

**FISHER, John,** *Magdalen College, Oxford.*—Brasen. Coll. Oxon. B.A. 1831, Magd. Coll. M.A. 1836, B.D. and D.D. 1844; Fell. of Magd. Coll. Oxon. [5]

**FISHER, John Hutton,** *Kirkby Lonsdale vicarage, Westmorland.*—Trin. Coll. Camb. Browne's Medallist for Greek Ode and Bell's Univ. Sch. 1815, 8th Wrang. and B.A. 1818, M.A. 1821; Deac. 1827, by Bp of Linc. Pr. 1828, by Bp of Ely; V. of Kirkby Lonsdale, Dio. Carl. 1831 (Patrons, Trin. Coll. Camb; Tithe—Imp. 984l 8s 11d, V. 304l; Glebe, 65 acres, and an estate of 149 statute acres in Ireland; V.'s Gross Inc. 550l and Ho; Pop. 1944); Fell. of Trin. Coll. Camb. 1820–31. [6]

**FISHER, John Turner,** *Hessenford, St Germans. Cornwall.*—Univ. Coll. Oxon. B.A. 1844; Deac. 1845, Pr. 1847; P.C. of St Anne, Hessenford, Dio. Exon. 1851 (Patron, Incumb. of St Germans; P.C.'s Gross Inc. 100l and Ho; Pop. 1001.) [7]

**FISHER, Osmond,** *Elmstead vicarage, Colchester, Essex.*—Jesus Coll. Camb. Wrang. and B.A. 1841, M.A. 1844; Deac. 1844, Pr. 1845; V. of Elmstead, Dio. Roch. 1857 (Patrons, Jesus Coll. Camb; V.'s Gross Inc. 315l and Ho; Pop. 908); Fell. of the Geological Society; late Fell. of Jesus Coll. Camb. 1845, Tut. 1853; formerly C. of Writhlington, Somerset, 1844; C. of All Saints, Dorchester, 1846; Author, single *Sermons,* Dorchester; *A Paper on the Purbeck Strata of Dorsetshire,* in the Cambridge Philosophical Society's Transactions, 1855. [8]

**FISHER, Richard,** *Steeple-Bumpstead vicarage (Essex), near Haverhill.*—Trin. Coll. Dub. Div. Prizeman, 1842 and 1843, B.A. 1845; Deac. 1845, by Bp of Salis. Pr. 1846, by Bp of B. and W; V. of Steeple-Bumpstead, Dio. Roch. 1849 (Patron, Ld. Chan; Tithe—App. 652l 2s 5d, V. 400l 2s 5d; Glebe, 3 acres; V.'s Gross Inc. 405l and Ho; Pop. 1295.) [9]

**FISHER, Robert,** *Shaw, Oldham, Lancashire.*—Brasen. Coll. Oxon. B.A. 1847, M.A. 1849; Deac. 1848, Pr. 1849, both by Bp of Linc; C. of Shaw. [10]

**FISHER, Robert Bailey,** *Basildon vicarage, Reading, Berks.*—Pemb. Coll. Oxon. B.A. 1805, M.A. 1834; V. of Basildon, Dio. Oxon. 1814 (Patrons, Rev W. Sykes and Simeon's Trustees; Tithe — Imp. 775l 6s, V. 215l 15s; Glebe, 19½ acres; V.'s Gross Inc. 234l and Ho; Pop. 798.) [11]

**FISHER, Samuel,** *Northwood, Hanley, Staffs.*—Trin. Coll. Dub. B.A. 1831; Deac. 1831, Pr. 1832; Incumb. of Hope, Staffs, Dio. Lich. 1845 (Patrons, the Crown and Bp of Lich. alternately; Incumb.'s Gross Inc. 210l; Pop. 4461.) [12]

**FISHER, Thomas,** *Bath.*—Trin. Coll. Camb. B.A. 1806, M.A. 1809; Deac. 1806, Pr. 1807; late R. of Luccombe, Somerset, 1839–57. [13]

**FISHER, Thomas,** *Little Waltham rectory, Chelmsford, Essex.*—Cains Coll. Camb. B.A. 1818, M.A. 1821; Deac. 1819, Pr. 1821, both by Bp of Lond; R. of Little Waltham. Dio. Roch. 1842 (Patrons, Exon. Coll. Oxon; Tithe—R. 673l 12s 6d; Glebe, 12 acres; R.'s Gross Inc. 630l and Ho; Pop. 651.) [14]

**FISHER, Thomas Ruggles,** *Liston rectory, (Essex), near Sudbury.*—King's Coll. Lond; Deac. 1853, Pr. 1854; R. of Liston, Dio. Roch. 1855 (Patron, R. Lambert, Esq; Tithe—R. 205l; Glebe, 18 acres; R.'s Gross Inc. 241l and Ho; Pop. 79.) [15]

**FISHER, Wilfred,** *Lodsworth, Petworth, Surrey.*—Ch. Ch. Oxon. B.A. 1855. M.A. 1858; Deac. 1838, by Bp of Oxon; C. of Lodsworth, 1858. [16]

**FISHER, William,** *Parwich, Ashbourne, Derbyshire.*—St Edm. Ha. Oxon. B.A. 1829; Deac. 1828, Pr. 1829, both by Bp of L. and C; P.C. of Parwich, Dio. Lich. 1849 (Patron, T. W. Evans, Esq. Allestree Hall, Derbyshire; Tithe—App. 135l, P.C. 10l; P.C.'s Gross Inc. 126l; Pop. 493); P.C. of Allsop-en-le-Dale, Derbyshire, Dio. Lich. 1849 (Patrons, certain Freeholders; P.C.'s Gross Inc. 52l; Pop. 60.) [17]

**FISHER, William,** ... ... ...—King's Coll. Lond. Theol. Assoc. 1839, Caius Coll. Camb. B.A. 1846, M.A. 1850; Deac. 1846, Pr. 1847; late V. of Hartlip, Kent, 1852-58; Author, occasional *Sermons.* [18]

**FISHER, William,** *Poulshot rectory, Devizes, Wilts.*—Ch. Ch. Coll. Oxon. B.A. 1819, M.A. 1821; R. of Poulshot, Dio. Salis. 1823 (Patron, Bp. of Salis; Tithe—R. 380l; Glebe, 80 acres; R.'s Gross Inc. 580l and Ho; Pop. 335); Can. Res. of Salis. Cathl. with Prebendal Stall of Ilfracombe annexed, 1834 (Value, 800l and Res.) [19]

**FISHER, William,** *Bishops Itchington, Southam, Warwickshire.*—Trin. Coll. Dub. B.A. 1843, M.A. 1846; Deac. 1846, Pr. 1847, both by Bp of Worc; C. of Bishops Itchington. [20]

**FISHER, William Frederick,** *Luccombe, Minehead, Somerset.*—Trin. Coll. Camb. B.A. 1850, M.A. 1853; Deac. 1852, Pr. 1853; C. of Luccombe, 1852. [21]

**FISHLAKE, John Roles,** *Little Cheverel rectory, Devizes, Wilts.*—Wadh. Coll. Oxon. 1st Cl. Lit. Hum. and B.A. 1810, M.A. 1814; Deac. 1813, Pr. 1814; R. of Little Cheverel, Dio. Salis. 1823 (Patron, Earl of Radnor; Land in lieu of Tithe, 190 acres; R.'s Gross Inc. 405l and Ho; Pop. 255); late Fell. of Wadh. Coll. Oxon; Author, *Translation of Buttman's Lexilogus,* Murray, 1836, 3rd edit. 1846: *Translation of Buttman's Catalogue of Irregular Greek Verbs,* ib. 1837, 2nd edit. 1844. [22]

**FISK, George,** *Great Malvern vicarage, Worcestershire.*—Corpus Coll. Camb. B.C.L. 1832; Deac. 1832, by Bp of Roch. Pr. 1833, by Bp of Carl; Preb. of Freeford in Lich. Cathl. 1843; V. of Great Malvern, Dio. Worc. 1856 (Patroness, Lady Emily Foley; Tithe—App. 1l 5s, Imp. 761l 16s 5d, V. 356l 19s 4d; V.'s Gross Inc. 350l and Ho; Pop. 5000); *Sermons* (preached at St Botolph, Camb.) 1 vol. 8vo. Deightons, 1835, 12s; *A Pastor's Memorial of the Holy Land,* 8vo. Hamilton and Adams, 6 edits. 7s 6d; *A Sevenfold Aspect of Popery,* Nisbet, 1852, 4s 6d; *Twelve Aspects of Christ,* 8vo. Sampson Low, 1854, 4s; *An Orphan Tale told in Rhyme,* ib. 2s 6d; various occasional *Sermons, Tracts, &c.* [23]

**FISKE, John Robert,** *Kettlebaston rectory, Lavenham, Suffolk.*—St Cath. Ha. Camb. B.A. 1828; Deac. 1828, Pr. 1831, both by Bp of Norw; R. of Kettlebaston, Dio. Ely, 1839 (Patron, William Dimes, Esq; Tithe—App. 3l 5s, R. 300l; Glebe, 17 acres; R.'s Gross Inc. 321l and Ho; Pop. 189.) [24]

**FISKE, Robert,** *Elmdon vicarage (Essex), near Royston.*—St John's Coll. Camb. B.A. 1840, M.A. 1843; Deac. 1841, Pr. 1842, both by Bp of Lond; R. of Wendon Lofts w Elmdon C. Dio. Roch, 1842 (Patron, J. Wilkes, Esq; Tithe—R. 406l 16s 3d; Glebe, 25 acres; R.'s Gross Inc. 430l and Ho; Pop. Wendon Lofts, 89, Elmdon, 743.) [25]

*The Victorian clergy:* Crockford's Clerical Directory *is a mine of information.*

## b) Coastguards

Kent's long coastline employed many coastguards. The service was formed in 1822 by the amalgamation of three anti-smuggling services. In 1831 it also incorporated the Coastal Blockade, at that time employing some 6,700 men. Records at TNA are scattered, the main series being succession books, 1816–78 (TNA: ADM 175) which give men's service and some personal details, and also officers' service registers, 1886–1947. Pension details are at TNA: ADM 23 and PMG 23.

## c) Customs

From the 1300s to the reign of Charles II the Exchequer administered the customs system, levying duties on imports and exports at rates determined by the government. Excise duties have been levied on the manufacture, sale or consumption of goods inside the country from 1642 when Parliament raised the first excise to pay its army. Commissioners were appointed at the Restoration and the hated excise officers then appeared throughout the country. Customs and Excise records survive from 1688 to the late Victorian period after which the two departments were merged in 1909. These include pay lists, 1675–1829 (TNA: CUST 18, 19), pension registers, 1803–1922 (TNA: CUST 39) and officers' records (TNA: CUST 50), the last containing much biographical information including age and place of birth.

## d) Government

Civil servants' records will be found at TNA, usually under the appropriate department. The Civil Service Commission was established in 1855 and required evidence of age to establish a pension entitlement; these down to 1930 are indexed at the SOG and include about 70,000 men born from the early 1800s onwards with names, addresses and dates of birth or baptism (with certificate sometimes attached). Many civil servants are listed in annual directories and almanacs, starting with the *Royal British Kalendar* and continuing from 1810 in the *British Imperial Calendar* (later the *Civil Service Year Book*). The names of those in government departments and the royal household have been published since 1669 in Chamberlayne's *Angliae Notitia* and *The Court and City Register*. Also useful for appointments are the *Foreign Office List*, *Colonial Office List*, *London Gazette* and *Whitaker's Almanac*. Records of the Treasury from the seventeenth century are at TNA and cover all

*Country Attorneys.*]  [ 268 ]  [The Law List.

**201. CANTERBURY, Kent, 55. County Ct. No. 50.**

Abbot, Wm. (and in *London*), with William Henry Cullen, proctors and notaries, and registrars of the commissary ct. of the archbishop, and deputy registrar of the archdeacon's court of Canterbury.  *Abbot & Sons.*

**Austin, George.  *Meredith, R. & Co.*

Cullen, Wm. Henry, sol., cl. to the guardians of Poplar union, and in *London*.  *E. J. Barron.*

De Lasaux, Thomas Thorpe, cor. for Kent and Canterbury, and cl. to coms. of pavement of Herne Bay, and cl. to coms. of land and ass. taxes for city of Canterbury, *G. Smith, 5, S. B.* and William Wright Eaden.  *George Booth.*

‡Fox, Charles James.  *Kingsford & Dorman.*

*Furley, Robert, cl. to the magistr. for Ashford, and sol. to Kent fire and life office, perp. com., steward of the royal manor of Wye and manors of Coningbrook and Boughton, Charles Mercer, steward of the manor of Ashford, and John Callaway, jun., cl. of the co. ct., Canterbury.  *S. C. Venour.*

*,**||‡Kingsford, Henry Coare, perp. com., and **||‡Thos. Norman Wightwick, perp. com. (firm Kingsford & Wightwick), sols. to Canterbury and Whitstable railway co., gas-light, &c. co., and to the Kent and Canterbury hospital, and cls. to co. magistr., to coms. of sewers for the eastern division of the county, to coms. of land tax, and to trustees of Dover, Sandwich, and the Ramsgate roads.  *Kingsford & Dorman.*

Mount, Richard Minter, cl. to the trustees of the Ashford, Canterbury, Faversham, and Hythe turnpike roads, the Whitstable road, and the Herne Bay road, perp. com., and **Allen Fielding.  *Kingsford & Dorman.*

Nutt, John, town cl., and cl. of peace, com. to adm. oaths, com. for affits., perp. com.  *Henry Dupleix.*

Plummer, Stephen, perp. com., ‡Stephen Plummer, jun., and Edward Plummer.  *H. Nethersole.*

Plummer, William.  *H. Nethersole.*

Rigg, Samuel.  *James Peachey.*

Sandys, Charles.  *Walker, Grant & Co.*

**‡Sankey, Robert, perp. com., *Richardson & Talbot,* and **‡Herbert Tritton Sankey, att. and not. and com. to adm. oaths (firm Sankey & Son, undersheriffs for the city of Canterbury).  *Kingsford & Dorman.*

**Walker, Robert, sol. to the conservative registn. soc., to the Kent and Canterbury permanent building soc., and com. for affits.  *G. Smith, 5, S. B.*

White, James, com. to adm. oaths, and com. for affits., cl. to the magistrs. of Sandwich.  *D. B. Smith, 19, E. S.*

‡**Wilkinson, Thos., perp. com., com. to adm. oaths, and com. in common law courts.  *J. Fluker.*

**202. CARDIFF, Glamorganshire, 160. County Ct. No. 30.**

Bird, John.  *Nicholls & Doyle*

Bradley, Wm. Alexander.  *J. Gregory & Sons*

*Canterbury attorneys: the Law List for 1855 provides useful details.*

aspects of central government finance. The Institute of Historical Research has published *Office-Holders in Modern Britain* which includes Admiralty, Board of Trade, Secretaries of State and Treasury, 1660–1780, and Home and Foreign Office, 1782–1870.

### e) Law

Lawyers (now solicitors or barristers), proctors, advocates, attorneys, judges and justices will appear in all kinds of reference works including directories, journals, admission registers, biographical dictionaries, printed pedigrees and the like. Barristers, who usually had no degree and included all judges, were admitted through one of the four Inns of Court (Lincoln's Inn, Middle Temple, Inner Temple and Gray's Inn), the records of which are mostly printed and show age and the name and address of the father. The names of all solicitors from 1775–1976 appear in *The Law List* (BL, SOG, TNA) and will reveal the name of the firm and its location or address. The *Oxford Dictionary of National Biography* may supply immediately a date of death and so facilitate probate searches. Solicitors' articles of clerkship, 1756–1874 (TNA: KB 105–107; CP 71) are on Ancestry.co.uk.

### f) Medicine

Before the twentieth century the medical profession was divided into physicians, surgeons and apothecaries, the last concerned with preparing medicines. Licences empowering the first two to practise were issued by bishops, and also by the Archbishop of Canterbury between 1580 and 1775, the fact being recorded in a bishop's register and noting name, parish, date and fee. The Lambeth Palace Library website has an index to physicians and surgeons licensed, 1535–1775. By law, physicians needed a degree from 1522, and are likely to be found among the records of the medical schools of the Scottish universities, or of the Royal College of Physicians which was founded in 1518 and whose fellows' and licentiates' lives are printed down to 1925. Surgeons (together with barbers) formed the Worshipful Company of Barber-Surgeons from 1540–1745, but separated thereafter as the status of surgeons increased; information about them should be sought from the Royal College of Surgeons (its excellent museum of the history of the profession is well worth visiting).

The Society of Apothecaries was founded in 1617, such men

originally treating most illnesses. Their records are at the Guildhall Library and, like most other guilds, include admission registers and apprentice bindings from 1617–1800s. They were licensed from 1815, and from that date include many physicians and surgeons who wished also to practise this further calling. All men licensed between 1815 and 1840 are indexed (SOG).

General practitioners developed in the earlier 1800s and were usually licentiates of the Society of Apothecaries or members of the Royal Colleges of Surgeons or Physicians. The British Medical Association was formed in 1823 and its Medical Directory first appeared in 1845, giving the names and addresses of practitioners. The Wellcome Library for the History and Understanding of Medicine at 183 Euston Road, NW1 has a fine collection of manuscripts and books relating to the entire medical profession, including doctors' obituaries.

Biographical dictionaries exist for many other trades and professions including architects, painters, furniture- and clock-makers, gunsmiths, MPs, printers, sculptors, surveyors, judges, musicians, writers and so on.

See also F. Boase's *Modern English biography*, which is especially useful after about 1850 before *Who's Who* started.

## G. THE SERVICES
### a) The Army
England had no regular standing army before the Civil War, raising troops only as required and placing them in infantry or cavalry regiments.

From the earliest times other ranks (privates, corporals and sergeants) were usually poorer men, sometimes even criminals. Most enlisted voluntarily for life, but in practice for twenty-one years, a period reduced to twelve in 1871, and were then discharged to pension. Many were in reality discharged early because of ill-health or the ending of hostilities.

A very few early documents survive but it is not until the mid-1700s that records are much fuller. Unless your ancestor was an officer, progress may well be very difficult without a known regiment, as the papers are archived by these units rather than centrally, so family stories or documents may be essential. Note that civil registration birth certificates from 1837 often state a father's regiment, as may deaths and wills. A child's given foreign birthplace in the census may alert you to

## 216   50th (or the West Kent) Regiment of Foot.

*The SPHINX, with the word " EGYPT."—" VIMIERA."—" CORUNNA."—*
*" ALMAREZ."—" VITTORIA."—" PYRENEES."—" NIVE."—" ORTHES."—*
*" PENINSULA."*

| Rank. | Name. | Rank in the Regiment. | Army. |
|---|---|---|---|
| Colonel | *Sir James Duff, Kt.* | 31Aug.1798 | Gen.    25Oct.1809 |
| Lieut. Col. | ⊚ John Bacon Harrison ✝ | 4Nov.1819 | 19June1812 |
| Major | { Emanuel Thomas Poe | 10Feb.1820 | 1Nov.1818 |
| | { Nicholas Wodehouse | 18Oct.1821 | |
| | ( William Mason | 19Nov.1807 | Major   19July1821 |
| | \| Holman Constance | 6July1815 | 26May1814 |
| | \| Edward Scott | 28May1818 | Major  12Aug.1819 |
| | \| James Bishop | 26Nov. | 27June1811 |
| Captain | { Thomas Ryan | 30Sept.1819 | |
| | \| Henry Fyge Jauncey | 3Nov. | |
| | \| William Turner | 4do. | |
| | \| Connell James Baldwin | 10Feb.1820 | |
| | ( Joseph Anderson | 3May1821 | 20Jan. 1814 |
| | ( George Bartley | 13Apr.1809 | |
| | \| Arthur Piggott Browne | 13Feb.1812 | |
| | \| Daniel Bateman | 25June1818 | |
| | \| Edward Johnston | 25Dec. | 4June1812 |
| | \| George M'Leod Tew | 30Sept.1819 | |
| Lieutenant | { Wm. Edward Crofton | 31Oct. | 17Dec.1812 Adjut. |
| | \| William Ross | 1Nov. | 27Jan. 1814 |
| | \| James H— Serjeantson | 2do. | |
| | \| George Flude | 29Dec. | |
| | \| James Weir | 30do. | |
| | \| Richard Seward | 27Jan.1820 | 13July 1815 |
| | ( James Briggs | 22June | 28July 1814 |
| | ( Thomas Ahmuty | 30Sept.1819 | |
| | \| Charles Willes | 2Nov. | 17Sept.1817 |
| | \| William Sheaffe | 4do. | |
| Ensign | { Henry Gill | 5do. | |
| | \| John Foy | 29Dec. | |
| | \| George Ross | 2Mar.1820 | |
| | ( James Barclay Ross | 19Oct. | |
| Paymaster | William Hen. Vinicombe | 6Jan.1820 | Lieut. 31Dec.1818 |
| Adjutant | William Edw. Crofton | 31Oct.1819 | Lieut. 17Dec.1812 |
| Quarter-Master | Benjamin Baxter | 5Oct.1804 | |
| Surgeon | ⚭ Pryce Jones | 17Feb.1820 | 7Sept.1815 |
| Assistant Surg. | Thomas Young | 10Aug.1820 | 9Sept.1813 |

*Facings black.—Lace silver.*

Agent, Messrs. Greenwood, Cox and Hammersley.

*West Kent Regiment of Foot:* The Army List *for 1822 gives interesting details of officers.*

military connections and to finding the birth in the GRO army regimental indexes which cover 1761–1924 in one sequence. The GRO holds regimental registers of marriages and burials, but these are only partially indexed and not searchable other than by personal application. It also holds the Chaplains' Returns for 1796–1880 and army births, marriages and deaths for men serving abroad, 1881–1955. If and when you achieve success with that elusive regiment and the rough period of your ancestor's service, you may then investigate the campaigns in which his regiment took part, perhaps through one of the many published histories or a regimental museum.

Much more information is available about officers, and often in published lists which will lead quickly to the regimental papers at TNA. Official army lists have been printed in overlapping series from the mid-1700s, are usually indexed and show as a minimum the dates of commission or promotion (good collections at TNA and the SOG) and in turn will direct you to service records (before 1922 at TNA, and thereafter at the Ministry of Defence, on which see just below).

The following, in summary, are the principal sources of further information, all held at TNA, Kew, and mostly online there or at Findmypast.co.uk. The 'burnt' and 'unburnt' documents (11 and 12 below) may be viewed at Ancestry.co.uk. Apart from the main sequence, the National Probate Index has additional soldiers' wills from 1850–1986 in a separate series.

1. Attestation and discharge papers ('soldiers' documents'), 1760–1913 (TNA: WO 97). None surviving for men killed in action
2. Discharge papers, 1817–88 (TNA: WO 12, WO 16, WO 25, WO 121)
3. Muster rolls and pay lists, 1732–1898 (TNA: WO 10–WO 16). Quarterly returns of unit locations with men's details
4. Description books, 1756–1900 (TNA: WO 25, WO 67). Personal details and physical description
5. Enrolment and casualty books, 1759–1925 (TNA: WO 68)
6. Casualty lists and returns, 1797–1910 (TNA: WO 25, WO 32). Include birthplace, trade and next of kin
7. Records of pensioners (both Chelsea and out-pensioners), 1715–1913 (TNA: WO 22, WO 23, WO 116, WO 117, WO 120)

8. Soldiers admitted to pension, 1838–96, certificates of service (TNA: WO 131)
9. Officers' service records, 1764–1914 (TNA: WO 76)
10. Household Cavalry service records, 1799–1920 (TNA: WO 400)
11. First World War, 1914–20, service records, 'the burnt documents' (TNA: WO 363)
12. First World War, 1914–20, pension records, 'the unburnt documents' (TNA: WO 364)

Records of officers who served after 1922 and of other ranks after 1920 are held by the Ministry of Defence, which will release information only to next of kin (or to agents with the kin's permission). Application is made through their website at a current cost of £30.

Apart from the usual GRO death certificates, French and Belgian death certificates for British soldiers who died in hospitals and elsewhere are at TNA: RG 35. The two works *Officers/Soldiers who died in the Great War* between them contain about 700,000 entries in 80 volumes (TNA, the SOG and elsewhere).

The justly famed Commonwealth War Graves Commission maintains the graves of over 1,500,000 men who died in the two world wars. Its impressive website allows details about those men, their graves, next of kin and other details to be accessed rapidly.

From the Anglo-Saxon period onwards formal inspections or 'musters' were taken of all able-bodied men aged 16–60. Those surviving for 1522–1640 are at TNA including the whole country for 1544, listed by hundred and parish; scattered Kentish ones for the 1500s–1700s are at the British Library or KHLC, the latter including Aylesford Lathe for 1581, and Faversham, New Romney, Queenborough, Sandwich and Tenterden for various dates (see *Gibson's Guide*). A man's income determined what arms or armour he had to provide, and so the rolls may indicate either his income or the arms.

The Militia Act of 1757 established militia regiments for each county and required each parish to provide a certain number of able-bodied men aged between 18 and 50 (reduced to 45 in 1762) for training. Usually there were insufficient volunteers, so a ballot system would produce the required conscripts. Ballot lists between 1757 and 1831 usually show a man's name, occupation and physical infirmities; from

*East Kent Militia: the Chilham overseers issue an account concerning the birth of a grandchild (CCA: U3/191/17/3). (Reproduced by kind permission of Canterbury Cathedral Archives and Library)*

1802 the number of his children and whether they were under or over 14; and from 1806 his age.

Militia units served in Britain or Ireland, men being engaged for three years (five after 1786), and in wartime on duty almost continuously anywhere in the country. This explains the large numbers of stray marriages and children's baptisms or burials whilst men were billeted in a camp (for example, Northgate Barracks in Canterbury or on Barham Downs, east of the city). Such entries in parish registers will generally note a man's regiment and rank.

When the French wars ended in 1815 most volunteer units were disbanded except for the yeomanry who were retained, often to help in counteracting local disorders. The militia ballot was suspended in 1829, and henceforth only volunteers were taken on. Muster books and pay lists for militia regiments, 1780–1925, are at TNA: WO 13 and WO 68, arranged by county. Attestation papers of militia men, 1769–1915, are at TNA: WO 96 and WO 97, arranged by regiment and surname.

RECORDS HELD LOCALLY
Kent Regimental records:

> Canterbury City muster lists, 1580–1795 (CCA: CC–N)
> East Kent militia returns, 1781–1876 (TNA: WO 13/1056–1081)
> West Kent militia returns, 1781–1876 (TNA: WO 13/1082–1107)
> Kent Artillery, 1853–76 (TNA: WO 13/1110–1113)
>
> Royal East Kent Yeomanry ('The Buffs'): regimental and
>   troop administration, 1795–1932 (KHLC: AG); persons killed or
>   dying overseas OAS (KHLC; SOG)
> Royal West Kent Regiment: regimental and troop administration,
>   1756–1961 (KHLC: B1)
> Militia officers, certificate and enrolment of property
>   qualifications for deputy lieutenants and commissioned officers,
>   1757–1879 (KHLC: Q/ROm)
> Militia Tax (St Augustine Division), 1678–90 (KHLC: Q/RTm)
> Wingham division ballot lists, 1764–85 (KHLC: L/M4)

**b) The Navy**
Britain's long and venerable history of maritime exploration, trade and

conquest means that many people have ancestors who were sailors or worked in dockyards and ports. As early as the reign of George I there were perhaps 20,000 men working as crew on merchant ships, and it is therefore quite likely that you may have an ancestor who was a a seaman.

Most records of officers and sailors down to about 1923 are at TNA. They are extensive, sometimes bewildering and not easy to use because of their dispersal among many different series. Officers are easily located in published lists and biographical dictionaries, especially *The Navy List* (1782–date). Ratings joining between 1853 and 1923 are also easily found in service records, but before 1853 a ship's name will be necessary, perhaps discoverable through the census, a GRO certificate or parish register. If you know the ship's name, you can turn immediately to the muster rolls for 1667–1878 (TNA: ADM 36–39 and ADM 41), which record the number of men on board, the ship's location and the issuing to each named individual of clothes, tobacco and other necessaries. The rolls also supply a man's place of birth, and date of joining and age at the time; a good picture of an individual's career may be built up by following the musters rolls through in a chronological sequence. W.R. O'Byrne's *Naval biographical dctionary* gives every officer of the rank of lieutenant and above, serving or retired, and alive in 1845. A valuable set of wills and administrations for all men joining the Royal Navy or Marines between 1786 and 1882 is at TNA: ADM 48 and online.

There was no systematic provision of pensions for naval personnel or their dependants until the late 1800s. The Chatham chest fund was established in 1590 (TNA: ADM 82) to provide sailors' pensions for the wounded and the dependants of those killed in action. Its administration was transferred to the Royal Greenwich Hospital in 1803, where there are registers of Chatham Chest payments, 1653–1799. Other Greenwich Hospital records include admissions and discharges of in-pensioners, 1704–1869 (TNA: ADM 73), applications for admissions to the hospital, 1737–1859 and out-pensioners' registers of application, 1789–1859 (TNA: ADM 6).

### ROYAL MARINES

A regiment of soldiers was formed in 1665, specifically to serve on ships, and replaced in 1698 by two regiments of troops called marines, who became a permanent force in 1755 with company divisions at Chatham, Plymouth and Portsmouth, and also at Woolwich from 1805. Nearly all records are at TNA in Admiralty class ADM, each division keeping its own papers which include births, marriages and deaths of marines and their families. Survival rates vary, and as a rule you will need to know the division your man served in to make progress. Certificate of service books, 1802–94, are searchable online (TNA: ADM 29). Officers were included in army lists from 1740, navy lists from 1814 and in *Hart's Army List* from 1840; their service records, 1793–1925 are in TNA class ADM 196. Also online are continuous service engagement books and registers of service, 1853–1923 (TNA: ADM 139).

A marine usually remained in the same company for his entire service. Attestation papers giving age, birthplace, trade and physical description for varying dates between 1790 and 1923 are in TNA: ADM 157, arranged by division, company and date of enlistment or discharge. There are also description books for varying dates, 1755–1940, giving much information, in TNA: ADM 158. After 1884 each marine was given a number by his division and records of service were introduced and filed under this number in TNA: ADM 159; they record date and place of birth, trade, religion, date and place of enlistment, physical description and service record.

## MERCHANT SEAMEN

Merchant shipping ultimately came under the responsibility of the Board of Trade, and all records are therefore at TNA in class BT. There are detailed indexed records of merchant seamen from 1835–57 (TNA: BT 112, 113, 116, 120; all on Findmypast.co.uk) and 1918–72, but for other periods you will need to ascertain a ship's name before investigating, perhaps from a will, the census, parish register or other source. The GRO marine register indexes of births, 1837–1930 and deaths, 1837–1965 may supply a ship's name immediately. Muster rolls will provide much information about an individual and survive for 1835–1994 in various sequences (TNA: BT 98).

Masters', engineers' and mates' tickets of competency from 1845, 1861 and 1883 respectively to about 1921 (TNA: various BT classes) supply date and place of birth and of certification. There are also boys' apprenticeship books, 1710–1811 (TNA: IR 1); from 1823 all merchant ships over 80 tons had to carry apprentices and these are indexed, 1824–1953 (TNA: BT 150). Agreements and crew lists, 1747–1860 are at TNA: BT 98 and online.

Trinity House dispensed charitable funds to seamen, their widows and dependants from 1514–1854. Petitions giving useful genealogical and career details survive for 1784–1854 at the London Guildhall Library, with films at the SOG and elsewhere. The Guildhall Library also holds registers of money paid to almspeople and out-pensioners, 1729–1946, giving names, ages and the reason for assistance being granted.

Lloyd's marine collection, also at the Guildhall Library, includes the *Mercantile Navy List*, the annual list of British-registered merchant vessels from 1857, which contains owners' names and addresses from 1865. *Lloyd's Register* from 1775 has very full details about each vessel. *Lloyd's Captains' Registers* lists the holders of masters' certificates from 1869–1948, giving date and place of birth or examination and ships served on. *Lloyd's List* from 1741 records ships' arrivals and departures for each port, as well as reported losses.

### RECORDS HELD LOCALLY
Crew Lists, all indexed (KHLC: RGS):

> Deal, 1863–83
> Dover, 1863–1913 and fishing vessels, 1884–1900
> Faversham, 1863–1909
> Folkestone, 1880–97
> Ramsgate, 1863–1913 and fishing vessels, 1884–1914
> Rochester, 1863–1913; calendared (MALSC: RGS)

Medway Navigation Company, 1740–1930 (MALSC: S/MN)

Shipping Registers (KHLC: RBS):

> Chatham Custom House, 1824–65; transaction books, 1863–1913
> Deal, 1825–78
> Dover, 1824–1994
> Faversham, 1824–1988
> Folkestone, 1848–1985
> Ramsgate, 1853–1992
> Sandwich, 1786–1854

## Bibliography

Chant, C., *The handbook of British regiments (1988)*

Crowder, N.K., *British army pensioners abroad 1772–1899* (1995)

Hallows, I.S., *Regiments and corps of the British army* (1991)

Hamilton-Edwards, G., *In search of army ancestry* (1977)

Holding, N., *World War I army ancestry* (3rd edn 1997)

List and Index Society, *Muster books and pay lists* (1984)

Macdougall, P., *Royal dockyards* (1989)

Murphy, G., *Where did that regiment go? The lineage of British infantry and cavalry regiments at a glance* (2009)

O'Byrne, W.R., *Naval biographical dictionary* (1849)

*Officers died in the Great War* (1919)

Pappalardo, B., *Using navy records* (2001)

——, *Tracing your naval ancestors* (2003)

Peacock, E., *The army lists of the roundheads and cavaliers . . . . the names of the officers in the Royal and Parliamentary armies of 1642* (1874)

Pols, R., *Dating old army photographs* (2011)

Rodger, N.A.M., *Naval records for genealogists* (1988)

Smith, K., Watts, C. and Watts, M., *Records of merchant shipping and seamen* (1998)

*Soldiers died in the Great War,* 80 vols (1919–21)

Spencer, W., *Records of the militia and volunteer forces 1757–1945* (1997)

——, *Army records: a guide for family historians* (2008)

Steppler, G.A., *Britons to arms! The story of the British volunteer soldier* (1992)

Thomas, G., *Records of the royal marines* (1994)

Watts, M.J. and C.T., *My ancestor was in the British army* (1995)

Western, J.R., *The English militia in the eighteenth century: the story of a political issue 1660–1802* (1965)

## H. TAX RECORDS

### a) Association Oath Rolls

Support for the Stuart cause remained strong after the Glorious Revolution of 1688, and in order to protect the life of the new King William III and avoid the possibility of a Catholic restoration in the event of his death, likely opposition were to be identified and removed from positions of influence. This was effected by an Act of 1696 (the 'Solemn Association') compelling all office-holders to take an oath of loyalty to

William and Mary and an oath that they would exact vengeance on the Jacobites in the case of a royal assassination. In fact, the oath rolls were open to all males to sign, and in most places all males of some age and standing were encouraged to take the oath, and their names, together with those of defaulters, were enrolled. They include clergymen, freemen, gentry, military and naval officers, office-holders and many others from Canterbury, Dover, Gravesend with Milton, Maidstone, Queenborough, Rochester and the Cinque Ports (TNA: C 213/129–37 and C 332).

Men accepting military or public office were required by the Corporation Act of 1661 and Test Act of 1672/3 to swear oaths of allegiance and royal supremacy before a justice, and to lodge a certificate at court confirming that they had received the sacrament. Catholics were excluded from official posts by a further declaration against transubstantiation. Records survive to 1828 when the acts were repealed (TNA: C 224, CP 37, E 196 and KB 22) and include good representation for Kent as it lay within the prescribed 30-mile radius of London. Most of these and other classes are online, some searchable by both surname and occupation group. Oaths of allegiance, test and abjuration sworn and enrolled in Chancery, 1673–1709 are at TNA: C 220/9.

### b) Hearth Tax

This was collected every six months on Lady Day (25 March) and Michaelmas (29 September) between 1662 and 1689 on properties worth 20s. or more. Paupers and certain exempted householders paid nothing, but otherwise the charge was 2s. on each fireplace, hearth or stove. The records are arranged by hundreds, liberties and boroughs and comprise lists drawn up by the parish constable and submitted to the justices at the quarter sessions. They record head of household, the number of hearths taxed (or sum paid) and comments on changes since the last collection. A rule of thumb is that one or two hearths were modest, three or four comfortable and six or more affluent. In the Kent returns for Lady Day 1664 2 per cent of houses had ten or more hearths, but hardly any twenty or more, the notable exceptions being Penshurst with twenty-one, Westenhanger Castle with sixty and Knole House with eighty-five.

After May 1664, landlords had to pay the tax for tenanted property if the occupier was absent, and anyone with two hearths was liable to pay even if they would otherwise have been exempt. The tax was never popular and there was widespread evasion, but one valuable aspect of the returns is that from 1663 paupers and other exempt people still had to be listed, although this provision was often ignored.

The Lady Day 1664 returns are the most complete, and in the case of Kent lack only Canterbury, the Cinque Ports and their associated towns, and the Liberty of Romney Marsh. A full transcript and comprehensive indexes are in D.W. Harrington's *Kent hearth tax assessment, Lady Day 1664*. At KHLC in class Q/RTh are partial county returns for 1662 and 1663, and also Canterbury for 1665, 1671 and 1673. There are also further Exchequer duplicates for various years (TNA: E 179).

### c) Land Tax

Land tax was collected form 1692–1963 on land with an annual value of more than 20s., Catholics being charged double until 1831. Commissioners surveyed and valued all property in towns and villages, after which the government took a rate varying from year to year on its needs. Increasingly, the tax came more and more from the annual value of land, usually fixed at 4s. in the pound, and was made perpetual in 1797. However, it was possible for landowners to redeem their tax by a lump sum and never pay again, although they were still included in the lists until 1832 as evidence of entitlement to vote. The lists consist of assessments and returns giving addresses, landowners or proprietors and (from 1772) occupiers of a property with the amounts paid. Care must be taken in interpretation as proprietors are not always freeholders, and occupiers may actually be tenants or sub-tenants; additionally, not all occupiers are always listed. Survival before 1780 is patchy, but thereafter until 1832 remarkably complete as payment was evidence of the qualification to vote, and duplicates were therefore lodged with the Clerk of the Peace who was responsible for producing voter lists. The introduction of electoral registers in 1832 rendered these records unnecessary for electoral purposes, although there are later, if incomplete, survivals. TNA has the whole county for 1798 at TNA: IR 23/35–8.

### d) Lay Subsidies

Various kinds of taxes were collected from the twelfth to seventeenth centuries by governments to pay the costs of administration and war. They were named lay subsidies because clerical property was exempt, although there were separate clerical ones. They were based on moveable personal property such as goods or crops above a minimum value, and sometimes also land or buildings, such thresholds effectively exempting the poor from liability. The many surviving and valuable lists are nearly all at TNA: E 179, for which an increasing TNA database should be consulted.

Two of the earliest and best preserved subsidies of 1327 and 1332 (the latter largely confined to better off householders) specified a quota to be levied, perhaps a tenth or smaller proportion of a man's property. Those of 1378–80 often give occupations and relationships between members of the household. From 1334–1523 the government took no interest in how much a man paid; townships were expected to raise a certain sum of tax, and so assessments now listed places and the total tax payable, rarely including names. The Tudors reversed matters in making great use of subsidies but also assessing individuals by taxing a man on the basis of his wages, the value of his goods or his income from land. The first of these was the Great Subsidy of 1523, levied for four years at 4*d*. in the pound, and applicable to everybody over 16 with income from land or taxable goods of £2 annually, or who earned £1 or more each year. The rolls are arranged by hundreds and give names and a man's taxable assets or tax actually paid, and are comprehensive enough to act as a basis for a simple family tree. Further returns survive for 1543, 1544 and 1545. All are now searchable at the TNA website.

### e) Marriage Duty Act

The raising of monies to fund a war with France led to the imposition of a tax from 1 May 1695, payable on a sliding scale, on births, marriages and burials, and in addition an annual tax was payable by bachelors over 25 and by childless widowers. Those in receipt of poor relief were exempt. The assessments were partly based on parish registers and should have listed the number of people in a parish in 1695.

Revenues derived from it were insufficient and led to its abolition in 1706. The outstanding county survival is KHLC: Q/CTz/2 (copies at CCA, KFHS), and amounts to a virtual census for about fifty eastern parishes between Thanet and Dover, all summarised as the 'Wingham Division'. There are also returns for New Romney, 1695–1706 (KHLC: NR/RTb 1–13).

## f) Poll Taxes

Poll taxes counted heads, and monies were raised on them in the fourteenth, seventeenth and eighteenth centuries, although, as so often, the poor were exempt. In 1377 a levy of 4*d*. per head was imposed on those aged over 14 (1*s*. on the clergy), and in 1379 on those aged over 16. In 1381 the Peasants' Revolt arose partly from the levy being raised in 1380 to 1*s*. on those aged over 15 – a peasant couple would with great difficulty be able to pay 2*s*. There were further regular annual collections between 1641 and 1703 and a quarterly one in 1694–5. Commissioners were appointed who then oversaw local inhabitants drawing up the assessment lists which give names in 1377 and 1381, and amounts paid in all three years. The records are all at TNA: E 179 and are searchable online. The first three returns are also in print (C.C. Fenwick (ed.), *The Poll Taxes of 1377, 1379 and 1381, Part One – Bedfordshire to Leicestershire*).

## g) Protestation Returns

A resolution of Parliament in 1641 asked for every male over 18 to take an oath in support of the Crown, Parliament and the Protestant religion. Lists of those men signing were prepared in each parish (sometimes actual signatures or marks) and sent to Parliament in 1642. Even those who generally would not comply (usually Catholics) were often listed, resulting in a virtual Commonwealth period census. The returns include about 100, mostly east Kent, parishes (HLRO: HL/PO/JO/10/1/92).

## h) Window Tax

This was levied between 1696 and 1851, although the later years saw widespread evasion and the blocking up of many windows. Houses with between seven and ten or more windows were chargeable, but some windows including those of a business premises attached to a residence were exempt. The tax fell on occupiers, not owners, paupers not paying Church or poor rates being exempt. The returns usually show names and addresses, the numbers of windows and tax paid. From 1784 other taxes, such as on servants and hair powder came within its aegis.

The *Gibson's Guide* lists window tax returns for these parishes, with runs of between about twenty and sixty years: Birchington, Canterbury city, Faversham, Folkestone, New Romney, Rodmersham, Sandwich, Thanet Sts John and Peter and the Wingham division.

### i) Miscellaneous

In 1641 when civil war broke out in Ireland, the government authorised sheriffs, churchwardens and parish overseers to collect gifts and receive loans for the relief of Protestant refugees. The lists of men's and women's names with amounts paid (TNA SP 28 and E 179) are, exceptionally, very comprehensive for Kent.

In 1661 subscriptions were collected for a 'free and voluntary present' to clear the debts of the newly restored Charles II. Payment was voluntary, but as the contributors' names were recorded, many people, especially the wealthier, did pay. The returns with names, and sometimes occupations, are at TNA: E 179.

There are other good runs of taxable commodities at KHLC:

Carriages, 1747–82
Coats of arms, 1793–1882
Dogs, 1796–1882
Game, 1784–1807
Hair powder, 1795–1861
Horses, 1784–1874
Male servants, 1777–1852
Silver plate, 1756–62
Uninhabited houses, 1851–1924

### Bibliography

Chandaman, G.D., *The English public revenue 1660–1668* (Oxford, 1975)

Dowell, S., *Taxation and taxes in England* (1884, repr. 1988)

Fenwick, C.C. (ed.), *The Poll Taxes of 1377, 1379 and 1381, Part One – Bedfordshire to Leicestershire* (1998)

Harrington, D.W., *Kent hearth tax assessment, Lady Day 1664* (2000)

Hoyle, R.W., *Tudor taxation records* (1994)

Noble, M., 'Land tax returns and urban development', *Local Historian*, 15 (1982)

Patten, J., 'The Hearth Taxes 1662–1689', *Local Population Studies*, 7 (1971)

Turner, M.E. and Mills, D.R. (eds), *Land and property: the English Land Tax 1692–1832* (1986)

Ward, W.R., *The English land tax in the 18th century* (1953)

——, *The administration of the window and assessed taxes 1696–1798* (1963)

# DIRECTORY OF ARCHIVES, LIBRARIES AND SOCIETIES

**Bexley Local Studies and Archive Centre**
Central Library, Townley Road, Bexleyheath DA6 7HJ
020 8303 7777
Monday–Wednesday, 10–5.30, Thursday, 10–7, Friday, 10–1, Saturday, 10–5
libraries@bexley.gov.uk

**The British Library (BL)**
96 Euston Road, London NW1 2DB
033 0333 1144
Monday, 10–8, Tuesday–Thursday, 9.30–8, Friday–Saturday 9.30–5
Department of manuscripts: Monday, 10–5, Tuesday–Saturday, 9.30–5
Customer-Services@bl.uk
Reader's ticket necessary

**Bromley Local Studies, Library and Archives**
Bromley Civic Centre, Stockwell Close, Bromley BR1 3UH
020 8461 7170
Monday–Friday, 8.30–5
localstudies.library@bromley.gov.uk

**Canterbury Cathedral Archives and Library (CCA)**
The Precincts, Canterbury CT1 2EH
01227 865330
Tuesday–Thursday and first Saturday of each month, 9.15–4.45
archives@canterbury-cathedral.org
CARN ticket necessary

### City of Westminster Archives
10 St Ann's Street, Westminster SW1P 2XR
020 7641 5180
Tuesday–Thursday, 10–7, Friday–Saturday, 10–5
archives@westminster.gov.uk

### College of Arms
130 Queen Victoria Street, London EC4V 4BT
Monday–Friday, 1–4
Email enquiries via www.college-of-arms.gov.uk

### Greenwich Heritage Centre
Artillery Square, Royal Arsenal, Woolwich, London SE18 6ST
020 8854 2452
Tuesday–Saturday, 9–5
heritage.centre@royalgreenwich.gov.uk

### Guild of One Name Studies (GOONS)
Box G, 14 Charterhouse Buildings, Goswell Road, London EC1M 7BA
080 0011 2182
guild@one-name.org

### Guildhall Library
Aldermanbury EC2V 7HH
020 7332 1868/1870
Monday, Tuesday, Thursday, Friday, 9–5.30, Wednesday, 9.30–7.30,
selected Saturdays, 9–5.30
guildhall.library@cityoflandon.gov.uk

### House of Lords Record Office (HOL)
Parliamentary Archives, Houses of Parliament, London SW1A OPW
020 7219 3074
Monday–Friday, 10–4
archives@parliament.uk

### Institute of Genealogical and Heraldic Studies (IHGS)
79–82 Northgate, Canterbury CT1 1BA
01227 768664
Email enquiries via www.ihgs.ac.uk

## Kent Archaeological Society (KAS)
c/o Maidstone Museum, St Faith's Street, Maidstone ME14 1LH
Email enquiries via www.kentachaeology.org.uk

## Kent Certificate Centre
The Mansion House, 39 Grove Hill Road, Tunbridge Wells TN1 1EP
030 0041 9300
certificates@kent.gov.uk

## Kent Family History Society (KFHS)
secretary@kfhs.org.uk
Branches:

> Ashford: peterrate@btinternet.com
> Canterbury: canterburykfhs@btinternet.com
> Deal: enquiries@dealkfhs.org.uk
> Maidstone: carol.paul74a@tesco.net
> Medway: email enquiries via www.kfhs-medway.org.uk
> Thanet: mikeandannlucas@tiscali.co.uk

## Kent History and Library Centre (KHLC)
James Whatman Way, Maidstone ME14 ILQ
030 0041 3131
Monday–Wednesday, Friday, 9–6, Thursday, 9–8, Saturday, 9–5
historyandlibrarycentre@kent.gov.uk
Library reader's card necessary

## Kent History Federation
chairman@kenthistoryfederation.org

## Lambeth Palace Library
Lambeth Palace Road, London SE1 7JU
020 7898 1400
Tuesday, Wednesday, Friday, 10–5, Thursday, 10–7.30
archives@churchofengland.org

## Lewisham Local History and Archive Centre
Lewisham Library, 199–201 Lewisham High Street, London SE13
   6LG
020 8314 8501
Monday, 10–4.45, Tuesday–Thursday, 9.30–4.45, Friday, 9.30–4,
Saturday, 9–4.45 (daily lunch closure, 12.45–2.15)
local.studies@lewisham.gov.uk

## London Metropolitan Archives (LMA)
40 Northampton Road, Clerkenwell, London EC1R OHB
020 7332 3820
Monday, 9.30–4.45, Tuesday–Thursday, 9.30–7.30, one Saturday
   a month
ask.lma@cityoflondon.gov.uk

## Medway Area Local Studies Centre (MALSC)
Clock Tower Building, Former Civic Centre Site, Strood ME2 4AU
01634 332714
Monday, Tuesday, Thursday, Friday, 9–5, Saturday, 9–4 (KFHS advice
   bureau Tuesday and Thursday, 9.30–12.30)
CARN ticket necessary
malsc@medway.gov.uk

## The National Archives (TNA)
Ruskin Avenue, Kew, Surrey TW9 4DU
020 8876 3444
Tuesday, Thursday, Friday, 9–7, Wednesday, Saturday, 9–5
Open access but reader's ticket necessary for production of
   documents
Email enquiries via www.nationalarchives.gov.uk

## North-West Kent Family History Society
membership@nwkfhs.org.uk
Branches at Bromley, Dartford and Sevenoaks

## Society of Antiquaries
Burlington House, Piccadilly, London W1J OBE
020 7479 7080
admin@sal.org.uk

**Society of Genealogists (SOG)**
14 Charterhouse Buildings, Goswell Road, London EC1M 7BA
020 7251 8799
Tuesday, Wednesday, Saturday, 10–6, Thursday, 10–8
genealogy@sog.org.uk
Annual membership or daily hourly/search fee

**Tunbridge Wells Family History Society**
Email enquiries via tunwells-fhs.co.uk

**Woolwich and District Family History Society**
suhiwfhs@tiscali.co.uk

# GENERAL BIBLIOGRAPHY

**Records and Archives**
Bond, M.F., *Guide to the records of Parliament* (1971)
Dale, J.K., *Introducing local studies* (1956)
Dunning, R., *Local history for beginners* (1973)
Durie, B., *Understanding documents for genealogy and local history* (2013)
Dymond, D., *Writing local history: a practical guide* (1988)
Emmison, F.G., *Introduction to archives* (1964)
——, *Archives and local history* (1965)
—— and Gray, I., *County records* (1961)
Galbraith, V.H., *An introduction to the use of the public records* (1952)
Harvey, P.D.A., *Editing historical records* (2001)
Iredale, D., *Enjoying archives* (1973)
——, *Local history research and writing* (1974)
Pugh, R.B., *How to write a parish history* (1954)
Redstone, L. and Steer, F.W., *Local records* (1953)
Rogers, A., *Approaches to local history* (2nd edn 1977)
Stephens, W.B., *Sources for English history* (1981)
West, J., *Town records* (1983)
——, *Village records* (3rd edn 1997)

**Reference Works**
Barrow, G.B., *The genealogist's guide* (1977)
Berry, W., *County genealogies: pedigrees of families in the county of Kent* (1830)
Besterman, T., *A world bibliography of bibliographies* (1950)
Boase, F., *Modern English biography* (1965, 2000)
*Burke's extinct peerage* (1841)
*Burke's family index* (1976)
*Burke's genealogical and heraldic history of the peerage, baronetage and knightage* (2004)
*Burke's guide to the royal family* (1973)
*Burke's landed gentry of Great Britain* (1921–date)

*Burke's peerage and baronetage* (1910–date)

Cave-Brown, J., 'Knights of the shire for Kent A.D.1275–1831', *Arch. Cant.*, 21 (1895)

Cheney, C.R. (ed.), *Handbook of dates for students of English history* (rev. edn 1955, repr. 1991)

Cokayne, G.C. (ed.), *The complete baronetage* (1900–6, repr. 1983)

——, *The complete peerage*, 15 vols (1910–64)

Coleman, J., *General index to printed pedigrees* (1866)

Cowper, J.M., *The roll of the freemen of the city of Canterbury from AD 1392–1800* (1903)

——, *Canterbury marriage licences 1568–1750*, 6 vols (1892–1906)

*Crockford's clerical directory* (1858–date)

*Debrett's peerage and baronetage* (1864–date)

Fitzhugh, T., *The dictionary of genealogy* (1985)

Foster, J., *Alumni Oxonienses 1500–1886* (1888–92)

Fryde, E.B. and Powicke, F.M. (eds), *Handbook of British chronology* (3rd edn 1986)

Gibson, J.S.W. et al., *Gibson Guides* (1980–2000s)
  *Bishops' transcripts and marriage licences*
  *Coroners' records in England and Wales*
  *Electoral registers 1832–1948; and burgess rolls*
  *Hearth tax, other later Stuart tax lists & Association Oath rolls*
  *Land tax and window assessments*
  *Local census listings 1522–1930*
  *Local newspapers 1750–1920*
  *Marriage, census and other indexes for family historians*
  *Militia lists and musters 1757–1876*
  *Poll books, c.1696–1782: a directory to holdings in Great Britain*
  *Poor law union records, 1: south-east England & East Anglia*
  *Protestation returns 1641–42, and other contemporary listings*
  *Quarter sessions records for family historians*
  *Specialist indexes for family historians*
  *A simplified guide to probate jurisdictions*
  *Tudor and Stuart muster rolls*
  *Victuallers' licences records for family historians*

Halliwell, J.O., *Dictionary of archaisms and provincialisms*, 2 vols (1860)

Herber, M., *Ancestral trails* (2nd edn 2004)

Hey, D., *The Oxford companion to local and family history* (1996)

Hull, F., *Guide to the Kent County Archives Offices* (1958); *1st supplement 1957–68* (1971); *2nd supplement 1969–80* (1983)

Humphery-Smith, C.R., *A genealogist's bibliography* (1985)

——, (ed.), *The Phillimore atlas and index of parish registers* (3rd edn 2003)

Jacobs, P.M., *Registers of the universities, colleges and schools of Great Britain and Ireland: a list* (1964)

Kidd, C. and Williamson, D., *Debrett's peerage, baronetage, knightage and companionage 1990* (1990)

Leeson, F., *A directory of British peerages* (2002)

Lewis, S., *Topographical dictionary of England,* 4 vols (1831–65)

*Lloyd's list* (1741–date)

*Lloyd's register* (1775–date)

Loveridge, P., *A calendar of fairs and markets held in the nineteenth century* (2003)

Marshall, G.W., *The genealogist's guide* (4th edn 1903)

Martin, C.T., *The record interpreter* (2nd edn, repr. 1982)

Mosley, C., *Burke's peerage and baronetage* (106th edn 1999)

Mullins, E.L.C., *Texts and calendars: an analytical guide to serial publications* (1958)

——, *Texts and calendars II: an analytical guide to serial publications 1957–1982* (1983)

Munby, L.M., *Dates and time: a handbook for local historians* (1997)

North West Kent Family History Society, *West Kent sources: a guide to genealogical research in the Diocese of Rochester* (3rd edn 1998)

——, *School records: a guide to the location of school records in the Diocese of Rochester* (2004)

*Oxford dictionary of national biography* (2004)

Pressat, R., *The dictionary of demography,* ed. C. Wilson (1988)

Purvis, J., *Dictionary of ecclesiastical terms* (1962)

Raymond, S.A., *Kent: a genealogical bibliography,* 2 vols (1998)

Richardson, J., *The local historian's encyclopaedia* (3rd edn 2003)

Riches, P.M., *An analytical biography of universal collected biography* (1934)

Royal Commission on Historical Manuscripts, *Principal family and estate collections: family names A–W,* RCHM guides to sources for British history, vols 10–11 (1996, 1999)

Sainty, J.C., *Office-holders in modern Britain 1660–1870,* 6 vols (1973–6)

Saul, P. and Markwell, F.C., *The family historian's enquire within* (5th edn 1995)

Shaw, W.A., *Knights of England* (1971)

Smith, K.L., *Genealogical dates: a user-friendly guide* (1994)

Venn, J. and J.A., *Alumni Cantabrigienses to 1900* (1922–54)

Walford, E., *County families of the United Kingdom 1860–1920* (1894–1920)

Webb, C., *Dates and calendars for the genealogist* (rev. edn 1994)

——, *London apprentices,* 38 vols (1996–2003)

West, J. (ed.), *Debrett's people of Kent* (1990)

*Whitaker's Almanack* (1868–date)

Whitmore, J.B., *A genealogical guide* (1953)

*Who's Who: an annual biographical dictionary* (1849–date)

Willis, A.J., *Canterbury marriage licences 1751–1837,* 3 vols (1967–71)

Woodcroft, B., *Alphabetical index of patentees of inventions 1617–1852* (1854)

Wright, D., *East Kent parishes: a guide for genealogists, local historians and other researchers in the Diocese of Canterbury* (2nd edn 2002)

——, *Bryan Faussett: Antiquary Extraordinary* (2015)

Youngs, F., *Guide to the local administrative units of England: Vol. 1, southern England* (1979)

# GAZETTEER OF KENT ANCIENT PARISHES

The following list shows every ancient Kent parish in existence in about 1830 followed by its Poor Law union/registration district and then the location of its original parochial records and parish map reference. Well-known but non-parochial places and a few Victorian parochial creations are cross-referenced.

**Abbreviations**

Bexley LSAC     Bexley Local Studies and Archives Centre
Bromley LSLA   Bromley Local Studies Library and Archives
CCA                  Canterbury Cathedral Archives
Greenwich HC  Greenwich Heritage Centre
KHLC              Kent History and Library Centre
MALSC           Medway Area Local Studies Centre

Acol (or Wood) – see Birchington
Acrise – Elham (CCA) G3
Addington – Malling (KHLC) G2
Adisham – Bridge (CCA) G3
Aldington – East Ashford (KHLC) F4
Alkham – Dover (CCA) G4
Allhallows – see Hoo, Allhallows
Allington – Malling (KHLC) D2
Appledore – Tenterden (KHLC) E4
Ash (next Ridley) – Dartford (MALSC) C2
Ash (near Sandwich) – Eastry (CCA) H2
Ashford – West Ashford (KHLC) E3
Ashurst – Tonbridge (KHLC) B4
Aylesford – Malling (KHLC) C2
Aylesham – see Nonington

Badlesmere – Faversham (CCA) F3
Bapchild – Milton (KHLC) E2
Barfrestone – Eastry (CCA) G3

Barham – Bridge (CCA) G3
Bearsted – Maidstone (KHLC) D3
Beauxfield – see Whitfield
Beckenham – Bromley (Bexley LSC) A2
Bekesbourne – Bridge (CCA) G2
Belvedere – see Erith
Benenden – Cranbrook (KHLC) D4
Bethersden – West Ashford (KHLC) E4
Betteshanger – Eastry (KHLC) H3
Bexley – Dartford (Bexley LSC) B1
Bexleyheath – see Bexley
Bickley – see Bromley
Bicknor – Hollingbourne (KHLC) D2
Bidborough – Tonbridge (KHLC) B3
Biddenden – Tenterden (KHLC) D4
Bilsington – East Ashford (KHLC) F4
Birchington – Thanet (CCA) H1
Bircholt – East Ashford (KHLC) F4
Birling – Malling (MALSC) C2
Bishopsbourne – Bridge (CCA) G3
Blackheath – see Charlton, Lewisham, Greenwich
Blackmanstone – Romney Marsh (KHLC) F5
Blean – Blean (CCA) F2
Bobbing – Milton (KHLC) E2
Bonnington – East Ashford (KHLC) F4
Borden – Milton (KHLC) E2
Borough Green – see Wrotham
Borstal – see Rochester
Boughton Aluph – East Ashford (KHLC) F3
Boughton Malherbe – Hollingbourne (KHLC) D3
Boughton Monchelsea – Maidstone (KHLC) D3
Boughton-under-Blean – Faversham (CCA) F2
Boxley – Hollingbourne (KHLC) D2
Brabourne – East Ashford (KHLC) F4
Brasted – Sevenoaks (KHLC) A3
Bredgar – Milton (KHLC) E2
Bredhurst – Hollingbourne (MALSC) D2
Brenchley – Tonbridge (KHLC) C3

Brents, The – see Davington
Brenzett – Romney Marsh (KHLC) E5
Bridge – Bridge (CCA) G3
Broadstairs – see Thanet St Peter
Brockley – see Lewisham
Bromley – Bromley (Bromley LSC) A2
Brompton – see Gillingham
Brook – East Ashford (CCA) F3
Brookland – Romney Marsh (KHLC) E5
Broomfield – Hollingbourne (KHLC) D3
Broomhill – see Lydd
Buckland (in Dover) – Dover (CCA) H3
Buckland (near Faversham) – Faversham (CCA) E2
Burham – Malling (MALSC) C2
Burmarsh – Romney Marsh (KHLC) F4

Canterbury, All Saints – Canterbury (CCA) G2
Canterbury, Christ Church – Blean (CCA) G2
Canterbury, Holy Cross – Bridge; Canterbury (CCA) G2
Canterbury, St Alphege – Canterbury (CCA) G2
Canterbury, St Andrew – Canterbury (CCA) G2
Canterbury, St Dunstan – Blean (CCA) F2
Canterbury, St George – Canterbury (CCA) G2
Canterbury, St Margaret – Canterbury (CCA) G2
Canterbury, St Martin – Canterbury (CCA) G2
Canterbury, St Mary Bredin – Canterbury (CCA) G2
Canterbury, St Mary Bredman – Canterbury (CCA) G2
Canterbury, St Mary Magdalene – Canterbury (CCA) G2
Canterbury, St Mary Northgate – Canterbury (CCA) G2
Canterbury, St Mildred – Canterbury (CCA) G2
Canterbury, St Paul – Canterbury (CCA) G2
Canterbury, St Peter – Canterbury (CCA) G2
Canterbury, St Stephen – see Hackington
Capel – Tonbridge (KHLC) C3
Capel le Ferne – Dover (CCA) G4
Catford – see Lewisham
Chalk – North Aylesford/ Strood (MALSC) C1
Challock – East Ashford (CCA) E3

Charing – West Ashford (KHLC) E3
Charlton (in Dover) – Dover (CCA) H4
Charlton (next Greenwich) – Lewisham/Woolwich (Greenwich LSC)
Chartham – Bridge (CCA) F3
Chart Sutton – Hollingbourne (KHLC) D3
Chatham – Medway (MALSC) D2
Chelsfield – Bromley (Bromley LSC) A2
Cheriton – Elham (CCA) G4
Chevening – Sevenoaks (KHLC) B3
Chiddingstone – Sevenoaks (KHLC) B3
Chilham – East Ashford (CCA) F3
Chillenden – Eastry (CCA) G3
Chislehurst – Bromley (Bromley LSC) A1
Chislet – Blean (CCA) G2
Cliffe at Hoo – North Aylesford/Strood; (MALSC) C1
Cliftonville – see Thanet, St John
Cobham – North Aylesford/Strood (MALSC) C2
Coldred – Dover (CCA) H3
Collier St – see Yalding
Cooling – Hoo/Strood (MALSC) D1
Cowden – Sevenoaks (KHLC) A4
Cranbrook – Cranbrook (KHLC) D4
Crayford – Dartford (Bexley LSC) B1
Crockenhill – see Eynsford
Crundale – East Ashford (CCA) F3
Cudham – Bromley (Bromley LSC) A2
Cuxton – North Aylesford/Strood (MALSC) C2

Darenth – Dartford (MALSC) B1
Dartford – Dartford (MALSC) B1
Davington – Faversham (CCA) E2
Deal – Eastry (CCA) H3
Denton (next Elham) – Dover (CCA) G3
Denton (near Gravesend) – North Aylesford (MALSC) C1
Deptford, St Nicholas – Greenwich (LMA) A1
Deptford, St Paul – Greenwich (LMA) A1
Detling – Hollingbourne (KHLC) D2
Ditton – Malling (KHLC) C2

Doddington – Faversham (CCA) E2
Dover, St James – Dover (CCA) H4
Dover, St Mary – Dover (CCA) H4
Downe – Bromley (Bromley LSC) A2
Dunkirk – see Boughton-under-Blean, Hernhill
Dymchurch – Romney Marsh (KHLC) F4

East Barming – Maidstone (KHLC) C3
Eastbridge – Romney Marsh (CCA) F4
Eastchurch – Sheppey (KHLC) E1
East Farleigh – Maidstone (KHLC) C3
East Langdon – Dover (CCA) H3
Eastling – Faversham (CCA) E2
East Malling – Malling (KHLC) C2
East Peckham – Malling (KHLC) C3
Eastry – Eastry (CCA) H3
East Sutton – Hollingbourne (KHLC) D3
Eastwell – East Ashford (KHLC) E3
East Wickham – Dartford (Bexley LSC) A1
Ebony – Tenterden (KHLC) E5
Edenbridge – Sevenoaks (KHLC) A3
Egerton – West Ashford (KHLC) E3
Elham – Elham (CCA) G3
Elmley – Sheppey (KHLC) E2
Elmsted – Elham (CCA) F3
Elmstone – Eastry (CCA) G2
Eltham – Lewisham (LMA) A1
Erith – Dartford (Bexley LSC) B1
Ewell – see Temple Ewell
Eynsford – Dartford (KHLC) B2
Eythorne – Eastry (CCA) H3

Fairfield – Romney Marsh (KHLC) E5
Falconhurst – see Hurst
Farnborough – Bromley (Bromley LSC) A2
Farningham – Dartford (KHLC) B2
Faversham – Faversham (CCA) F2
Fawkham – Dartford (MALSC) B2

Folkestone – Elham (CCA) G4
Foots Cray – Bromley (Bexley LSC) A1
Fordcombe – see Penshurst
Fordwich – Bridge (CCA) G2
Forest Hill – see Lewisham
Frindsbury – North Aylesford/Strood (MALSC) C1
Frinsted – Hollingbourne (KHLC) E2
Frittenden – Cranbrook (KHLC) D4

Gillingham – Medway (MALSC) D2
Godmersham – East Ashford (CCA) F3
Goodnestone (next Faversham) – Faversham (CCA) F2
Goodnestone (next Wingham) – Eastry (CCA) G3
Goudhurst – Cranbrook (KHLC) C4
Grain – Hoo/Strood (MALSC) E1
Graveney – Faversham (CCA) F2
Gravesend – Gravesend (MALSC) C1
Great Chart – West Ashford (KHLC) E4
Great Mongeham – Eastry (CCA) H3
Greenhithe – see Swanscombe
Greenwich – Greenwich (LMA) A1
Groombridge – see Speldhurst
Guston – Dover (CCA) H3

Hackington – Blean (CCA) G2
Hadlow – Tonbridge (KHLC) C3
Halling – North Aylesford/Strood (MALSC) C2
Halstead – Sevenoaks (KHLC) B2
Ham – Eastry (CCA) H3
Hamstreet – see Orlestone
Harbledown – Bridge (CCA) F2
Harrietsham – Hollingbourne (KHLC) D3
Hartley – Dartford (MALSC) C2
Hartlip – Milton (KHLC) D2
Harty – Sheppey (KHLC) F2
Hastingleigh – East Ashford (CCA) F3
Hawkhurst – Cranbrook (KHLC) D4
Hawkinge – Elham (CCA) G4

Hayes – Bromley (Bromley LSC) A2
Headcorn – Hollingbourne (KHLC) D3
Herne – Blean (CCA) G2
Herne Bay – see Herne
Hernhill – Faversham (CCA) F2
Hever – Sevenoaks (KHLC) B3
Hextable – see Sutton-at-Hone
Higham – North Aylesford/Strood (MALSC) C1
High Halden – Tenterden (CCA) E4
High Halstow – Hoo/Strood (MALSC) D1
Hildenborough – see Tonbridge
Hinxhill – East Ashford (KHLC) F3
Hither Green – see Lewisham
Hoath – Blean (CCA) G2
Hollingbourne – Hollingbourne (KHLC) D3
Hoo, Allhallows – Hoo/Strood (MALSC) D1
Hoo, St Mary – Hoo/Strood (MALSC) D1
Hoo, St Werburgh – Hoo/Strood (MALSC) D1
Hope – Romney Marsh (KHLC) F5
Horsmonden – Tonbridge (KHLC) C4
Horton Kirby – Dartford (MALSC) B2
Hothfield – West Ashford (KHLC) E3
Hougham – Dover (CCA) H4
Hucking – Hollingbourne (KHLC) D2
Hunton – Maidstone (KHLC) C3
Hurst – East Ashford (KHLC) F4
Hythe – Elham (CCA) G4

Ickham – Bridge (KHLC) G2
Ide Hill – see Sundridge
Ifield – North Aylesford/Strood (MALSC) C1
Ightham – Malling (KHLC) B2
Ivychurch – Romney Marsh (KHLC) E5
Iwade – Milton (KHLC) E1

Kemsing – Sevenoaks (KHLC) B2
Kenardington – Tenterden (KHLC) E4
Kennington – East Ashford (KHLC) F3

Keston – Bromley (Bromley LSC) A2
Kidbrooke – see Charlton
Kilndown – see Goudhurst
Kingsdown (near Dartford) – see West Kingsdown
Kingsdown (near Deal) – see Ringwould
Kingsdown (near Sittingbourne) – Milton (CCA) E2
Kingsnorth – West Ashford (KHLC) E4
Kingston – Bridge (KHLC) G3
Kippington – see Sevenoaks
Knockholt – Bromley (KHLC) A2
Knowlton – Eastry (KHLC) H3

Lamberhurst – Ticehurst (KHLC) C4
Langley – Hollingbourne (KHLC) D3
Langton Green – see Speldhurst
Leaveland – Faversham (CCA) E3
Lee – Lewisham (Lewisham LSC) A1
Leeds – Hollingbourne (KHLC) D3
Leigh – Sevenoaks (KHLC) B3
Lenham – Hollingbourne (KHLC) E3
Lewisham – Lewisham (Lewisham LSC) A1
Leybourne – Malling (KHLC) C2
Leysdown – Sheppey (KHLC) F1
Lidsing – see Chatham
Linton – Maidstone (KHLC) D3
Littlebourne – Bridge (CCA) G2
Little Chart – West Ashford (KHLC) E3
Little Mongeham – Eastry (CCA) H3
Loddington – see Maidstone
Longfield – Dartford (MALSC) C2
Loose – Maidstone (KHLC) D3
Lower Halstow – Milton (KHLC) D2
Lower Hardres – Bridge (CCA) G3
Luddenham – Faversham (CCA) E2
Luddesdown – North Aylesford/Strood (MALSC) C2
Lullingstone – Dartford (KHLC) B2
Luton – see Chatham
Lydd – Romney Marsh (KHLC) F5

Lydden – Dover (CCA) G3
Lyminge – Elham (CCA) G4
Lympne – Elham (KHLC) F4
Lynsted – Faversham (CCA) E2

Maidstone – Maidstone (KHLC) D3
Marden – Maidstone (KHLC) D3
Margate – see Thanet, St John
Markbeech – see Hever
Matfield – see Brenchley
Meopham – North Aylesford/Strood (MALSC) C2
Mereworth – Malling (KHLC) C3
Mersham – East Ashford (KHLC) F4
Merston – see Shorne
Midley – Romney Marsh (KHLC) E5
Milstead – Milton (KHLC) E2
Milton (next Gravesend) – Gravesend (MALSC) C1
Milton Chapel – Bridge (CCA) F2
Milton Regis – Milton (KHLC) E2
Minster-in-Sheppey – Sheppey (KHLC) E1
Minster-in-Thanet – Thanet (CCA) H2
Molash – East Ashford (CCA) F3
Monks Horton – Elham (KHLC) F4
Monkton – Thanet (CCA) H2
Mottingham – see Eltham
Murston – Milton (KHLC) E2

Nackington – Bridge (CCA) G3
Nettlestead – Maidstone (KHLC) C3
Newchurch – Romney Marsh (KHLC) F4
New Cross – see Deptford, St Paul
Newenden – Tenterden (KHLC) D5
Newington (next Hythe) – Elham (CCA ) G4
Newington (near Sittingbourne) – Milton (KHLC) D2
Newnham – Faversham (CCA) E2
New Romney – Romney Marsh (KHLC) F5
Nonington – Eastry (CCA) G3
Northbourne – Eastry (CCA) H3
North Cray – Bromley (Bexley LSC) B1

Northfleet – North Aylesford/Strood (MALSC) C1
Norton – Faversham (CCA) E2
Nurstead – North Aylesford/Strood (MALSC) C2

Oare – Faversham (CCA) E2
Offham – Malling (KHLC) C2
Old Romney – Romney Marsh (KHLC) F5
Orgarswick – Romney Marsh (KHLC) F4
Orlestone – East Ashford (KHLC) E4
Orpington – Bromley (Bromley LSC) A2
Ospringe – Faversham (CCA) E2
Otford – Sevenoaks (KHLC) B2
Otham – Maidstone (KHLC) D3
Otterden – Hollingbourne (CCA) E3
Oxney – Dover (CCA) H3

Paddlesworth (next Folkestone) – Elham (CCA) G4
Paddlesworth (next Snodland) – Malling (KHLC) C2
Patrixbourne – Bridge (CCA) G3
Pembury – Tonbridge (KHLC) C4
Penshurst – Sevenoaks (KHLC) B4
Petham – Bridge (CCA) F3
Pevington – see Pluckley
Plaxtol – Malling (KHLC) C2
Pluckley – West Ashford (CCA) E3
Plumstead – Lewisham/Woolwich (LMA) A1
Postling – Elham (CCA) G4
Poulton – Dover (CCA) G4
Preston (next Faversham) – Faversham (CCA) F2
Preston (next Wingham) – Eastry (CCA) G2

Queenborough – Sheppey (KHLC) E1

Rainham – Milton (MALSC) D2
Ramsgate – see Thanet, St Lawrence
Reculver – Blean (CCA) G2
Ridley – Dartford (MALSC) C2
Ringwould – Dover (CCA) H3
Ripple – Eastry (CCA) H3
River – Dover (CCA) H3

Riverhead – see Sevenoaks
Rochester Cathedral – Medway (MALSC) C2
Rochester St Margaret – Medway (MALSC) C2
Rochester St Nicholas – Medway (MALSC) C2
Rodmersham – Milton (KHLC) E2
Rolvenden – Tenterden (KHLC) D4
Rosherville – see Northfleet
Ruckinge – East Ashford (KHLC) F4
Rusthall – see Speldhurst
Ruxley – see North Cray
Ryarsh – Malling (KHLC) C2

St Margaret's at Cliffe – Dover (CCA) H3
St Mary Cray – Bromley (Bromley LSC) B2
St Mary in the Marsh – Romney Marsh (KHLC) F5
St Mary Platt – see Wrotham
St Nicholas at Wade – Thanet (CCA) G2
St Paul's Cray – Bromley (Bromley LSC) A1
St Stephen's Canterbury – see Hackington
Saltwood – Elham (CCA) G4
Sandgate – see Cheriton
Sandhurst – Cranbrook (KHLC) D5
Sandwich St Clement – Eastry (CCA) H2
Sandwich St Mary – Eastry (CCA) H2
Sandwich St Peter – Eastry (CCA) H2
Sarre – see St Nicholas at Wade
Seal – Sevenoaks (KHLC) B3
Seal Chart – see Kemsing
Seasalter – Blean (CCA) F2
Sellindge – Elham (KHLC) F4
Selling – Faversham (CCA) F2
Sevenoaks – Sevenoaks (KHLC) B3
Sevington – East Ashford (KHLC) F4
Shadoxhurst – West Ashford (KHLC) E4
Sheerness – see Minster-in-Sheppey
Sheldwich – Faversham (CCA) F2
Shepherdswell – Dover (CCA) G3
Shipbourne – Malling (KHLC) B3

Sholden – Eastry (CCA) H3
Shooters Hill – see Eltham; Plumstead
Shoreham – Sevenoaks (KHLC) B2
Shorncliffe – see Cheriton
Shorne – North Aylesford/Strood (MALSC) C1
Shortlands – see Beckenham
Sibertswold – see Shepherdswell
Sidcup – see Foot's Cray/Chislehurst
Singlewell – see Ifield
Sissinghurst – see Cranbrook
Sittingbourne – Milton (KHLC) E2
Smallhythe – see Tenterden
Smarden – West Ashford (KHLC) E3
Smeeth – East Ashford (KHLC) F4
Snargate – Romney Marsh (KHLC) E5
Snave – Romney Marsh (KHLC) F4
Snodland – Malling (MALSC) C2
Southborough – see Tonbridge
Southfleet – Dartford (MALSC) B1
Speldhurst – Tonbridge (KHLC) B4
Stalisfield – Faversham (CCA) E3
Stanford – Elham (CCA) F4
Stansted – Malling (KHLC) B2
Staple – Eastry (CCA) G2
Staplehurst – Maidstone (KHLC) D3
Stelling – Elham (CCA) G3
Stockbury – Hollingbourne (KHLC) D2
Stodmarsh – Bridge (CCA) G2
Stoke – Hoo/Strood (MALSC) D1
Stonar – Thanet (CCA) H2
Stone (next Dartford) – Dartford (MALSC) B1
Stone (next Faversham) – Faversham (CCA) E2
Stone-in-Oxney – Tenterden (KHLC) E5
Stourmouth – Eastry (CCA) G2
Stowting – Elham (KHLC) F3
Strood – North Aylesford/Strood (MALSC) C2
Sturry – Blean (CCA) G2
Sundridge – Sevenoaks (KHLC) B3

Sutton (near Dover) – Eastry (CCA) H3
Sutton-at-Hone – Dartford (MALSC) B1
Sutton Valence – Hollingbourne (KHLC) D3
Swalecliffe – Blean (CCA) G2
Swanley – see Sutton-at-Hone
Swanscombe – Dartford (MALSC) B1
Swingfield – Elham (CCA) G3
Sydenham – see Lewisham

Temple Ewell – Dover (CCA) H3
Tenterden – Tenterden (KHLC) E4
Teston – Maidstone (KHLC) C3
Teynham – Faversham (CCA) E2
Thanet, St John – Thanet (CCA) H1
Thanet, St Lawrence – Thanet (CCA) H2
Thanet, St Peter – Thanet (CCA) H2
Thanington – Bridge (CCA) F2
Throwley – Faversham (CCA) E3
Thurnham – Hollingbourne (KHLC) D2
Tilmanstone – Eastry (CCA) H3
Tonbridge – Tonbridge (KHLC) B3
Tonge – Milton (KHLC) E2
Tovil – see Maidstone
Trottiscliffe – Malling (KHLC) C2
Tudeley – Tonbridge (KHLC) C3
Tunbridge Wells – Tonbridge (KHLC) B4
Tunstall – Milton (KHLC) E2

Ulcombe – Hollingbourne (KHLC) D3
Underriver – see Seal
Upchurch – Milton (KHLC) D2
Upnor – see Frindsbury
Upper Hardres – Bridge (CCA) G3

Waldershare – Eastry (CCA) H3
Walmer – Eastry (CCA) H3
Waltham – Bridge (CCA) F3
Warden – Sheppey (KHLC) F1
Warehorne – East Ashford (KHLC) E4

Wateringbury – Malling (KHLC) C3
Weald – see Sevenoaks
West Barming – see Nettlestead
Westbere – Blean (CCA) G2
Westbrook – see Thanet, St John
Westcliffe – Dover (CCA) H3
Westerham – Sevenoaks (KHLC) A3
West Farleigh – Maidstone (KHLC) C3
Westgate – see Thanet, St John
West Hythe – Romney Marsh (KHLC) F4
West Kingsdown – Dartford (KHLC) B2
West Langdon – Dover (CCA) H3
West Malling – Malling (KHLC) C2
Westmarsh – see Ash (near Sandwich)
West Peckham – Malling (KHLC) C3
Westwell – West Ashford (KHLC) E3
West Wickham – Bromley (Bromley LCS ) A2
Whitfield – Dover (CCA) H3
Whitstable – Blean (CCA) F2
Wickhambreaux – Bridge (CCA) G2
Willesborough – East Ashford (KHLC) F3
Wilmington – Dartford (MALSC) B1
Wingham – Eastry (CCA) G2
Wittersham – Tenterden (KHLC) E5
Womenswold – Bridge (CCA) G3
Wood (or Acol) – see Birchington
Woodchurch – Tenterden (KHLC) E4
Woodnesborough – Eastry (CCA) H2
Woolwich – Greenwich/Woolwich (LMA) A1
Wootton – Dover (CCA) G3
Wormshill – Hollingbourne (KHLC) E2
Worth – Eastry (CCA) H2
Wouldham – Malling (MALSC) C2
Wrotham – Malling (KHLC) C2
Wychling – Hollingbourne (CCA) E3
Wye – East Ashford (CCA) F3

Yalding – Maidstone (KHLC) C3

# INDEX

adoption, 20

alehouses, *see* victuallers and alehouses

apprentices, 115–16, 149

architecture, *see* Kent

army, *see* military records

assize courts, 163–4

Bank of England wills, *see* probate records

banks and bankruptcy, 151–2

banns, 64

baptisms, 64
  indexes of, 62

bargain and sale, 175

bastardy, 117

bell-founding, 152–3

Bernau Index, 162

bibliographies
  army and navy, 195
  cathedral and church courts, 100
  census returns, 55
  civil registration, 50
  computer genealogy, 40
  crime and punishment, 165
  directories, 103
  Domesday Book, 167
  general genealogy, 23–5
  general history, 14–17
  heraldry, 170–1
  house histories, 105–6
  journals, 25–6
  Latin and palaeography, 35

manors, 180–1

maps, 147–8

monumental inscriptions, 74

names, 35–6

newspapers, 108–9

Nonconformity, 113

parish chest, 127

parish registers, 69–70

Poor Law, 133

probate, 91

tax records, 200

trades and industry, 157–8

births, 47, 48

Bishop's Transcripts, 67–9

bonds, *see* probate records

borough records, 92–6

brewing, 153

brick-making, 153

burials, 65–7
  indexes of, 63

calendar and dates, 38

castles, 5, 7

cathedral and church court records, 96–100

Catholics, 110, 111

cement-making, 153–4

cemeteries, 72–4

census returns, 13–14, 21, 50–5

Chancery Court, *see* courts

changes of name, 20

Channel crossings, 10

charity, 119

Charter Rolls, 173

Chatham Chest, 192
Christianity, early, 3–4
churches, *see* Kent
churchwardens, 119–20
civil registration, 45–9
civil servants, 183–5
clergy, 181
Close Rolls, 173
cloth-making, 154
coal-mining, 154–5
coastguards, 183
College of Arms, 167–8
Compton census, 109
computer genealogy, 39–40
constables, 120–1, 137
copperas, 155
coroners, 164
county maps, *see* maps
courts
  Chancery, 162
  Exchequer, 162
  Justice and Appeal, 162
  Requests, 162
  Star Chamber, 162
  crime and punishment, 161–5
customs officers, 183

dates, *see* calendar and dates
Death Duty Records,
  *see* probate records
deaths, 49
debtors, 138
Deeds of the Exchequer, 177
defences, *see* Kent
dioceses, foundation of, 3
directories, 100–3
Dissolution of the Monasteries, 7
divorce, 59–60

dockyards, 155
Domesday Book, 165–7

education, *see* schools and
  education
electoral registers, 159–60
enclosure, 7, 121–3, 150
estate maps, *see* maps
Exchequer Court, *see* courts
Exchequer deeds, *see* Deeds of
  the Exchequer

family trees, deposited, 29
  construction of, 33–4
final agreements, 172
fishing, 155
forenames, 28
freeholders, 137
freemasons, 137
freemen, 149
fuller's earth, 154

gamekeepers, 137
gavelkind, 6–7
GOONS, 29
GRO indexes, 45–7
guilds, 148–9
gunpowder, 156

handwriting, 29
hearth tax, 196
heraldry, 167–71
history
  oral, 33
  social, 30
hospitals, 133–5
house histories, 103
house tax, 138

Huguenots, 149–50

indexes, 21
Indictment Rolls, 138
Inquisitions Post Mortem, 174–5
intestacy, *see* probate records
inventories, *see* probate records
iron-making, 156

jurisdictions, probate, *see* probate
   records
jurors, 138
Justice and Appeal Court, *see*
   courts
justices, 138

Kent
   Anglo-Saxon, 3–4
   architecture, 8–9
   churches, 9
   defences, 8
   mediaeval, early, 5–6
   Norman, 4–5
   population figures, 4, 8, 13–14,
     50
   Roman, 2
Kent Certificate Centre, 50

land, 171–8
land division, 6–7
land tax, 136, 138, 197
landscapes, 14
Latin, 28–9
law courts, 161
lay subsidies, 197–8
lease and release, 176
legal profession, 185
living relatives, tracing, 33

Manorial Documents Register,
   178–9
manorial records, 178–81
maps, 143–7
   county, 143
   estate, 104, 143–4
   Ordnance Survey, 104, 147
   surveys, 145
   tithe, 104, 146–7
   town, 147
Marriage Duty Act, 198
marriage licences, *see* parish
   registers
marriages, 47–9
   indexes of, 62
medical profession, 185–6
memorabilia, family, 33
merchant seamen, 193
Methodists, 111–12
military records, 186–91
minute books, 138
monumental inscriptions, 70–2
musters, 189–91

Napoleonic wars, 12
National Probate Index, *see*
   probate records
naval records, 191–4
newspapers, 106–8
Nonconformity, 109–13

oath rolls, 139, 195–6
Old Bailey, 164
order books, 139
Ordnance Survey, *see* maps

paper-making, 156–7
parish chest, 113–27

parish registers, 56–67
  copies of, 61
  history of, 56–9
  indexes, 62–3
  marriage licences, 59, 64
  searching, 63–7
Patent Rolls, 173
peerage, 21
petty sessions, 137, 139
photographs, 31
Pipe Rolls, 173
place-names, 18–19, 37
police, 13
poll books, 159
poll tax, 199
Poor Law, 128–30
population figures, *see* Kent
Prerogative Court of Canterbury
  (PCC), *see* probate records
prisoners, 139
prisons, 13, 163
probate records, 75–91
  1858 and after, 83–5
  1858 and before, 85–91
  Bank of England wills, 88
  bonds, 80
  Death Duty Records, 87–8
  east Kent, 90–1
  history of, 76–80
  intestacy, 80, 81
  inventories, 80
  jurisdictions, 78
  National Probate Index, 83
  PCC, 64–5
  reasons for not finding, 88
  west Kent, 89–90
  wills, assessment and
    recording, 81–2

process records, 139
professions, the, 181–6
protestation returns, 199

Quakers, 109, 111
quarrying, 157
quarter-sessions, 135–40

railways, 10–11
rates, 122
recognisance rolls, 139
registration districts, 46
regnal years, 38–9
religious houses, 6, 7
Requests Court, *see* courts
roads, *see* turnpikes
rope-making, 155
royal marines, 192
royalty, 21

schools and education, 140–3
seaside resorts, 11–12
servant tax, 140
Sessions Papers, 139–40
settlement and removal, 122–6
silk-weaving, 157
social history, *see* history
Star Chamber Court, *see* courts
State Papers Domestic, 177
stillbirths, 49
Supreme Court of Judicature,
  *see* Court of Justice and Appeal
surnames, 19, 27–8, 37
surveys, *see* maps
surveyors, 126
'Swing' riots, 12–13

tax records, 195–200

tithes, early, 140
tithe maps, *see* maps
title deeds, 104, 176–7
town maps, *see* maps
trades and industry, 148–58
transportation, 163–4
turnpikes and roads, 9–10, 146

vestry minutes, 126–7
victuallers and alehouses, 140

views of frankpledge, 178
voters, 158–60

watering places, 11
wills, *see* probate records
window tax, 140, 199
workhouse records, 130–3